ASSATA

AN AUTOBIOGRAPHY

Assata Shakur

Lawrence Hill Books

AS-
SA-
TA

Library of Congress Cataloging-in-Publication Data

Shakur, Assata.
Assata, an autobiography.
1. Shakur, Assata. 2. Afro-Americans—Biography. 3. Black Panther Party—Biography. 4. Black Nationalism—United States. 5. Racism—United States. 6. United States—Race relations. I. Title.
E185.97.S53A3 1987
973′.0496073024 87-23772
ISBN 1-55652-074-3, previously 0-88208-222-1.

Cover design: Joan Sommers Design

Originally published in the United Kingdom by Zed Books Ltd.
Published in the United States by Lawrence Hill Books
An imprint of Chicago Review Press, Incorporated
814 North Franklin Street
Chicago, Illinois 60610
ISBN 1-55652-074-3

Printed in the United States of America

Contents

Foreword by ANGELA Y. DAVIS vii
Foreword by LENNOX S. HINDS xi
Trial Chronology xix

Chapter 1 3
Chapter 2 18
Chapter 3 45
Chapter 4 71
Chapter 5 80
Chapter 6 99
Chapter 7 118
Chapter 8 131
Chapter 9 141
Chapter 10 148
Chapter 11 160
Chapter 12 173
Chapter 13 195
Chapter 14 208
Chapter 15 216
Chapter 16 234
Chapter 17 241
Chapter 18 244
Chapter 19 253
Chapter 20 257
Chapter 21 260

Postscript 266

Foreword

In the 1970s, as Assata Shakur awaited trial on charges of being an accomplice to murder, I participated in a benefit at Rutgers University in New Brunswick, New Jersey, to raise funds for her legal defense. At the time, Assata was being held nearby in the Middlesex County Correctional Facility for Men. Lennox Hinds, a member of the Rutgers faculty, had invited me to be one of the featured speakers at the benefit. Lennox was a leader of the National Conference of Black Lawyers and represented Assata in a federal lawsuit contesting the appalling conditions of her confinement in the New Jersey prison. He had previously worked on my case, and we had both served in the leadership of the National Alliance Against Racist and Political Repression since its founding in 1973. Attending the benefit event were Rutgers faculty members, a sizeable number of black professionals, and local activists who were the mainstay of numerous campaigns to free the political prisoners of that era.

It was an upbeat event, imbued with the optimism of the times. My own recent acquittal on charges of murder, kidnapping, and conspiracy stood as a dramatic example of how we could successfully challenge the government's offensives against radical antiracist movements. However powerful the forces arrayed against Assata—the FBI's counterintelligence program, and the New York and New Jersey police organizations—no one could have persuaded us then that we were not capable of building a triumphant movement for Assata's freedom. This benefit was one small step in that direction, and, as we left the event, we were quite satisfied with the three thousand dollars we raised that afternoon.

By then, every radical activist had learned to assume that our public meetings were subject to routine police and/or FBI surveillance. Yet we were entirely unprepared for what seemed like a reenactment of the 1973 events for which Assata faced charges of murder. Assata, Zayd Shakur, and Sundiata Acoli had been stopped on the New Jersey Turnpike by state troopers who claimed that they had a faulty tail light. The encounter left Assata critically wounded and two others—state trooper Werner Forster and Assata's friend Zayd Shakur—dead. As a group of us left the benefit and drove down a county road toward Lennox Hinds's house, where we were having a small after-party, we were quite startled when local police signaled for our car to stop. My friend Charlene Mitchell, at that time the executive director of the Alliance, was told to step out of the car, along with the driver and the other person riding with us. As the policemen taunted us by clearly placing their hands on their holstered guns, I was instructed to remain in the otherwise empty automobile. Lennox, whose car we had been following, immediately doubled back and approached the police with his attorney's identification card in hand, explaining that he was our lawyer. This caused the officers to become more visibly nervous, including one who pulled a riot gun from his police car and proceeded to aim at Lennox from close range. All of us froze. We knew only too well that any innocent gesture could be construed as a reach for a weapon and that this confrontation could easily become a recapitulation of the events that had left Assata with a murder charge.

The spurious explanation given by police for the ambush was a warrant for my arrest (later proven false). Though they allowed us to leave, it was only shortly after we arrived at Lennox's that we discovered they had already called for reinforcements and literally surrounded the house. With one of the first black woman judges in New Jersey and several other prominent community figures at the house, we were nonetheless compelled to call on higher powers, in the form of Congressman John Conyers in Washington. We figured a request for a federal escort out of the state of New Jersey might put some pressure on the local police. These were the kinds of measures—and friends—needed in such a volatile time.

I relate this incident in detail because it may help readers of Assata's autobiography not only to focus on the political role of the police during the 1970s but also to better understand important historical aspects of the routine racial profiling associated with current police practices. Such a historical perspective is especially important today when brazen expressions of structural racism—such as the pattern of mass imprisonment to which communities of color are subjected—are rendered invisible by the prevailing moral panic over crime. And if this were not enough, we find that at the same time such remedies as affirmative action programs and such safety nets as social welfare are being consistently disestablished.

When Richard Nixon raised the slogan of "law and order" in the 1970s, it was used in part to discredit the black liberation movement and to justify the deployment of the police, courts, and prisons against key figures in this and other radical movements of that era. Today, the ironic coupling of a declining crime rate and the consolidation of a prison industrial complex that makes increased rates of incarceration its economic necessity has facilitated the imprisonment of two million people in the United States. In this ideological context, political prisoners like Assata Shakur, Mumia Abu-Jamal, and Leonard Peltier are represented in popular political discourse as criminals who deserve either to be executed or to spend the rest of their lives behind bars.

During the late 1990s, the racist hysteria directed against Assata was resuscitated when the New Jersey State Police reputedly prevailed upon Pope John Paul II to use the occasion of his first trip to Cuba as pressure for Fidel Castro to extradite Assata. As if this were not enough, New Jersey governor Christine Todd Whitman offered a $50,000 reward—later doubled—for Assata's return, and Congress passed a bill calling on the government of Cuba to initiate extradition procedures.

In an open letter to the Pope, Assata asks a question that should concern all of us: "Why, I wonder, do I warrant such attention? What do I represent that is such a threat?" We would all do well to seriously ponder her questions. Why, indeed, was she constructed by the government and mass media as a consummate enemy in the 1970s, only to reemerge at the turn of the century as a singular target of governors, Congress, and the Fraternal Order of Police? What has she been made to represent? What ideological work has this representation performed?

In the 1970s, Assata Shakur's image was deployed on official FBI wanted posters and in the popular media as visual evidence of the terrorist motivations of the black liberation movement. Black militants were assumed to be enemies of the state and were associated with communist challenges to capitalist democracy. The protracted search for Assata, during which she was demonized in ways that are now unimaginable, served further to justify the imprisonment of vast numbers of political activists, many of whom remain locked up today.

Twenty-five years later, the retailoring of the image of Assata as enemy is even more damaging, omitting the original political context and representing her as a common criminal—a bank robber and murderer. This lifting of her image out of the past for very contemporary purposes serves to justify the consolidation of a vast prison industrial complex, which Assata herself has described as ". . . not only a mechanism to convert public tax money into profits for private corporations [but also] an essential element of modern neoliberal capitalism." In her view, this new formation serves two purposes: "one, to neutralize and contain huge segments of potentially rebellious sectors of the population, and two, to sustain a system of super-exploitation, where mainly black and Latino captives are imprisoned in white rural, overseer communities."

As the above quotation reveals, Assata remains very much engaged with contemporary radical politics specific to the United States, even though she has been unable to visit this country since her escape from prison and her decision to settle in Cuba many years ago. As you read her extraordinary autobiography, you will discover a woman who has nothing in common with the hostile representations that refuse to expire. I urge you to reflect on what it must mean for her to have been unable to attend her mother's funeral or to visit with her new grandchild. As you follow her life story, you will discover a compassionate human being with an unswerving commitment to justice that travels easily across racial and ethnic lines, in and out of prison and across oceans and time. She speaks to all of us, and especially to those of us who are sequestered in a growing global network of prisons and jails. At a time when optimism has receded from our political vocabulary, she offers invaluable gifts—inspiration and hope. Her words remind us, as Walter Benjamin once observed, that it is only for the sake of those without hope that hope is given to us.

ANGELA Y. DAVIS
University of California, Santa Cruz
March 2000

Foreword

The publication of this extraordinary autobiography provides a rare opportunity to see behind the carefully orchestrated distortions of fact concerning the life and motivations of Assata Shakur. Writing simply and vividly about the racism that permeated her childhood and young womanhood—those ordinary experiences of Black people in the United States that have driven millions to despair and many to rebellion—Assata leads us all to understand more about the society we live in. Clearly, it was the racism riddling every aspect of the early life of this sensitive, intellectually gifted, and life-passionate child, as she struggled to establish her own identity, that led her to seek solutions to the catastrophic impact of racism and economic oppression on all people of color in the United States. It is racist America that provides the context for the making of this Black revolutionary.

People struggling for self-determination are a phenomenon of the twentieth century. These struggles are frequently understood and supported by people of goodwill in the United States—when the struggles take place in South Africa, El Salvador, the Philippines, or Palestinian refugee camps. Assata Shakur's own words, as she writes about her struggles for growth and meaning in the streets of New York and in the South as a child and as a woman, present as clear a case for self-determination and development in the United States as do the lives of her brothers and sisters throughout the world. For although her book is intensely personal, it is also absolutely political. She writes about her experiences not as a historical icon seeking to crystallize the "Official Life" but as one whose experiences searching for change can provide a key to her own life and to all those others, who, as she so vividly puts it, "have been locked by the lawless. Handcuffed by the haters. Gagged by the greedy," and for whom "a wall is just a wall and nothing more at all. It can be broken down."

As a lawyer, teacher, and student of history, I know that while Assata's story may be unique in its energy, creativity, and passion for life and principle, it is typical of the ways the United States has responded historically to individuals that the government sees as political threats to domestic tranquility.

Since Assata touches only lightly on the events that led to her being a target for police fire on the New Jersey Turnpike in 1973 and on the flimsy evidence on which she was finally convicted in 1977, I will attempt to sketch some of the details that contributed to the fearsome image generated by the state and perpetrated in the media.

I first met Assata Shakur in 1973, as she lay in the hospital, close to death, handcuffed to her bed, while state, local, and federal police attempted to question her. As the national director of the National Conference of Black Lawyers, an organization that has been called on to defend political activists in the Black community since its founding in 1968, I was no stranger to the carefully orchestrated disinformation campaigns that federal, state, and local law enforcement agencies had engaged in against Black activists under the leadership of the Federal Bureau of Investigation.

Prior to meeting Assata, we had represented Angela Davis, had initiated inquiries into the 1969 police executions of Black Panther leaders Fred Hampton and Mark Clark and the 1971 police attack and indictments of the leadership of the Republic of New Afrika, and had defended many other Black men and women who had been identified as targets of the FBI. The FBI's systematic surveillance of and attacks on Black groups and individuals were orchestrated by its counterintelligence program (COINTELPRO), which was directed specifically against what the FBI termed "Black nationalist hate groups." COINTELPRO's first targets were Martin Luther King and thousands of less prominent civil rights activists. Elsewhere,* I have written extensively about COINTELPRO and the criminal disruption and destruction of Black leaders and groups that were the specific goals of this government program. The pertinent and unimpeachable documents collected in the Church committee report of the Senate Select Committee to Study Governmental Operations with Respect to Intelligence Activities were also reprinted in that book. In addition, the findings of the Domestic Intelligence Subcommittee, headed by Senator Walter Mondale, which were published by the U.S. Government Printing Office in 1976, provided incontrovertible documentation of this government-sponsored conspiracy against the civil and human rights of all sorts of political activists and, most particularly, Black people.

It is important to remember that Assata Shakur's decision to join the Black Panthers occurred soon after J. Edgar Hoover ordered the forty-one FBI offices to intensify their efforts "to expose, disrupt, misdirect, discredit, and otherwise neutralize" Black na-

*Lennox S. Hinds, *Illusions of Justice: Human Rights Violations in the United States*, University of Iowa, 1978.

tionalist organizations and their leaders. The Student Nonviolent Coordinating Committee (SNCC), the Southern Christian Leadership Conference (SCLC), the Nation of Islam, and above all, the Black Panthers were specifically targeted, as were, among many Blacks, Stokely Carmichael, Rap Brown, Elijah Muhammad, Fred Hampton, Mark Clark, and, as we shall see, Assata Shakur, also known as JoAnne Chesimard.

As is now clear,* a carefully orchestrated intelligence and counterintelligence campaign was conducted by the FBI in cooperation with state and local law enforcement agencies designed to criminalize, defame, harass, and intimidate Assata beginning at least in 1971. By the time Assata Shakur was shot and captured on the New Jersey Turnpike on May 2, 1973, she was wanted for a number of most serious crimes.

Massive prejudicial publicity had been generated by the Federal Bureau of Investigation and the New York City Police Department to create an image of dangerousness and to convict her in every aspect of the mass media before any trial. Orders had been issued to apprehend her, dead or alive. She spells out the dread and terror when she writes:

> Everywhere i went it seemed like i would turn around to find two detectives following behind me. I would look out my window and there, in the middle of Harlem, in front of my house, would be two white men sitting and reading the newspaper. I was scared to death to talk in my own house.

Assata could no longer go home. She was on the FBI's Most Wanted list, accused of being armed, of being a bank robber and, subsequently, of being a kidnapper and murderer. A photograph alleged to be Assata Shakur taken at the scene of a bank robbery in August 1971 appeared in a full-page advertisement in the New York *Daily News* on July 10, 1972. It was a duplicate of a poster placed in every bank in the city and state of New York and post offices and subway stations. This advertisement announcing "Wanted for Bank Robbery, $10,000 Reward" was printed above four photographs, one of them the picture of a woman allegedly taken during the 1971 bank robbery. Beneath the picture, in bold capital letters, was the name "JoAnne Deborah Chesimard."

During her trial for this bank robbery, which ended in acquittal, a jury found that it was not a picture of Assata Shakur (JoAnne

*The information presented here is based on federal and state court records and files, FBI memoranda, secret service files, police records, and information in the media.

Chesimard). The photograph had been released by the FBI and the U.S. Attorney's office to the New York Clearing House Association (a bank's association), which placed the ad and posters. Even after Assata had been acquitted of this bank robbery in January 1976, another advertisement offering the same reward for unapprehended bank robbers appeared in the *Daily News* in March 1976. This time, however, the photograph was a recognizable mug shot of Assata, with the word "APPREHENDED" across her face. This poster appeared two months after her acquittal on the August 1971 charge, two years after her acquittal on the September 1972 bank robbery charge, and while no bank robbery charges were outstanding against her.

On February 12, 1973, four months before Assata was apprehended on the New Jersey Turnpike, *New York* magazine published an article under the title "Target Blue," written by Robert Daley, an excerpt of this book of the same title. The cover of the magazine depicted a uniformed police officer. The subtitle was "The Story Behind the Police Assassinations." The article purported to provide intimate details about the Black Liberation Army, whose activities, the article claimed, were cop killing, bank robbing, and efforts to overthrow the U.S. Government. Above a picture of Assata Shakur were the words "Gunmen of the Black Liberation Army," and she was described by former Deputy Police Commissioner Daley as the "mother hen who kept them together, kept them moving, kept them shooting." Notwithstanding this trial by media, the only indictment against Assata for killing a police officer was dismissed in October 1974 for lack of evidence.

As the chart that follows this essay shows, on May 2, 1973, when the shooting on the New Jersey Turnpike occurred, Assata was "wanted" for all these crimes. The irony is that not one of the charges led to conviction. When she was apprehended, shot down on the New Jersey Turnpike, leading to her only conviction, she should have enjoyed the presumption of innocence that the Fifth Amendment to the U.S. Constitution is supposed to grant to any of us when accused.

On May 2, 1973, Assata, Sundiata Acoli, and Zayd Malik Shakur were traveling south on the New Jersey Turnpike in a white Pontiac. They were stopped by New Jersey state trooper James Harper for reasons consistent with the FBI COINTELPRO guidelines, which directed that activists be arrested for minor traffic violations. The Pontiac allegedly had defective taillights. Harper's testimony, however, leaves open the suggestion that the Pontiac was simply a target.

Harper testified that when he first saw the Pontiac he was two miles north of the turnpike administration building, headquarters for the troopers. He followed the car for two miles until it was close to the administration building before he pulled it over because "the light was better and there was more security." The Pontiac was traveling at normal speed in the center lane. Harper first passed it in the left lane, observed the driver, and "made a mental note of his description." He then moved to the right lane and let the Pontiac pass him, at which time he "made a mental note of the sex and race of the passengers." He then approached the Pontiac in the left lane, motioned the driver (Sundiata) to pull over, and called the administration building for assistance. When trooper Robert Palenchar was directed to assist Harper, he commented over his radio, "Meet you at the pass, partner," and sped to the administration building at 120 miles an hour. Trooper Werner Foerster also went to assist in this "stop" for which, Harper testified, only a summons would have been issued.

Over the years, I was to learn much about the selective, arbitrary, and ferocious ways the law and its processes would be applied against Assata Shakur from the moment I met her in that hospital in May 1973 where she clung to life.

I can certainly not improve on Assata's account of her experiences before, during, and after her numerous trials, but I must point out that she *understates* the awfulness of the conditions in which she was incarcerated. As she mentions, even a hearing officer appointed by Middlesex County, at the instruction of one of the federal judges before whom we argued our suits on the inhumanity of the conditions in which she was held, found the conditions shocking.

In the history of New Jersey, no woman pretrial detainee or prisoner has ever been treated as she was, continuously confined in a men's prison, under twenty-four–hour surveillance of her most intimate functions, without intellectual sustenance, adequate medical attention, and exercise, and without the company of other women for all the years she was in their custody. We filed one civil rights lawsuit after another complaining of the barbarous treatment selectively meted out to her, with limited success. As you read her story, imagine the effect these conditions must have had on this proud and sensitive woman.

Another bitter irony of her situation is that during the course of those years awaiting trial in New Jersey, the many other charges that caused her to become a fugitive, leading to the shootout on the New Jersey Turnpike, were dropped for lack of evidence, were dismissed, or resulted in acquittal, and yet the physical conditions under which she was held worsened, at best. Once again, the manipulation of facts by the media became a substitute for reality—none of the acquittals or dismissals was publicized. The massive security precautions for the pending New Jersey trial were the major stories on the front pages of the local newspapers, day after day, in the community from which the jury was selected.

The sheer number of these baseless charges supports the contention held by many people that the extraordinary efforts of the state of New Jersey to get Assata Shakur convicted, notwithstanding the flimsy evidence, were undertaken to justify the fabricated image of mad-dog killer that had failed, so humiliatingly, to get her convicted in New York state and federal courts.

Assata was convicted in New Jersey as an accomplice to the murder of state trooper Werner Foerster and of atrocious assault on James Harper with the intent to kill. Under New Jersey law, if a person's presence at the scene of a crime can be construed as "aiding and abetting" the crime, that person can be convicted of the substantive crime itself. The state of New Jersey convicted Sundiata Acoli for these same murders after Assata was severed from the proceedings because of her pregnancy. The jury at Assata's trial for the same offenses was permitted to speculate that her "mere presence" at a scene of violence, with weapons in the vehicle, was sufficient to sustain a conviction—even though three neurologists testified at the trial that her median nerve had been severed by gunshot wounds, rendering her unable to pull a trigger, and that her clavicle had been shattered by a shot that could only have been made while she was seated in the car with her hands raised. Other experts testified that the neutron activation analysis administered by the police right after the shootout showed no gun residue on her fingers, meaning she had not shot a weapon. She was also convicted of possession of weapons—none of which could be identified as having been handled by her—and of the attempted murder of state trooper Harper, who had sustained a minor injury at the shootout.

It had been and is my view that it was the racism in Middlesex County, fueled by biased, inflammatory publicity in the local press before and throughout the trial, fanned by the documented government lawlessness, that made it possible for the white jury to convict Assata on the uncorroborated, contradictory, and generally incredible testimony of trooper Harper, the only other witness to the events on the turnpike. Harper's testimony as well as that of all the other state's witnesses was riddled with inconsistencies and discrepancies. On three separate official reports, including his grand jury testimony, Harper said that he saw Assata take a gun from her pocketbook, while in the car, and shoot him. He admitted, on cross-examination during both Sundiata's trial and Assata's trial, that he never saw Assata with a gun and did not see her shoot him—that, in fact, he had lied.

In addition, the judge refused to permit the defense to present any testimony on COINTELPRO. The truth is very simple. Assata Shakur did not receive a fair trial in Middlesex County, New Jersey. She had been convicted in the press and in the minds of the general public from the moment she was apprehended in New Jersey and over and over again until the trial. The conviction in court was but a formality.

Dear Sister, thank you for sending us your vital voice and sharing your passion and commitment with us. Meanwhile, we in this society must remind ourselves again how we threaten our own interests and rights when we condone by our silence the government's use of surveillance, attacks on the legitimacy of political activists, and the use of the criminal law to suppress and punish political dissent.

In 1975, Attorney General Edward H. Levi, under the direction of President Carter and in consideration of the Church committee's findings, designed the first set of guidelines to keep the FBI within the Constitution in its investigations of individuals and groups allegedly dangerous to national security. The Levi guidelines, while not heartily applauded by civil libertarians, did attempt to restrain the unbridled use of the government's power to penetrate and disrupt organizations.

By 1983, Attorney General William French Smith, under President Reagan, had rescinded the Levi guidelines, and each year since then protections of the Bill of Rights have been further eroded. For example, the FBI is now free to investigate persons or groups accused of *advocating* criminal activity. Clearly, the federal government is continuing the unrestrained abuse of power by which it attempted to destroy Assata Shakur and other Black individuals and groups by surveillance, rumor, innuendo, eavesdropping, arrest and prosecution, incarceration, and murder throughout the sixties and seventies.

As long as members of Congress, still intimidated by ABSCAM, are afraid to antagonize the FBI, and as long as FBI guidelines are drafted internally by the FBI and as long as the Justice Department is subject to the political imperatives of the President, monitored only within the system but without public accountability, we are all in danger of the kinds of repression and government secrecy that victimized Martin Luther King, Malcolm X, Viola Liuzzo, Medgar Evers, Fred Hampton, Obadele Imari, Assata Shakur, and many other brothers and sisters whose ideas and advocacy are threatening to the administration. We are all potential victims.

I encourage you now to enter the heart and soul of Assata Shakur who, despite all that has happened to her, preserves fresh idealism and confidence in the power of principled people to make change together for the common good of the peoples of the world.

LENNOX S. HINDS
New York City

TRIAL CHRONOLOGY

DATE OF ALLEGED CRIME AND CHARGE	*JURISDICTION STATE-FEDERAL*	*DATE OF ARRAIGNMENT*	*TRIAL DATE*	*DISPOSITION*
April 5, 1971 Armed robbery Hilton Hotel New York City	N.Y. State Supreme Court County of New York	Nov. 22, 1977	No trial	Dismissed
Aug. 23, 1971 Bank robbery Queens	U.S. Eastern District Brooklyn	July 20, 1973	Jan. 5, 1976 to Jan. 16, 1976	Acquittal
Sept. 1, 1972 Bank robbery Bronx	U.S. Southern District New York City	Aug. 1, 1973	Dec. 3, 1973 to Dec. 14, 1973	Hung jury
			Dec. 19, 1973 to Dec. 28, 1973	Acquittal
Dec. 28, 1972 Kidnap of drug dealer	N.Y. State Supreme Court County of Kings	May 30, 1974	Sept. 6, 1975 to Dec. 19, 1975	Acquittal
Jan. 2, 1973 Murder of drug dealer	N.Y. State Supreme Court County of Kings	May 29, 1974	No trial	Dismissed
Jan. 23, 1973 Attempted murder of policemen (ambush)	N.Y. State Supreme Court County of Queens	May 11, 1974	No trial	Dismissed
May 2, 1973 Murder of state troopers New Jersey Turnpike	Superior Court Middlesex County	May 3, 1973	Oct. 9, 1973 to Oct. 23, 1973	Change of venue
		Jan. 1, 1974 to Feb. 1, 1974	Mistrial because of Assata's pregnancy	
		Jan. 15, 1977 to March 25, 1977	Convicted	

Affirmation

I believe in living.
I believe in the spectrum
of Beta days and Gamma people.
I believe in sunshine.
In windmills and waterfalls,
tricycles and rocking chairs.
And i believe that seeds grow into sprouts.
And sprouts grow into trees.
I believe in the magic of the hands.
And in the wisdom of the eyes.
I believe in rain and tears.
And in the blood of infinity.

I believe in life.
And i have seen the death parade
march through the torso of the earth,
sculpting mud bodies in its path.
I have seen the destruction of the daylight,
and seen bloodthirsty maggots
prayed to and saluted.

I have seen the kind become the blind
and the blind become the bind
in one easy lesson.
I have walked on cut glass.
I have eaten crow and blunder bread
and breathed the stench of indifference.

I have been locked by the lawless.
Handcuffed by the haters.
Gagged by the greedy.
And, if i know any thing at all,
it's that a wall is just a wall
and nothing more at all.
It can be broken down.

I believe in living.
I believe in birth.
I believe in the sweat of love
and in the fire of truth.

And i believe that a lost ship,
steered by tired, seasick sailors,
can still be guided home
to port.

Chapter 1

There were lights and sirens. Zayd was dead. My mind knew that Zayd was dead. The air was like cold glass. Huge bubbles rose and burst. Each one felt like an explosion in my chest. My mouth tasted like blood and dirt. The car spun around me and then something like sleep overtook me. In the background i could hear what sounded like gunfire. But i was fading and dreaming.

Suddenly, the door flew open and i felt myself being dragged out onto the pavement. Pushed and punched, a foot upside my head, a kick in the stomach. Police were everywhere. One had a gun to my head.

"Which way did they go?" he was shouting. "Bitch, you'd better open your goddamn mouth or I'll blow your goddamn head off!"

I nodded my head across the highway. I was sure that nobody had gone that way. A few of the cops were off and running.

One pig said, "We oughta finish her off." But the others were all busy around the car, searching it. They were pulling and prodding.

"Ya find the gun?" they kept asking each other. Later, one of them asked another, "Should we put'er in the car?"

"Naw. Let'er lay in the gutter where she belongs. Just get'er out of the way."

I felt myself being dragged by the feet across the pavement. My chest was on fire. My blouse was purple with blood. I was convinced that my arm had been shot off and was hanging inside my shirt by a few strips of flesh. I could not feel it.

Finally the ambulance came and they moved me into it. Being moved was agony, but the blankets were worth it. I was so cold. The medics examined me. I tried to talk, but only bubbles came out. I was foaming at the mouth.

"Where's she hit?" they asked each other as if i wasn't there. They concluded their examination. I was relieved.

"Let's move it," one of them said.

"O.K., but wait a minute," said the driver and he got out. "Hit twice," i heard him say. "We gotta wait." The driver slammed the door.

He said something else but i didn't understand it. Time passed. I was floating off again. It felt so weird, like a dream, a nightmare. More time passed. It seemed like forever. I was in and out, in and out.

A rough voice asked, "Is she dead yet?" I floated off again. I heard another voice. "Is she dead yet?" I wondered how long the ambulance had been sitting there. The attendants looked nervous. The bubbles in my chest felt like they were growing bigger. When they burst, my whole chest shattered. I faded again and it was down South in the summertime. I thought about my grandmother. At last the ambulance was moving. "If i live," i remember thinking, "i'll only have one arm."

The hospital is glaring white. Everybody i see is white. Everyone seems to be waiting. All at once they are in motion. Blood pressure, pulse, needles, etc. Two detectives come in. I know they're detectives because they look like detectives. One of them has a face like a bulldog, with jowls hanging down the sides. They supervise the nurse as she cuts off my clothes. After a while, one of them dabs my fingertips with what look like Q-tips. Later i find out that this is the neutron activation test to determine whether or not i have fired a weapon. Another one then tries to fingerprint me, but he has trouble because my hand is dead.

"Gimme the dead man's kit." He puts my fingers into spoon-looking things used to fingerprint dead people. They begin to ask me questions, but a bunch of doctors come in. One of them, who appears to be the head doctor, examines me. He pokes and prods, throwing me around like a rag doll. then, like he is going to kill me, he jerks me around so that i'm on my stomach. The pain is like an electric shock. I moan.

"Don't cry now, girlie," he says. "Why'd you shoot the trooper? Why'd you shoot the trooper?"

I want to kick him in his face. I know he would kill me if he had the chance. I can see the scalpel slipping. One of the other doctors says something about calling the operating room. "Hell no!" is all i can think of. "Hell no!"

After a while, they all leave. Then a Black nurse comes into the room. I am glad as I could be to see her. She bends over me.

"What is your name?" she asks. "What is your name?"

I think about it and decide to say nothing. If i tell them my name they will know who i am and they will kill me for sure.

"What is your name?" she keeps asking, enunciating each syllable in the way that people talk to someone who has trouble hearing or understanding. "What is your name? What is your address? Where do you live?" Her voice is getting louder. "We need your signature, miss," she says, waving a piece of paper in front of me. "We need your permission for treatment, in case we have to operate." She repeats the same thing, over and over. "Who shall we contact in case of emergency?" (I think that's kind of funny.) "What is your name? Where do you live?" I close my eyes, wishing she would go away. She keeps right on talking.

I drift off, thinking about my arm. It is still there.

"Nerve damage. Paralyzed," i heard them say. It has never occurred to me. It isn't that bad, i remember thinking. I can live with that if i have to.

More voices, other voices, grating my ears and my consciousness.

"She can talk," one is saying. "The doctor says she can talk. Where were you going? What is your name? Where were you coming from? Who was in the car with you? How many of you were there? I know she can hear me."

I keep my eyes closed. One of them leans down real close to me. I feel his breath on my cheek. And smell it.

"I know you can hear me and I know you can talk, and if you don't hurry up and start talking, I'm gonna bash your face in for you."

My eyes fly open in spite of myself. Immediately they are all in my face, throwing question after question at me. I say nothing. After a while, i close my eyes again.

"Oh, she doesn't feel good," one of them says in a sweet, mocking voice. "Where does it hurt? Here? Here? HERE?"

With each *here* comes a crash. I look around wildly, but no one is there. More thumps and punches, but none of them hurts as bad as my chest is hurting. I try to scream but i know immediately that that's a mistake. My chest erupts and i think i am gonna die. They go on and on. Questions and bangs. I think they will never stop.

A woman's voice. "Telephone."

"Thank you," one of them says, giving me an ugly grin. They are gone.

Another pig comes in. A Black pig. In uniform. He comes closer and i see that he is not a cop but a hospital security guard. He stands not too far from where i am lying and i can see he is not at all hostile. His face breaks into a kind of reserved smile and, very discreetly, he clenches his fist and gives me the power sign. That man will never know how much better he made me feel at that moment.

The detectives come back with a nurse. They begin to move the stretcher. My mind races. Where are they taking me? The only place i can think of is the operating room. When we arrive at the X-ray room, i'm thankful. Because i have to move around, the X-rays are painful, but the technician is cool. X-rays are over and i am rolled down the hallway, determined to keep my eyes closed. All of a sudden, flashes of light. My eyes pop open. This time they are taking my picture.

The police photographer asks, "Don't you wanna give us a smile? Come on. Give us a smile."

I close my eyes again. We are moving. The stretcher stops. One of the pigs tells the nurse he has a headache. She volunteers to get him something.

The stretcher is moving again. Where the hell are they taking me? Again the light is changing and, although my eyes are closed, i can feel the difference. It feels like i'm in the dark. I can't take it any longer and i look. The room is dark, but there is some light. My eyes slowly adjust. There's something lying next to me. I can see an outline. Something in plastic. Something—my mind slowly realizes that it is a man in a plastic bag. And that the man is Zayd. My body stiffens. My mind spins.

One of the troopers says, "That's what's gonna happen to you before the night is over if you don't tell us what we want to know."

I say nothing, but inside i'm raging. "Dogs! Swine! Filthy pigs! Dirty slimy scum! Bastards! Sons of bitches!" I rage on and on. "I wouldn't tell you the right time of day," i remember thinking. "I wouldn't tell you that shit stinks!"

The night crawls along. Nurses, doctors, and troopers. I am still scared, but i am just as angry and evil as i am scared. The detectives are in and out and, when nobody is there except them, they get in their digs and bangs. But after a while i don't think about them too much. I am thinking about living, about surviving, thinking about what is going to happen next. They are gonna do what they are gonna do and there isn't much i can do about it. I just have to be myself, stay as strong as i can, and do my best. That's all. There is nowhere to run and i am in no shape to try. I realize how isolated and vulnerable i am. What if i really do need an operation? I need help from the outside world. I have to try to get word out to someone. The Black nurse has been back and forth, asking me the same questions. Each time i have closed my eyes until she goes away. I decide to ask her to get in touch with my people the next time she comes by. Maybe she will be cool. She is my best shot; the guard is long gone.

I doze off for a little while. When i wake up, a nurse and a priest are standing over me. The priest is mumbling and seems to be rubbing something on my forehead. At first i don't understand what he is doing. Then it dawns on me. Last rites. Last rites are for the dying.

"Go away," i say out loud. I don't have the strength to say anything else. But i know i don't want anybody's last rites. I am not going to die, and even if i do die, i'm not going to die nobody's hypocrite.

The Black nurse comes back and starts her questions again. Before she can get started good, i beckon her to come closer. There is no one else around. I ask her to get in contact with my lawyer (who is also my aunt). I give her my name and ask her to make the call herself. She has a hard time understanding me and keeps asking me to repeat my name. I can barely talk, and each time she asks me to repeat myself, i feel like screaming. Then it occurs to me that Assata is foreign to her ears. She has probably never heard the name before. So i give her my slave name. Then i give her the number and she is off and running.

Two minutes later the detectives are on me like white on rice. They threaten and plead, reason and offer me the world. They hurl question after question at me, acting crazier than before. One plays the nice cop who is trying to save me from the bad cop, if only i will cooperate. I am tired and their act is even tireder. I can see exhaustion in their faces. The whole night is coming down on me. Their voices begin to sound far away. I can't take it anymore. They can go to hell. I am going to sleep. This time i am going out for real.

When i wake up the stretcher is moving. After a little while we arrive at the intensive care part of the hospital. The place is packed with nurses. I am elated. All i want to do is sleep. Soon i'm drifting off again.

I wake up and it's the next day. The doctors are making their rounds. One of them, an intern i think, is very kind to me. They examine me and spend the rest of the morning doing blood tests, X-rays, EKGs, etc., etc.

Soon i learn that they're going to move me again. I also find out that i'm in middlesex county hospital. I hear the nurses talking. They are glad i am being moved because the police are driving them crazy.

When they come to move me it looks like a police parade. The rooms i am moved to are called the Johnson Suite. I can't believe it. I have never imagined that hospitals have rooms like this. There is a sitting room, a huge hospital-equipped room (where i am kept), a den, a kitchen, a full bathroom and another little room whose purpose i will never learn. They transfer me to the bed and handcuff one of my legs to the side rail.

I keep looking around. It is elegant and clearly for rich people. I am probably the first Black person who has ever been in this room. And the only reason i am there is for security. They have sealed off the doors and no one can enter except through the sitting room next door where three state troopers are stationed. Two regulars and one sergeant.

The police radio in the room cackles all day long. "A carload of suspicious-looking coloreds in a white Ford coupe." "A suspicious-looking Negro walking near the hospital in a blue jacket and sneakers." No suspicious-looking white people are reported. From listening to the police talk next door, and to the radio, i learn that the hospital is saturated with state troopers. They seem to be under the impression that somebody is going to try and break me out. I feel better. The Demerol has me flying a little and makes it easier for me to lie in the contorted position i am forced into because of the cuff on my leg.

Later that afternoon, it begins again. Detectives and more detectives. Questions and more questions. This time the questions are different. Now they want to know about the Black Liberation Army: how big is it; what cities is it in; who is in it, etc., etc. But the main focus of their questions centers around "the guy that got away." I am delighted! I figure that Sundiata is somewhere safe by now, cooling out.

They are more careful where and how they hit me now. I guess they don't want to leave any marks. One sticks his fingers in my eyes. I don't know what he has on his fingertips, but whatever it is burns like hell. I think I am gonna be blind forever. He says he will keep doing it until i am completely blind. I close my eyes and hold them as tight as i can. He strikes me a few more times. Some of the stuff gets into my eyes anyway. Burning tears pour down my face and my whole head is throbbing. I think he is going to keep on, but he begins to curse me, calling me all kind of nigger bitches. Finally, he and the others leave.

On one of those first days, a white doctor comes to examine me. He acts very nice, sweet as pie. He examines me slowly, the whole time making friendly conversation. I wonder what kind of specialist he is since i haven't seen him before and i know he isn't one of the regulars. He says he knows how terrible i must feel and makes a big deal of protesting that i am chained to the bed. He keeps on talking and, after a while, pulls a chair close to the bed. Then he starts to ask friendly little questions. The conversation goes something like this:

"Those guys on the turnpike are rough. They'll give you a ticket for anything. I take the turnpike every day. You live in jersey? I live in Newark. You ever been there? You must really be lonely up here. I'll bet you really need someone to talk to. I went to medical school in New York. You're from there, aren't you?"

I get suspicious and say nothing to him. I tell him i want to go to sleep and he leaves. I never saw him again, but to this day i'm convinced he was some kind of police or FBI agent.

On the third or fourth day, most of my troubles came to an end. Well, not really, but the punch, bang, poke, and prod part of my troubles ended. A nurse with a German accent came to my aid. She was one of the morning nurses, very professional and exacting, to the point that she could be a pain in the neck. But she was a lifesaver. It was she who had first protested the tightness of the handcuff on my leg. My leg had begun to swell and she had insisted they loosen it and that the cuff be covered with gauze. Of course, as soon as she was gone they tightened it again, but the gauze helped somewhat. I could tell by the little things she said and did that she knew what was going on. One morning she came in as usual and, after she had finished her normal routine, she reached behind the bed, pulled at something, and then handed me an electric call button on a cord.

"Anytime you need me or need anything from the nurses, just press this button," she said. "Don't be afraid to use it," she added, giving me a knowing look.

I could have kissed her. Later, when she returned to the room, after the troopers realized i had the call button, one came in behind her.

"Is there any way to disconnect that thing?" he asked. "She might hurt someone with it or hurt herself."

"No," she said, "there is no way to remove it. If you pull it out, it will just keep ringing in the nurses' station. She is having difficulty breathing and she needs it."

"Right on!" i thought. "Das ist richtig."

After that, whenever the police came within two feet of my bed, i would push the button. Finally, they gave up the idea of beating on me and contented themselves with threats and other kinds of harassment. A favorite was to stand in the door and point their guns at me. Each day was my last day on earth. Each night was my last night. After a while, i became accustomed. Immune. Sometimes they would cock a gun i didn't know was empty, give a long, impassioned speech, and then pull the trigger. Other times i was invited to a game of Russian roulette. they all expressed a bitter hatred for me. They were state troopers and i was accused of killing one of them.

Every day there were three shifts of police. When they changed shifts, the two troopers would salute the sergeant. Some saluted an army salute, but others saluted like the nazis did in Germany. They held their hands in front of them and clicked their heels. I couldn't believe it. One day one of them came in and gave me a speech about how he fought in World War II on the wrong side. He went on and on and there was no question that he believed everything he said. He talked about how messed up the world is. How decent people couldn't walk the streets. He said that if Hitler had won, the world wouldn't be in the mess it is in today, that niggers like me, no-good niggers, wouldn't be going around shooting new jersey state troopers.

He went on to say that the white race had invented everything because they were smart and worked hard, that other races wanted to riot and use terrorism to take everything the white race had worked so hard to get. I had a hard time keeping my mouth shut. He talked about empires, the Roman, the Greek, the Spanish, the British. He told me white people created empires because they were more civilized than the rest of the world. White people created ballet and opera and symphonies. "Did you ever hear of a nigger writing a symphony?" he asked. Every day he gave me a speech about nazism. Sometimes other nazis would join in. I asked him if there were a lot of nazis in the state troopers, but he just laughed and kept on talking.

When i was in the Black Panther Party, we used to call the police "fascist pigs," but i had called them fascists not because i believed they were nazis but because of the way they acted in our communities. As many times as i had referred to police as fascists, these shocked me by the truth of my own rhetoric. I later learned that the state troopers in new jersey was started by a German, that their uniforms were patterned after some type of German uniform (very similar to the uniforms South African police wear), that they are notorious for stopping Black, Hispanic, and long-haired people on the turnpike and beating, harassing, and arresting them.

The nazis headed the harassment campaign against me. They spit in my food and turned down the thermostat in the room until it was freezing. For a while their campaign centered on keeping me from sleeping. They stamped their feet on the floor, sang songs all night, played with their guns, shouted, etc. I told the nurses about it, but it was no use.

I could deal with whatever they were putting out, but how long would this go on? I had heard nothing from the outside world, and i didn't even know if anybody knew where i was or whether i was dead or alive. My chest was feeling better, but i still could hardly breathe. I thought i was past the point of needing an operation, but i wasn't sure if it was because of the painkillers they had given me or because i was really getting better.

Every day i asked them to contact my lawyer, and every day they said they had tried but there was no answer. I knew that was a lie because Evelyn had an answering service. Every day i asked them to contact my family. The response to this was usually obscene.

"Oh, you got a family, do you? Is your mother a nigger whore like you? We don't allow no pickaninnies at this hospital."

They went on and on about my family until they found something else to go on and on about. Whoever said that no news is good news had to be out of his mind.

Well, there was news, but it wasn't good news. They told me they had arrested Sundiata. At first i didn't believe them, but they were too glib and arrogant. I knew something had happened.

"We got your friend," they said, "and he's singing like a bird. Yeah, he's singing like a bird, and he's giving you all the weight. It's a good thing for you he didn't know what color undies you had on or he would have told us that. We know where you were coming from. We know where you were going. We know that you stopped at a Howard Johnson. He even told us what you ordered and that you just love potato chips."

"What?" i thought. "How did they know that?" Then i remembered that we had bought potato chips at a Howard Johnson on the turnpike. Maybe someone had seen me and remembered.

"Yes, Clark Squire tells us that you took the trooper's gun and shot him in the head. Now, you wouldn't do a thing like that, would you? Well, JoAnne, you're in a hell of a fix. If I were you, I wouldn't let him get away with it. It's a low-down thing to do, giving all the weight to a woman. I'll make a deal with you. You tell us everything that happened and I promise we'll go light on you. I just don't like to see you get a bad break, that's all. You know, you're facing a lot of time in prison, the way things stand, if he testifies against you. You could get life in prison or even the chair, but all you have to do is tell us what happened and we'll see to it that you do just a couple of years and go home. You're young. You don't want to rot away your whole life in prison, do you? Maybe you think you owe something to the cause. You think he's thinking about the cause now? No, he's singing his head off, trying to give you all the weight. They're all the same. They talk all this shit about Black people, equal rights, civil rights, but when it comes down to the wire, all they care about is their hide. He's thinking about his hide and you better think about yours. You think the cause gives a damn about you? Your own people don't give a damn about you. To them you're just a common criminal. Now I'm giving you this one chance to save yourself and come clean. If you don't take it, you're a fool."

They really did think Black people were stupid. Their line had to be the oldest in the book. He was sitting there like he just knew his corny little speech had done the trick. I said nothing. If you don't say anything to them, they have nothing to turn around and use against you. "Divide and conquer" has always been their motto.

When they realized i wasn't going to talk, they began to leave. Then one came back. "Oh," he said, "I almost forgot to read you your rights." He pulled out this little card and read from it. " 'You have the right to remain silent. . . . You have the right to . . . etc.' I wouldn't want you to say that we didn't read you your rights."

Thursday afternoon. They're letting me make a phone call. I don't believe it. I call my aunt. She's not in. The answering service answers. I don't know who else to call. The only lawyers whose names i know worked on the Panther 21 trial. I call them at random. No one is in, but secretaries promise to give them messages. I'm disappointed but i feel a lot better. Things are looking up.

It is Friday. From the activity in the room next door, i can tell something is up. Voices and whispers. They are back and forth, in and out, arranging this, moving that. The police radio is jumping. What is happening? Whatever it is, it can't be too bad, i think. They are leaving me alone. In a little while a policewoman comes in. She is in a brown uniform and her insignia says "Sheriff's Department."

She's Black or Hispanic. I can't tell exactly, except that she isn't white. Then some more police come in, dressed in uniforms similar to hers. Then more police. They are state troopers. One of them moves to the door and stands at attention. Then some men in suits come in. Then a man comes in with a stenographic machine.

"The Honorable Joseph F. Bradshaw, State of New Jersey, County of Middlesex. All rise."

Then this judge walks in with a black robe on. One of the men in a suit reads the charges against me:

> We are here today to serve complaints upon you for the matters arising out of the shooting of May 2 of 1973. I will read you the complaints, leave copies with you of the charges that will be pending against you. The Judge will then advise you on the arraignment of such rights you may have. . . .
>
> . . . you are charged under Complaint Number 119977, by Detective Taranto, New Jersey State Police, who says on the 2nd of May, 1973, within the confines of the Township of East Brunswick, County of Middlesex, that you unlawfully and illegally resisted a lawful arrest being made by New Jersey State Trooper James Harper by discharging a dangerous pistol and wounding the said James Harper and fleeing the scene of the incident, all in violation of N.J.S. 2A:85-1. . . .
>
> You are also charged, . . . under complaint Number S 119979, by Detective Sergeant Taranto of the New Jersey State Police, who says that on the 2nd of May, 1973, within the Township of East Brunswick, County of Middlesex, that you did commit an Atrocious Assault and Battery upon New Jersey State Trooper James Harper by shooting, wounding and maiming the said James Harper with a hand gun then and there discharged by the defendant, all in violation of N.J.S. 2A:90-1.
>
> In the Second Count you are charged by the said officer who says that defendant Joanne Deborah Chesimard did on the aforementioned date and place unlawfully and illegally assault the said James Harper with intent to kill, murder and slay him by use of a hand gun then and there held by the defendant, all in violation of N.J.S. 2A:90-2.
>
> It further charges in the Third Count that the aforementioned defendant did at the above mentioned time and place commit an unlawful and illegal assault and battery on a law enforcement officer, to wit, one James Harper, a duly sworn Trooper of the New Jersey State Police, by discharging a firearm and wounding the said James Harper, all in violation of N.J.S. 2A:90-4. . . .
>
> In S 119980 you are charged with illegally and unlawfully committing the crime of murder by willfully and with malice

aforethought shooting, killing and slaying New Jersey State Trooper Werner Foerster, all in violation of N.J.S. 2A:113-1 and N.J.S. 2A:85-14. . . .

You are further being charged under S 119981 with one count, wherein Detective Sergeant Taranto charges you on the 2nd day of May, 1973, within the Township of East Brunswick, County of Middlesex, that you did unlawfully, illegally and with malice aforethought cause or affect the murder of James Coston a/k/a Zayd Shakur, while resisting or avoiding a lawful arrest then and there being affected by New Jersey State Trooper James Harper, all in violation of N.J.S. 2A:113-2. . . .

You are charged with S 119982 by State Police Sergeant Louis Taranto, that on the 2nd day of May, 1973, in the Township of East Brunswick, County of Middlesex, you unlawfully and illegally possessed on your person, under your custody and control, an illegal weapon, to wit, one Browning 9 milimeter automatic pistol, one Browning automatic .380 caliber, one .38 caliber Llama automatic pistol, serial number 24831, all without having obtained any necessary permit for the carrying of same, in violation of N.J.S. 2A:151-41 (a). . . .

You are further charged in Complaint S 119983, wherein Detective Sergeant Taranto says on the 2nd day of May, 1973, in the Township of East Brunswick, County of Middlesex, that you did unlawfully and illegally and forcibly take from the person of New Jersey State Trooper Werner Foerster a .38 caliber revolver by violence,to wit, by shooting, slaying and killing the same Werner Foerster, all in violation of N.J.S. 2A:141-1.

The Second Count of that Complaint charges you with committing that act while being armed, in violation of N.J.S. 2A:151-5. . . .

. . . you are being charged by State Trooper Detective Sergeant Taranto, Complaint S 119984, who says on the 2nd day of May, 1973, in the Township of East Brunswick, County of Middlesex, that you did illegally, unlawfully conspire with James Coston, a/k/a Zayd Shakur and one John Doe to commit the crime of murder of the said Trooper Werner Foerster, and in the affectuation of said conspiracy did execute the following overt acts:

1. That the said defendant Joanne Deborah Chesimard did have in her possession a pistol with which to affectuate the ends of the conspiracy on the above-mentioned time and . . . at the above-mentioned place.

2. The above named defendant Joanne Deborah Chesimard in concert with and by common scheme and plan did assault Trooper James Harper and otherwise discharge her weapon at the said Trooper James Harper with the intent to affect the ends of the

conspiracy by otherwise wounding, maiming or killing him, all in violation of N.J.S. 2A:98-1 and N.J.S. 2A:113-1.

I think he will never stop. Half of the charges i don't even understand. I interrupt the proceedings. "I don't have a lawyer here," i protest. "I would like to have a lawyer present." They ignore me and keep on reading.

"How do you plead?" they ask me.

"I would like to have a lawyer present. Don't i have a right to a lawyer?"

"That will not be necessary," the judge says coldly. "Enter a plea of not guilty for the defendant."

And just as quickly as they entered, the procession departs.

Later the same policewoman comes back. She stands rigidly against the wall. Her face is a mask. "Oh, no!" i think. "Court again? What are they gonna do, railroad me here and now?" I imagine myself being tried right there in the bed with no lawyer.

The door opens. It is Evelyn—my lawyer and aunt. She is the most beautiful sight in the world. She embraces me and sits down next to me. As usual, she is business first.

"I only have five minutes," she tells me. "They told me that I couldn't see you. I had to go to court and get a court order to see you. The judge would give us only five minutes apiece. Your mother and sister are outside. So talk fast."

We look up. The police are practically standing in our mouths.

"I would like to talk with my client in private," Evelyn says. "Would you please move back. This is an outrage. This is an attorney-client visit and we have a constitutional right to privacy."

The police move back one inch. I tell Evelyn about the kangaroo court in the morning. My mouth moves so fast it's like one of those old-style movies, but a talkie. I can see from the expression on her face that i must look horrible.

"How are they treating you?" she asks.

I don't have time to tell her the whole story, but i have to let her know what is going on. I don't know what they will do next. I have to try to get someone to put pressure on them to stop. I tell her some of it, but i just can't tell her the worst things. Her face looks so pitiful and every time i tell her something else, her hands shake.

"Try to do what you can," i say.

"Time's up. Time's up, miss!"

Evelyn makes her futile protests. "I need to talk with my client. This is just not enough time."

"Sorry, miss. Time's up!" They move toward her like they are going to beat her up.

Then she is gone. I brace myself for my mother and my sister. It has been such a long time since i have seen them. I don't know what to expect.

My mother comes in. She looks worried but strong. She kisses me.

"I'm proud of you," she says.

The words spin around me, weaving a warm blanket of love. I am so happy. I can hardly contain myself. My mother is proud of me. She loves me and she is proud of me.

Too soon the time with my mother is up. My sister comes in. She has her hair wrapped in a turban and she looks so pale. As soon as she sees me, she breaks out crying. Tears stream down her already puffy face. I can tell she has been crying a lot.

"I love you," she says simply.

We don't do a lot of talking, but i feel so very close to her during those few minutes.

"Time's up." Again. And then she is gone.

I lie there full of emotion. All of this is so hard on my family. They look vulnerable and shaken. This is maybe harder on them than it is on me. I wish there was something i can do to make them happy.

Two Black nurses were very kind to me. When they were on duty, they would go out of their way to make sure i was all right. They made frequent trips to my room, for which i was especially grateful during those first days.

"If you need anything, just ring," they said knowingly.

One night one of the nurses came in and gave me three books. I hadn't even thought about reading. The books were a godsend. They had been carefully selected. One was a book of Black poetry, one was a book called *Black Women in White Amerika,* and the third was a novel, *Siddhartha,* by Hermann Hesse. Whenever i tired of the verbal abuse of my captors, i would drown them out by reading the poetry out loud. "Invictus" and "If We Must Die" were the poems i usually read. I read them over and over, until i was sure the guards had heard every word. The poems were my message to them.

When i read the book about Black women, i felt the spirits of those sisters feeding me, making me stronger. Black women have been struggling and helping each other to survive the blows of life since the beginning of time. And when i read *Siddhartha,* a peace came over me. I felt a unity with all things living. The world, in spite of oppression, is a beautiful place. I would say "Om" softly to myself, letting my lips vibrate. I felt the birds, the sun, and the trees. I was in communion with all the forces on the earth that truly love people, in communion with all the revolutionary forces on the earth.

I was definitely getting better. They were even unchaining me so that i could hobble to the bathroom every now and then, with the help of the nurse. I was still weak and, when i returned from the bathroom, i would flop on the bed as if i had just accomplished a great physical feat. But at least now i knew what was wrong with me. During those first days i could barely ask, and when i did, they acted as if my condition were some top secret information i was not privy to. I had three bullet holes. There was a bullet in my chest (it's still there); an injured lung with fluid in it, a broken clavicle, and a paralyzed arm with undetermined damage to the nerves. I kept asking if i would be able to use my hand again. One or two doctors said, flatly, no. The others said, "Maybe yes, maybe no."

Anyway, i was gonna live.

STORY

You died.
I cried.
And kept on getting up.
A little slower.
And a lot more deadly.

Chapter 2

The FBI cannot find any evidence that i was born. On my FBI Wanted poster, they list my birth date as July 16, 1947, and, in parentheses, "not substantiated by birth records."

Anyway, i was born. I am the older of two children. My sister, Beverly, was born five years later. The name my momma gave me was JoAnne Deborah Byron. I am told that i was a fat, happy baby and that i was talking in complete sentences when i was about nine months old. They say that i was lazy, though, that i talked way before i learned to walk. Everybody says that i had my days mixed up with my nights and kept everybody up all night. (I'm still pretty much a night owl.) The only other tale i remember hearing about my babyhood was that i would scream at the top of my lungs whenever anybody wearing furs or feathers came near me. (I'm still not too fond of furs and feathers.)

My mother and father were divorced shortly after i was born. I lived with my mother, my aunt (now Evelyn Williams), my grandmother (Lulu Hill), and my grandfather (Frank Hill) in a house in the Bricktown section of Jamaica, New York. The only thing i remember about that house is the backyard, which i loved, and the huge dog next door. I remember the dog well because he terrified me. To my young eyes he looked like a giant, a canine version of King Kong or Mighty Joe Young. (I'm still not too wild about dogs.) When i was three years old, my grandparents sold the house and moved down South. I moved with them.

We moved into a big wooden house on Seventh Street in Wilmington, North Carolina. It was the house my grandfather had grown up in. It had a wraparound porch with a big green swing and, of course, rosebushes in the front yard and a pecan tree in the back. My grandfather originally thought that the house had belonged to my great-grandfather, Pappa Linc (short for Lincoln), but they found out he had only been given the use of the house for his lifetime. Pappa Linc had worked as a chauffeur for one of the most prominent white families in Wilmington and, the story goes, had been a prominent member of the Black community. He and my great-grandmother, Momma Jessie, had worked hard all their lives, had raised eleven children in that house, and had died under the impression that the house was theirs. Fine print and white lawyers have a way of robbing Black people of what is theirs. My grandparents were forced to buy the house again.

"Who's better than you?"
"Nobody."
"Who?"
"Nobody."
"Get that head up."
"Yes."
"Yes, who?"
"Yes, Grandmommy."
"I want that head held up high, and i don't want you taking no mess from anybody, you understand?"
"Yes, Grandmommy."
"Don't you let me hear about anybody walking over my grandbaby."
"No, Grandmommy."
"I don't want nobody taking advantage of you, you hear me?"
"Yes, i hear you."
"Yes, who?"
"Yes, Grandmommy."

All of my family tried to instill in me a sense of personal dignity, but my grandmother and my grandfather were really fanatic about it. Over and over they would tell me, "You're as good as anyone else. Don't let anybody tell you that they're better than you." My grandparents strictly forbade me to say "yes ma'am" and "yes sir" or to look down at my shoes or to make subservient gestures when talking to white people. "You look them in the eye when you talk to them," i was told. "And speak up like you've got some sense." I was told to speak in a loud, clear voice and to hold my head up high, or risk having my grandparents knock it off my shoulders.

My grandparents were big on respect. I was to be polite and respectful to adults, to say "good morning" or "good evening" as i passed the neighbors' houses. Any kind of back talk or sass was simply out of the question. My grandparents didn't even permit me to answer questions with a simple "yes" or "no." Instead I had to say "yes, Grandmother" or "no, Grandfather." But when it came to dealing with white people in the segregated South, my grandmother would tell me, menacingly, "Don't you respect nobody that don't respect you, you hear me?" "Yes, Grandmother," i would answer, my voice almost a whisper. "Speak up!" she would tell me repeatedly, something she seemed hell-bent on making me do. She would send me to the store with clear instructions on what to bring back. I was, under no circumstances, to come home with inferior goods, something which happened all too often to Black people in the South. "You tell them that you don't want any garbage, and you'd better not come back with any," she would warn me. If the store owner sold me something that my grandmother didn't like, i would have to return to the store and get the thing changed or get my money back. "You speak up loud and clear. Don't let me have to go down to that store." Scared to death of the fuss my grandmother would make if she had to go to the store herself, i would hurry back to the store, prepared to raise almighty hell.

Whenever my grandmother heard about somebody being mistreated, especially if it was a man mistreating a woman, she would glare at me and say, "Don't you let anybody mistreat you, you hear? We're not raising you up to be mistreated, you hear? I don't want you taking no mess off of nobody, you understand?" "Yes, Grandmother," i would answer, for what seemed like the millionth time, wondering why my grandmother liked to repeat herself so often. The tactics that my grandparents used were crude, and i hated it when they would repeat everything so often. But the lessons that they taught me, more than anything else i learned in life, helped me to deal with the things i would face growing up in amerika.

But a lot of times, for my grandparents, pride and dignity were hooked up to things like position and money. For them, being "just as good" as white people meant having what white people had. They would tell me to go to school and study so that i could have a nice house and nice clothes and a nice car. "White people don't want to see us with nothing," they would tell me. "That's why you've got to get your education so that you can be somebody and have something in life." Becoming "somebody" in life just didn't mean too much to me. I wanted to feel happy, to feel good. My awareness of class differences in the Black community came at an early age. Although my grandmother taught me more about being proud and strong than anyone i know, she had a lot of Booker T. Washington, pull yourself up by the bootstraps, "talented tenth" ideas. She had worked hard and had made a decent living as a pieceworker in a factory, but she had other ideas for me. She was determined that i would become part of Wilmington's talented tenth—the privileged class—part of the so-called Black bourgeoisie.

One of her first steps was to sternly forbid me to play with "alley rats." It was impossible for me to obey her orders since i had absolutely no idea what an alley rat was. I often became the unwitting object of my grandmother's fury, charged with the crime of alley rat playing. My grandmother, writhing with annoyance, would threaten me with untold punishments if i continued my evil ways. I received strict orders to abandon my penchant for alley rats and play with "decent children." But we could never agree on who "decent children" were. Decent children, to my grandmother, were a whole 'nother story.

"Decent children" came from "decent families". How did you know what a decent family was? A decent family lived in a decent house. How did you know what a decent house was? A decent house was fixed up nice and had a sidewalk in front of it. Decent families didn't let their kids play in the street with no shoes on and didn't let their kids say "ain't." Little did my grandmother know that *ain't* was my favorite word once i got two feet out of her hearing range. My grandmother had a little alley rat right under her roof and she didn't even know it. Alley rats supposedly lived in alleys, in run-down shacks, but my grandmother would often call one of my friends an alley rat even if the kid didn't live in an alley.

Dutifully, to put some sense in my head, she would take me to visit "decent children." These decent little souls were invariably the offspring of Wilmington's Black doctors, lawyers, preachers, and undertakers. Schoolteachers, barbershop owners, and the editor of the "colored" newspaper were also decent. In most of these "decent" little play sessions, the other kids and I would stand around looking at each other awkwardly. Sometimes we would get it on and have some fun. But more often than not, it would be glare-at-each-other time or show-and-tell time (the kids showing me their toys and such while the grownups oohed and aahed). The worst times were eating at the preacher's house, where they would take an hour saying grace, or playing ball with the undertaker's daughter. She always wanted to play ball and i was scared to death that the ball was going to roll into the part where they kept the dead people and end up in the mouth of some corpse. My grandmother would have caught a shitfit if she had known that one of her favorite little decent kids' favorite game was playing show and tell with his ding-a-ling and threatening to pee on everybody.

After these visits, my grandmother would chirp for a week about how nice my little decent friends were and about how nicely we had played together, while i would groan silently and keep the expression on my face one shade away from insolence. My grandmother and i waged a standoff battle damn near until i was grown. It wasn't that i wanted to defy her, it was that i just liked who i liked. I didn't care what kind of house my friends had or whether or not they lived in alleys. All that mattered was whether i liked them. I was convinced then, and i'm still convinced, that in some things kids have a lot more sense than adults.

But, to my young mind, life in Wilmington was exciting. There were always new places to go and new cousins, aunts, and uncles to meet. One of my favorite relatives was Aunt Lou. She was Momma Jessie's sister and she lived across town. She was my grandfather's only remaining relative in Wilmington, the rest having moved up North or out West. Aunt Lou had a magic house, full of all kinds of flavors, textures, smells, and things. There were whole worlds in her house to explore. She would always feed me something good to eat and then let me run wild.

I didn't know until i was grown that Aunt Lou had a son. His name was Uncle Willie and he died before i was born. Uncle Willie was something of a legend around Wilmington during the twenties, thirties, and forties. Whenever he came to town, they say, Aunt Lou would plead and moan and worry until he was in safer territory up North. They say that he would tear down the "colored" and "white only" signs and break the Jim Crow laws at whim. He would go around demanding his rights and denouncing the oppression of Black people, and it is logical that no one who loved him felt the least bit comfortable until he was long gone. They called him "Wild Willie" or "that crazy Indian" (he was supposedly Black and Cherokee), but people called him that because of his nature. They say he had a lot of friends and that he died of natural causes.

The rest of the relatives i met came from my grandmother's side. My grandmother's family lived in Seabreeze, outside of Wilmington, close to Carolina Beach. Their last name was Freeman, and they were famous for being high-strung, quick-tempered, and emotional. They seldom worked for anybody, choosing instead to live on the land their father had left them. They worked as farmers and fishermen, and they owned small stores. I have also heard that they were in the bootleg business. My grandmother's father was a Cherokee Indian. He died when my grandmother was very young. Nobody knows too much about him, except that, somehow, he acquired a great deal of land and left it to his children. The land was very valuable because much of it bordered either on the river or on the ocean. Everybody had a different theory about what my great-grandfather had done to acquire it. But it was because of this land that my grandparents had moved down South.

In 1950, the year we moved to Wilmington, the South was completely segregated. Black people were forbidden to go many places, and that included the beach. Sometimes they would travel all the way to South Carolina just to see the ocean. My grandparents decided to open a business on their land. It consisted of a restaurant, lockers where people could change their clothes, and an area for dancing and hanging out.

The popular name for the beach was Bop City, although my grandparents insisted on calling it Freeman's Beach. Throughout my childhood, the name Freeman had no particular significance. It was a name just like any other name. It wasn't until i was grown and began to read Black history that i discovered the significance of the name. After slavery, many Black people refused to use the last names of their masters. They called themselves "Freeman" instead. The name was also used by Africans who were freed before slavery was "officially" abolished, but it was mainly after the abolition of chattel slavery that many Black people changed their names to Freeman. After learning this, i saw my ancestors in a new light.

For me, the beach was a wonderful place, and to this day there is no place on this earth that i love more. I have never seen a beach more beautiful than it was then, before they decided to build a canal right through the property of my grandparents. It is now just a pale shadow of what it used to be, most of it destroyed by erosion. But back then there were majestic sand dunes covered with tall sea grass where my cousins and i would build forts, houses, and, sometimes, cities. When time permitted, we spent hours hiding and making sneak attacks on one another. The sand was fine and clean and, in the beginning of summer, we could find just about every imaginable kind of sea shell. When the sun got too hot, we would sit in the old blue jeep my grandfather drove and play with frilly things like paper dolls and teacups. After i learned to read, i would sit in the sun, under the huge hats my grandmother always made me wear, and read one book after another.

Every other week my grandfather went to the "colored" library on Red Cross Street and the librarian would send ten or so books for me to read. As soon as i finished reading them, my grandfather would go and get another batch. My imagination was vivid. With fragments of pirates and the Bobbsey Twins floating around, i would sit looking out at the ocean and think about everything. I imagined all the places i had read about on the other side of the ocean and wondered if i would ever see them. And, of course, i daydreamed about all kinds of stuff, most of it silly.

But my days were not spent simply daydreaming. My grandparents were firm believers in work. They had worked all of their lives and there was no way they were gonna tolerate any "lazy-good-for-nothin's" around them. Every day there were chores to do and there was no playing until they were completed. I did things like putting the potato chips on the racks, putting sodas in the cooler, wiping the tables clean, etc. When customers were there, i would sell small stuff like potato chips, Nabs, pickles, and pickled pigs' feet. I would also set the tables and bring customers things they needed. But my main job was collecting fifty cents for parking. Because there was no road to our beach (the paved road ended with the white section), my grandparents had to pay for a dirt road and parking lot to be laid over the sand. Truckloads of dirt were brought and a steamroller mashed it down so that it was hard enough to drive on. This was an expensive process, so my grandparents decided to charge fifty cents for parking. I could count and make change at a very early age, so it was my job to collect the fifty cents. During the week it wasn't too time-consuming, but on the weekends, if the weather was nice, it was an all-day job.

Cars and buses of people came from all over North Carolina, South Carolina, and Virginia. There were church groups, school groups, social clubs, women's clubs, boy scouts, and girl scouts. All kinds of people would come to the beach, some with a little money and some that you could tell were real poor. In all the years i spent on that beach, only one or two people hassled me. Most of them treated me very kindly, just like i was their kid.

The people who came to the beach fascinated me. I loved to see them come and go. After a while, i would recognize the regulars and it didn't take me too long to learn their names. Some of them gave me tips, which i usually spent on the picolo (jukebox). There were lots of lovers and i spent some of my time spying on them in the parking lot, but they weren't too interesting. All they did was squirm a lot. Checking license plates (i could recognize almost all of the states' license plates on sight) and collecting bugs (i had a huge collection) were much more interesting. But watching families was better, on their picnics with their fried chicken, potato salads, and watermelons. Some of them looked so happy you could tell they didn't get a chance to go to many picnics. And i was always on the watch for kids to play with when I wasn't busy.

Then there were the goodtimers. Their cars smelled like whiskey. They would dance a lot, eat a lot, spend a lot on the picolo, and many times i would wonder if they had made it home all right.

A lot of poor people came to the beach. Sometimes the floors of their raggedy old cars or trucks were half rotted out. Usually a lot of little children were with them and they wouldn't have bathing suits. They went swimming in whatever clothes they had worn to the beach, and half the time the little kids wore nothing. Then there were those who came to put on airs, usually in the evening, all dressed up, to eat dinner.

Many would say, "I can't stand the sun," "I'm too Black already, I ain't goin' out in no sun." It was amazing the number of people who said they were too Black already. We looked at them like they were crazy because we loved the sun. But the umbrellas for rent went like hotcakes. Some people draped clothes and blankets around the umbrellas so that no light penetrated whatsoever. One lady always put a paper bag on her head and poked holes in it for her eyes. Some of the women refused to go near the water because they were afraid their hair would "go bad."

One of the moving things for me was when someone saw the ocean for the first time. It was amazing to watch. They would stand there, in awe, overpowered and overwhelmed, as if they had come face to face with God or with the vastness of the universe. I remember one time a preacher brought an old lady to the beach. She was the oldest-looking person i had ever seen. She said that she just wanted to see the ocean before she died. She stood there in one spot for so long she looked like she was in a trance. Then, with the help of the preacher, she hobbled around, picked up the mundane shells, and put them into her handkerchief as if they were the most precious things in the world.

I loved to eat (still do) and the beach was right up my alley. Right now, when i think of the fried chicken and fish dinners, my mouth starts to water. But what really sends me off is remembering those seafood platters with fish, shrimps, oysters, deviled crab, clam fritters, and french fries with lettuce and tomatoes on the side. If my memory is any good, i think they sold for $1.50.

Next to food, music was my love. Fats Domino, Nat King Cole, Chuck Berry, Little Richard, the Platters, Brook Benton, Bobby "Blue" Bland, James Brown, Dinah Washington, Maxine Brown, Big Maybelle were some of the people I listened to during those beach years. I loved to dance. They would play that music and i would dance my natural heart out. That was another way i collected tips. People would egg me on, "Go on, gal, go. Boy, looket that little girl dance." But i loved to see people dance, too. Many a time my grandmother or grandfather had to call me out of the trance i was in watching somebody dance instead of doing my chores.

At night, my cousins, who sometimes came over to work on the beach, told ghost stories. They loved to tell them to me because i would get scared out of my wits. They would tell me about people who came back from the dead, about snakes that could crawl a hundred miles an hour and beat you to death with their tails, and about red phantoms and haints and all kinds of other horrible things. My imagination was vivid, and before the night was over the sea grass turned to monsters and the wind made ghost howls.

Sometimes even my grandmother and grandfather would get into the ghost story sessions. My grandfather's favorite one goes like this: He was driving home in a terrible storm one night. It was lightning and thundering like crazy. He saw lightning hit a tree ahead of him and saw the tree fall across the road. He tried to stop, but it was too late. He braced himself to hit the tree, but nothing happened. The car went smoothly through it as if it weren't there. He turned around and, sure enough, the tree was still lying across the road. He swears that the story is true and i'm convinced that he thoroughly believes it is.

We were, however, visited by real, live ghosts. They were the phantoms of the parking lot. It seems that the white citizens of Wilmington and Carolina Beach were not at all happy that my grandparents had dared to build on the land and to start a "colored" business. We were too close for their comfort. So they would visit us from time to time to express their disapproval. I don't know for a fact that they were card-carrying members of the Klan, but, judging from their behavior, i think they were. But then, of course, they weren't wearing their sheets. They could've just been red-blooded amerikan boys out for some good clean fun. The parking lot was made of dirt, and cars spinning around on it at breakneck speed would ruin it in no time. Two or three of them would ride around the parking lot, spinning and skidding, while they shouted curses and racist insults. One time they fired guns in the air. I remember seeing them and hearing them out there and wondering what they were gonna do next. More than once i saw my grandfather go to where he kept his gun and carry it quietly to where he had been sitting. Somehow this made me more afraid, because i knew that he, too, thought they were scary.

Finally my grandfather put a big fat chain, almost as big as the kind used to anchor ships, across the road at the entrance to the parking lot. This soon eliminated our nightly visitors.

One night, as my grandmother and i were fastening the chain in place and locking it, a white man drove up to the lot and, in an arrogant tone of voice, ordered my grandmother to open the gate so that he could turn his car around. My grandmother, looking very dignified, said, "No, I can't let you do that." Then, in a nicer voice, he asked my grandmother again to open the gate. "No," she said again. "Come on now, auntie, I got a mammy in my house. Now open the gate and lemme turn around." "Wha'd you say?" asked my grandmother. "I said I got a mammy in my house, now come on, open up." My grandmother leaned over in the man's face. "I don't care how many mammies you got in your house. I don't care if you've got a hundred mammies in your house, you're gonna back out of here tonight. And I want you off of my property now! Right now!"

That man turned as red as a redneck can turn and started to back his car up. The road was very narrow, barely wide enough for one car, and there was no way he could turn around without getting stuck in the sand. He backed up for more than a quarter of a mile. As we looked at him backing up, my grandmother and i laughed so hard the tears fell from our eyes.

Every day when we drove from the house on Seventh Street to the beach, we passed a beautiful park with a zoo. And every day i would beg, plead, whine, and nag my grandmother to take me to the zoo. It was almost an obsession. She would always say that "one day" she would take me, but "one day" never came. I would sit in the car pouting, thinking how mean she was. I thought that she had to be the meanest woman on the face of the earth. Finally, with the strangest look on her face, she told me that we were not allowed in the zoo. Because we were Black.

When we were on the beach we shopped at Carolina Beach. It had an amusement park, but of course Black people were not permitted to go in. Every time we passed it i looked at the merry-go-round and the Ferris wheel and the little cars and airplanes and my heart would just long to ride them. But my favorite forbidden ride had little boats in a pool of water, and every time i passed them i felt frustrated and deprived. Of course, peristent creature that i am, i always asked to be taken on the rides, knowing full well what the answer would be. One summer my mother and sister and i were walking down the boardwalk. My mother was spending part of her summer helping my grandparents in the business. As soon as we neared the rides, i went into my usual act. I continued, ad nauseam, until my mother, grinning, said. "All right now, I'm gonna try to get us in. When we get over there, I don't want to hear one word out of either of you. Just let me do the talking. And if they ask you anything, don't answer. Okay? Okay!"

My mother went over to the ticket booth and began talking. I didn't understand a word she was saying. The lady at the ticket window kept telling my mother that she couldn't sell her any tickets. My mother kept talking, very fast, and waving her hands. The manager came over and told my mother she couldn't buy any tickets and that we couldn't go into the park. My mother kept talking and waving her hands and soon she was screaming this foreign language. I didn't know if she was speaking a play language or a real one. Several other men came over. They talked to my mother. She continued. After the men went to one side and had a conference, they returned and told the ticket seller to give my mother the tickets.

I couldn't believe it. All at once we were laughing and giggling and riding the rides. All the white people were staring at us, but we didn't care. We were busy having a ball. When i got into one of those little boats, my mother practically had to drag me out. I was in my glory. When we finished the rides we went to the Dairy Queen for ice cream. We sang and laughed all the way home.

When we got home my mother explained that she had been speaking Spanish and had told the managers that she was from a Spanish country and that if he didn't let us in she would call the embassy and the United Nations and i don't know who all else. We laughed and talked about it for days. But it was a lesson i never forgot. Anybody, no matter who they were, could come right off the boat and get more rights and respect than amerikan-born Blacks.

My first school experience was Mrs. Perkins's school in Wilmington. It was a little two-room school on Red Cross Street where i learned the fundamentals of reading, writing, and arithmetic. I was four years old. Mrs. Perkins's school was the closest thing to nursery school that Black people in Wilmington had, but she didn't play that baby play stuff. We were there to learn. I was prone to colds, however, and i guess the potbellied stove in the school didn't give off enough heat. I was out sick more than i was in school. But i learned enough so that when i went to first grade, everything was easy. I could already read.

I spent most of first grade in New York with my mother, the rest of the first and all of the second down South with my grandparents. I went to Gregory Elementary School in Wilmington. My teachers knew my grandparents well and gave them daily reports of my progress. The teachers were strict and believed solemnly in the paddle, but we learned.

Of course, our school was segregated, but the teachers took more of an interest in our lives because they lived in our world, in the same neighborhoods. They knew what we were up against and what we would be facing as adults, and they tried to protect us as much as they could. More than once we were punished because some children had made fun of a student who was poor and badly dressed. I'm not saying that segregation was a good system. Our schools were inferior. The books were used and torn, handed down from white schools. We received only a fraction of the state money allotted to white schools, and the conditions under which many Black children received an education can only be described as horrible. But Black children encountered suppport and understanding and encouragement instead of the hostile indifference they often met in the "integrated" schools.

There was a big dirt yard next to the school where we would play and fight. We grew up fighting; it was really hard to get through school without a few fights, just to survive. But i always wondered what made people fight. Especially after we learned about wars. I used to look out on the remains of the sunken ship that tilted up in front of our beach and wonder how people had died in it. It was covered with green moss and i imagined skeletons floating around inside. The ship had been sunk during the Civil War and i always wondered if it carried Northerners or Southerners. Back in those days i used to think the Northerners were the good guys.

But I never could make much sense out of war. I remember being taught that World War I was the war to end all wars. Well, we know that was a lie because there was World War II. I remember a teacher telling us that World War I was started because Prince Ferdinand, somewhere in Austria, got killed. (When we learned history, we were never taught the real reasons for things. We were just taught useless trivia, simplistic facts, key phrases, and miscellaneous, meaningless dates.) I couldn't understand it. What were people all the way in amerika doing in a war because some prince got killed in Austria? I could just imagine going home and telling my grandmother that i got in a fight because some dude in Europe got killed.

They made war sound so glorious in school, so heroic. But the wars we had on the way home from school and in the playground were anything but glorious. Besides the cuts and scratches we received on our battleground, we were likely to get spanked for fighting or for getting our clothes dirty. I was pretty lucky in that respect. When my grandmother would discover that i was all in one piece she wouldn't make too much of a fuss. I guess i looked pretty much the same after a fight as i did any other day when i came home from school. I was a natural tomboy and a natural slob. My blouse was always hanging out of my skirt, one of my socks always fell down in my shoe, and my hair always flew wild around my head. I always managed to get something torn and dirty and, because i was awkward and clumsy, i always looked like a victim of about fifty wars.

Most of our fights started over petty disputes like stepped-on shoes, flying spitballs, and the contested ownership of pens and pencils. But behind our fights, self-hatred was clearly visible.

"Nappy head, nappy head, I catch your ass, you goin' be dead."

"You think you Black and ugly now; I'm gonna beat you till you purple."

"You just another nigga to me. Ima show you what I do with niggas like you."

"You better shut your big blubber lips."

We would call each other "jungle bunnies" and "bush boogies." We would talk about each other's ugly, big lips and flat noses. We would call each other pickaninnies and nappy-haired so-and-so's.

"Act your age, not your color," we would tell each other.

"You gon thank me when I'm through with you, Ima beat you so bad, I'm gon beat the black offa you."

Black made any insult worse. When you called somebody a "bastard," that was bad. But when you called somebody a "Black bastard," now that was terrible. In fact, when i was growing up, being called "Black," period, was grounds for fighting.

"Who you callin' Black?" we would say. We had never heard the words "Black is beautiful" and the idea had never occurred to most of us.

I hated for my grandmother to comb my hair. And she hated to comb it. My hair has always been thick and long and nappy and it would give my grandmother hell. She has straight hair, so she was impatient with mine. When she combed my hair she always remembered something i had done wrong the day before or earlier that day and popped me in the head with the comb. She would always tell me during these sessions, "Now, when you grow up, I want you to marry some man with 'good hair' so your children will have good hair. You hear me?" "Yes, Grandmother." I used to wonder why she hadn't followed her own advice since my grandfather's hair is far from straight, but i never dared ask. My grandmother just said what everybody knew was a common fact: good hair was better than bad hair, meaning that straight hair was better than nappy hair.

When my sister Beverly was little, i remember teasing her about her lips. She has big, beautiful lips, but back then we looked at them as something of a liability. I never thought of them as ugly—my sister has always seemed very pretty to me—but her lips were something good to tease her about. I once told her, "With those big lips, the only thing you've got going for you is your long hair; you better never cut it off." I will never know how much damage all my "teasing" did to my sister. But i was only saying what everybody knew: little, thin lips were better than big, thick lips. Everybody knew that.

There was one girl in our school whose mother made her wear a clothespin on her nose to make it thin. There were quite a few girls who tried to bleach their skin white with bleaching cream and who got pimples instead. And, of course, we went to the beauty parlor and got our hair straightened. I couldn't wait to go to the beauty parlor and get my hair all fried up. I wanted Shirley Temple curls just like Shirley Temple. I hated the smell of fried hair and having my ears burned, but we were taught that women had to make great sacrifices to be beautiful. And everybody knew you had to be crazy to walk the streets with nappy hair sticking out. And of course long hair was better than short hair. We all knew that.

We had been completely brainwashed and we didn't even know it. We accepted white value systems and white standards of beauty and, at times, we accepted the white man's view of ourselves. We had never been exposed to any other point of view or any other standard of beauty. From when i was a tot, i can remember Black people saying, "Niggas ain't shit." "You know how lazy niggas are." "Give a nigga an inch and he'll take a mile." Everybody knew what "niggas" like to do after they eat: sleep. Everybody knew that "niggas" couldn't be on time; that's why there was c.p.t. (colored people's time). "Niggas don't take care of nothin'." "Niggas don't stick together." The list could go on and on. To varying degrees we accepted these statements as true. And, to varying degrees, we each made them true within ourselves because we believed them.

I entered third grade in P.S. 154 in Queens. The school was almost all white, and i was the only Black kid in my class. Everybody in my family was glad i was going to school in New York. "The schools are better," they said. "You'll get a better education up North than in that segregated school down South."

School up North was much different for me than school down South. For one thing, the teachers (they were all white—i don't remember having any Black teachers until i was in high school) were always grinning at me. And the older i got, the less i liked those grins. I didn't have a name for them then, but now i call them the "little nigga grins."

My third grade teacher was young, blond, very prissy, and middle class. Whenever i came into the room she would show me all thirty-two of her teeth, but there was nothing sincere about her smile. It never made me feel good. There was always something unnatural and exaggerated about her behavior with me. On my first or second day in class she was teaching us penmanship. "Does anyone know how to make a capital *L* in script?" she asked. Nobody raised a hand. Timidly, i did. "You know how to do it?" she asked incredulously. "Yes," i told her, "we had that last year down South." "Well, come and write it on the blackboard, then," she told me. I wrote my pitiful little second grade *L* on the blackboard. After looking at me and nodding, she made a big, fancy *L* next to mine.

"Is this what you're trying to make, JoAnne?" Her expression was smug. The whole class broke out laughing. I wanted to go somewhere and hide. After that, it seemed that every time i mentioned something i learned down South she got mad. She never saw my raised hand. When she couldn't ignore it, like when no one else raised theirs, she would say something like "Oh, do you know the answer, JoAnne?"

Every holiday a class was assigned to put on a play. There were plays for Columbus Day, Halloween, Thanksgiving, Christmas. Our class had George Washington's birthday, and our play was about his cutting down this cherry tree when he was a little boy. I was selected to be in the play. I was tickled pink and so proud. I was cast as one of the cherry trees. The teacher put some green crepe paper over my head and told me to stand at the back of the stage where i was to stay until the end of the play. Then the cherry trees were supposed to sway from side to side and sing: "George Washington never told a lie, never told a lie, he never told a lie. George Washington never told a lie, and the truth goes marching on."

I didn't know what a fool they had made out of me until i grew up and started to read real history. Not only was George Washington probably a big liar, but he had once sold a slave for a keg of rum. Here they had this old craka slavemaster, who didn't give a damn about Black people, and they had me, an unwitting little Black child, doing a play in his honor. When George Washington was fighting for freedom in the Revolutionary War, he was fighting for the freedom of "whites only." Rich whites, at that. After the so-called Revolution, you couldn't vote unless you were a white man and you owned a plot of land. The Revolutionary War was led by some rich white boys who got tired of paying heavy taxes to the king. It didn't have anything at all to do with freedom, justice, and equality for all.

Again, in the fourth grade, i was the only Black kid in my class. My teacher, Mr. Trobawitz, was cool, though, and a very good teacher. He had modern ideas about teaching, and instead of making us read those old boring readers, he had us read real books and write reports about them. His class was always interesting. He told us all kinds of jokes and stories and he seemed to be sincerely concerned about us. That year we were learning about the Civil War and about Lincoln's freeing the slaves. Like all the other teachers, Mr. Trobawitz taught us "fairy-tale history," but at least he made it interesting. That year i was crazy about Lincoln. I memorized the entire "O Captain! My Captain!" by Walt Whitman and recited it to the class.

Little did i know that Lincoln was an archracist who had openly expressed his disdain for Black people. He was of the opinion that Black people should be forcibly deported to Africa or anywhere else. We had been taught that the Civil War was fought to free the slaves, and it was not until i was in college that i learned that the Civil War was fought for economic reasons. The fact that "official" slavery was abolished was only incidental. Northern industrialists were fighting to control the economy. Before the Civil War, the northern industrial economy was largely dependent on southern cotton. The slave economy of the South was a threat to northern capitalism. What if the slaveholders of the South decided to set up factories and process the cotton themselves? Northern capitalists could not possibly compete with slave labor, and their capitalist economy would be destroyed. To ensure that this didn't happen, the North went to war.

When i was still in the fourth grade, i fell off a swing and broke my leg. Mr. Trobawitz came to my house and gave me lessons and assignments. When i returned to school, Mr. Trobawitz had left to teach in college. Everybody in the class was sad. A bird-beaked, stick-to-the-book, teach-by-rote teacher replaced him. She made us go back to reading in the readers and changed the desks around so that once again we were sitting in rows. I didn't like her and she bored me to death.

One time our class had a dance. It was a big event for me since i loved to dance. The white kids couldn't dance for nothing. They looked like a bunch of drunken kangaroos, hopping all over the place, out of time with the music. I sat there with my hand over my mouth trying to suppress my laughter. I ached to get out there and show them how to do it. But nobody asked me to dance. I don't think it ever occurred to them, and, if it did, they knew better. Dancing with a "nigger" was surely good for a week or so of teasing. But these whites were not at all out in the open with their racism. It was undercover, like their parents' racism. Anyhow, i just sat there, looking at them flop around until this one kid (i'll never forget his name: Richard Kennedy; he was a poor Irish kid with red hair) came over to where i was sitting and said, "If you give me a dime, i'll dance with you." The sad part of the story is that i almost gave him the dime.

In the fifth grade, i was put into the class of the school's most notorious battle-ax, Mrs. Hoffler. I knew from the first day it was going to be a long, hot year. The only good thing was that there was another Black kid in the class. The teacher put us in the back, next to each other. His name was David something, but i called him David Peacan. The teacher was one of those military types and her classes resembled boot camp. We were told where to sit, how to sit, and what kind of notebooks, pens, pencils, etc., to use. She permitted no talking and gave tons of homework. Her punishment for everything was extra homework. Whenever somebody got caught talking or doing anything she disapproved of, she gave extra homework. When you didn't have your homework, she gave extra homework. And every time she gave you extra homework she wrote your name on the blackboard and refused to remove it until you had turned in the "punishment." By the time i left her class my name covered practically the entire blackboard.

David and i were her favorite targets. The whole class would be in an uproar, but we were the only ones she saw with our mouths open. The more she rode our backs, the more rebellious i became. I would sit in the back of the class and make jokes about her.

One day when we were talking and giggling, she came up and pulled David out of his seat by the ear, twisting it until the whole side of his face was red and contorted with pain. I made up my mind right then and there that she wasn't going to do it to me. A few days later, she came after me. When she put her hands on me, i kicked her or hit her. I don't remember which. Anyway, the next thing i knew i was in the principal's office being sent home with a note. I was scared to death my mother would find out, so i signed the note myself and brought it to school the next day. My signature didn't fool anybody. To make a long story short, when my mother found out i confessed everything and i told her about Mrs. Hoffler. I think she had some idea about what was going on because she had seen a change in me. I had always been very quiet and obedient in school. My mother went to the school, talked to the teacher and the principal, and demanded i be moved to another class. It's a good thing she wasn't one of those parents who believe the teacher is always right because i don't know what would have happened. I guess the fact that she's a teacher and is acutely aware of the racism and hostility that Black children are exposed to from the time they enter school had something to do with it.

I don't remember the name of my other fifth grade teacher except that it was a mile long and began with a Z, but she was very nice and a very good teacher. She introduced us to art, literature, and philosophy. I remember studying the French Revolution in her class. She made names like Marie Antoinette, Charlotte Corday, and Robespierre come alive. She talked about philosophers like Rousseau who influenced the thinking of the period and about how the French Revolution was influenced by the amerikan Revolution. She even showed us pictures of the art and architecture of the period. She was the first teacher (one of a very few) who taught subjects as if they related to each other.

Before i was in her class, i would never have imagined that history was connected to art, that philosophy was connected to science, and so on. The usual way that people are taught to think in amerika is that each subject is in a little compartment and has no relation to any other subject. For the most part, we receive fragments of unrelated knowledge, and our education follows no logical format or pattern. It is exactly this kind of education that produces people who don't have the ability to think for themselves and who are easily manipulated.

As we grew older, the differences between the Black and white, the poor and rich students grew bigger and bigger. Once a new teacher told us to make mobiles as homework. Most of us brought in cardboard, wood, or paper mobiles. One kid brought in a mobile made out of metals—not just one kind of metal, but metals of different colors. I was in awe of this kid who had the resources to cut all those different, perfectly formed geometric shapes. Calder would have taken notice.

The school was in a largely Jewish, middle-class neighborhood. There was a little island of Black people in the middle, and that was where i lived. It was almost completely segregated from the white section. The school was right in the middle. In most of the Black families the mother and father both worked, and many worked two or three jobs and weren't able to spend a lot of time in the school. But some of the white parents were there for every little thing from trips to cookie selling. And talk about pushy parents! To this day, i believe that some of them did most of their kids' homework. Black kids wrote a composition or a book report on plain lined paper and handed it in. Some of the white kids presented their reports bound in expensive binders, some were typed, and each page was covered with plastic. I could just imagine asking my mother to type my homework for me or to give me money to buy binders and plastic sheets. She would surely have thought i had gone crazy. The white kids came to school with all kinds of junk: expensive pen and pencil sets, compasses, and one kid even had a slide rule, which i doubt he had the faintest idea how to use.

The older they grew, the more snobbish the white kids became. They were always talking about what they had and what their parents had bought them. One girl, Marsha, horribly ugly to me, was always dressed like some kid in the movies or on TV. She was one of the super-snobs in the class. One day she came to school with weird-looking mittens on. She said they were made of chinchilla and that it was the most expensive fur in the world. I raced home to ask my mother. I just knew she had to be lying because i had never even heard of chinchilla and everybody i knew thought that mink was the most expensive fur on the market. I was really shocked when my mother told me she was telling the truth.

Every year when we came back to school, we would inevitably be told to write a composition entitled "My Summer Vacation." Usually we stood in front of the room and read our compositions aloud. I was always fascinated by some of the places these kids had been to during the summer: places like Spain, England, Brazil, and Bermuda. Some of them even brought slides and movies of their trips. After they finished talking, i wouldn't even want to read my compositon about being down South with my grandparents.

One of the things that had been drilled into my head since birth was that we were just as good as white people. "You show those white people that you are just as good as they are," i was told.

This meant that i was to get good marks in school, that i was to always be neat and clean when i went to school, that i was to speak as "properly" as they did, and that i would show them whenever i could that Black people (we called ourselves Negroes then) could do whatever white people could do and that we could appreciate what white people appreciated.

I was supposed to be a child version of a goodwill ambassador, out to prove that Black people were not stupid or dirty or smelly or uncultured. I carried out this mission as best i could to show that i was as good as they were. I never questioned the things they thought were good. White people said classical music was the highest form of music; white people said that ballet was the highest form of dance; and i accepted those things as true. After all, wasn't i as cultured as they were? And everything that they wanted, i wanted. If they wanted poodle jackets, i wanted a poodle jacket. If they wanted a Star of David necklace, i wanted a Star of David necklace. If they wanted a Revlon doll, i wanted a Revlon doll. If they could act snobby, then i could act snobby. I saved my culture, my music, my dancing, the richness of Black speech for the times when i was with my own people. I remember how those kids would talk about gefilte fish and matzos. It would never have occurred to me to talk about black-eyed peas and rice or collard greens and ham hocks. I would never have given them an opportunity to ridicule me. Anyway, half the white people thought that all we ate was grits and watermelon. In many ways i was living a double existence.

I became interested in television in the fifth or sixth grade. Or, rather, i should say that that was about the time television started to corrode my brain. You name any stupid show that existed back in those days and it was probably one of my favorites. "Ozzie and Harriet," "Leave It to Beaver," "Donna Reed," "Father Knows Best," "Bachelor Father," "Lassie," etc. After a while i wanted to be just like those people on television. After all, they were what families were supposed to be like.

Why didn't my mother have freshly baked cookies ready when i came home from school? Why didn't we live in a house with a backyard and a front yard instead of an ole apartment? I remember looking at my mother as she cleaned the house in her old raggedy housecoat with her hair in curlers. "How disgusting," i would think. Why didn't she clean the house in high heels and shirtwaist dresses like they did on television? I began to resent my chores. The kids on television never had any work to do. All they did was their homework and then they went out to play. They never went to the laundromat or did the shopping. They never had to do the dishes or scrub the floor or empty the garbage. They didn't even have to make their own beds. And the kids on television got everything they wanted. Their parents never said, "I don't have the money, I can't afford it." I had very little sympathy for my mother. It never occurred to me that she worked all day, went to school at night, cooked, cleaned, washed and ironed, raised two children, and, in her "spare" time, graded tests and papers and wrote her thesis. I was furious with her because she wasn't like Donna Reed.

And, of course, the commericals took another toll. I wanted everything i saw. My mother always bought Brand X. I would be so exasperated when we went shopping. I wanted her to buy Hostess Twinkies and Silvercup white bread. Instead, she bought whole wheat bread and apples. She would never get good cereals like Sugar Crunchies and Coco Puffs. She always bought some stuff that was supposed to be good for us. I thought she was crazy. If Hostess Twinkies were good enough for the kids on TV, then why weren't they good enough for me? But my mother remained unmoved. And i remained disgusted. I was a puppet and i didn't even know who was pulling the strings.

One year everybody was wearing buttons on their coats. Some had writing on them and others had pictures of movie stars. I went somewhere with my mother and my aunt, and they asked me if i wanted a button. I picked out one with Elvis Presley on it. All the kids at school thought Elvis Presley was cool. I wore that button religiously, all winter, and that summer, when i went down South, i went to see one of Elvis Presley's movies.

In Wilmington, at that time, there was only one movie theater where Black people were allowed to go. It was called the Bailey Theater. Once you bought your ticket, you went up a long staircase on the side of the theater to the second balcony, the "colored" section. Shame on you if you were nearsighted. The movie was like all the rest of Elvis's movies—forgettable! When it was over, i went downstairs. All the white kids were leaving with pictures of Elvis Presley that they had bought. I started to walk to my grandparents' restaurant on Red Cross Street, but then i turned around and walked back. If the white kids could have a picture of Elvis, then so could i. At least i was gonna try. I knew it would be absolutely no use to go to the ticket booth and ask the woman anything. She would most assuredly say no. So i walked right on past her, straight into the white section of the theater. What a surprise it was! It was just like the movies in New York. They had soda machines, a butter popcorn machine, and all kinds of candy and potato chips and things. Upstairs in the "colored" section, they had some old, stale plain popcorn and a few candy bars and that was it.

The moment i walked in, all the action stopped. Everybody's eyes were on me. I walked over to the counter where they were selling the pictures. Before i could open my mouth, the salesgirl told me, "You're in the wrong section; just go outside and go up the stairs on the side."

"I want to buy a picture of Elvis Presley," i said.

"What'd you say, again?" she drawled.

"I want to buy a picture of Elvis Presley," i repeated. "They don't have any upstairs."

"Well, I don't know," she said. "I'll have to get the manager." She said something to the other woman behind the counter and then left. By this time a crowd had gathered around me.

"What's she doing in here?" they kept asking each other. "Now, she knows better," somebody was saying. "Look, Ma, a colored girl." "Ya get lost, honey?" "What's she want?" "Don't they have no pictures in the colored section?" "What's she need with a picture anyway?"

The crowd was all around me, gawking. It seemed like the manager would never come.

"Can't she read? Don't she know that we don't allow no colored in here?" "I don't know what it's about. Something about a picture." "Came walking right in here bold as day."

Finally the salesgirl came back. A man was with her. All eyes were fixed on the manager. He took one look at me and another at the crowd forming around me.

"Give her the picture and get'er out of here," he told the salesgirl. Hurriedly, she sold me the picture.

"All right, folks, it's all over now. Go on about your business."

I took my picture and went prancing out into the daylight. I was feeling good. It seemed funny when i thought about it. The looks on those crakas' faces, all puffed up like balloons. I had a good time, laughing all the way to my grandparents' restaurant. And of course the minute i got there, i told everybody what happened. I was just so proud. I took my picture and put it on the back counter right next to the funeral parlor calendar. The picture stayed there a few days until Johnnie from the cab stand across the street came and told me that Elvis had said the only thing a Black person could do for him was to buy his records and shine his shoes. Quietly, i slid the picture into obscurity, then oblivion. (Later i read that Elvis had given Spiro Agnew a gold-plated .357 Magnum and had volunteered to work for the FBI.)

Evelyn, my aunt, was the heroine of my childhood. She was always taking me places and "exposing me to things," as she called it. She took me to museums—i think we visited just about every museum in the city of New York. She turned me into a real art lover. Before i was ten, i could recognize a Van Gogh on sight, and i knew what cubism, surrealism, and abstract expressionism were. Picasso, Gauguin, Van Gogh, and Modigliani were my favorite artists. I didn't know the name of one Black artist in those days. Very few, if any, museums exhibited the work of Black artists, so i just assumed that Black people weren't too good at painting. But i learned about African art from my mother. From the time i can remember, my mother always had African sculpture in the house. It was the only kind she had. I always loved those pieces and it really annoyed me when i took art history in school and the teacher referred to African art as primitive. In fact, if the art was by anyone else but a white person, it was called primitive art.

In addition to museums, Evelyn would take me to see plays and movies, and we would experiment with all kinds of restaurants. We would go to parks, go bicycle riding, and it was Evelyn who gave me my first rowboat lesson. She was very sophisticated and knew all kinds of things. She was right up my alley because i was forever asking all kinds of questions. I wanted to know everything. She would give me a book and say, "Read this," and i would eat up that book like it was ice cream.

It was Evelyn who took me to see my first show at the Apollo. We saw Frankie Lymon and the Teenagers. I was walking on clouds. After that, as soon as i learned to ride the subway by myself, i went to the daytime shows. If my mother and my aunt had known, they would have had a fit. I guess people wondered what this little girl was doing in the Apollo all by herself, but nobody ever bothered me. I was always pretty lucky that way.

Barbara was a little girl who lived next door to us in Queens. She was my main friend and foe for quite a while. One day i saw her leaving her house wearing a white dress and a little white veil like a bride wears. Everything she had on was white, all the way down to her shoes. She even had a little white Bible in her hands. I thought she was gonna be in a Tom Thumb wedding like they have down South. So i went up to her and asked her who she was marrying. She said she was making her first communion, that she was Catholic.

Well, i became an instant convert. I wanted to wear a white dress and dress up like a bride, too. And Catholics even got out early from school on Wednesdays. I raced home to tell my mother. My mother was very permissive where religion was concerned. She gave us carte blanche to be Catholics, Baptists, Methodists, or whatever. So i started going to mass and to catechism classes on Wednesday.

The Catholic Church was like no other church i had ever been to. Down South i always went to church. But those services were rich with music and emotion. I would sit caught up in the music and watch those people who had "got happy" or "got the spirit" jumping around all over the place. I was never holy-holy, but i had liked going to church. In the Black churches that i had been in, the air was charged. The music rocked and the preacher preached and sang at the same time. People felt free to do what they needed to do. If they felt like dancing, they danced; if they felt like praying, they prayed; if they felt like screaming, they screamed; and if they felt like crying, they cried. The church was there to give them strength and to get them through the long week ahead of them. Where we lived in Queens, there was no Black church.

The Catholic Church was different. It was silent and cold. The music was terrible and you couldn't understand nine-tenths of the service. But what fascinated me was the spookiness of it. They had so much weird stuff attached to their religion. When you walked in the door, you had to cross yourself with holy water; then, before you could sit down, you had to genuflect. And throughout the mass, you were forever up and down, sitting, standing, and kneeling. And there was so much stuff to learn. The stations of the cross, rosary beads, lighting candles, going to confession. It was all so spooky i just knew that this had to be the real god. The nuns really tripped me out. They walked around with rings on their fingers saying they were married to God. That was really weird. And they could never have children or "do it," and people said they had bald heads under their habits. I was simply overwhelmed.

The catechism class was nothing like Sunday school. They never told good stories about Jesus and we never sang "Yes, Jesus Loves Me." In catechism class, we learned all about the saints—it seemed like they had a million of them. And then there was the Virgin Mary. They made a big deal out of her. They even had us praying to her. I would do it, but that story was always kind of hard for me to swallow. Nothing about the Catholics was simple; they even had different kinds of hell. They had a special one for babies and then they had one in between and then they had the sho nuff, sho nuff hell.

They even had two kinds of sin. I can still hear that nun, as if it were yesterday. Now, a venial sin is a sin that's not so bad; it's a white sin. But a mortal sin is terrible; it is a black sin.

The night before i was to make my first communion, i had to run to the church with my baptismal certificate. They needed it to prove i had been baptized. My mother had had a hell of a time finding it. I was tickled to be going because they told me to bring it to the convent where the nuns lived. I had been dying to see what it looked like inside. It was just as cold and lifeless as the church. When i gave the nun my baptismal certificate, she looked at it and almost jumped out of her chair. "Oh, no, this won't do," she said. "This is not a Catholic baptismal certificate. You weren't really baptized."

"What?" i said. "I was too baptized."

"No, you weren't," she said. "It's not a Catholic baptism, so it doesn't count. You'll have to be baptized tonight or you can't make your first communion tomorrow."

I was not ready for that one. I caught an instant attitude. She was talking about my godparents like they were dirt under her feet. They called my mother and told her she had to come to the church. Then they got these total strangers from somewhere and told me they were supposed to be my godparents and they baptized me. I never saw those people again, and if you ask me their names i couldn't tell you. I had had a godmother all my life and here they were telling me she wasn't my godmother because she wasn't Catholic. They really made me mad that day, but i didn't say too much about it. I really wanted to make my first communion. I did and, later, my confirmation, but i never looked at them the same.

The sixth grade passed along rather uneventfully. There was another Black in my class, Gail. We became friendly, but my relationships with the white kids deteriorated even more. They made it pretty evident that they didn't care too much for me, and i made it clear right back that i didn't care for them. The thing i disliked most about them was their assumptions about me. For one thing, they automatically assumed that i was stupid, and they would really act surprised when i showed i had some brains. One of the biggest fights i had was when this kid in my class couldn't find some pen that his father had given him and accused me of stealing it. I waited for him outside the classroom and as soon as he came out the door, i jumped on him like a crazy person. Some teachers broke us up. "I'm surprised at you," they kept saying. "I never thought you'd act that way." I was usually very quiet and well behaved. They acted like i had jumped on that boy for nothing, and they couldn't understand why i was so angry. As a matter of fact, even i didn't understand. Then.

Outside of school was a whole 'nother matter. When i wasn't doing homework or chores, i would go "exploring." My bicycle was one of the great loves of my life. I would jump on it and ride all over Queens. Sometimes on Saturdays or Sundays i would ride all day long, leaving early in the morning and returning as late as i was allowed to. And if i wasn't on my bicycle, i was somewhere playing with my friends. We played everything from house to handball. I played with the boys more than with the girls because the boys had better games. I loved punch ball and handball, anything that involved running. The playground was right across the street from my house and i took full advantage of everything that was there. I played hopscotch, marbles, and cowboys and Indians. I always wanted to be an Indian and would hide over or under something and leap out shrieking at the top of my lungs. I guess i was unusual in that respect, because most of the kids wanted to be cowboys.

I was always rough and clumsy and i played everything as if my life depended on it. Some of the girls didn't like to play with me because they said i was too rough. And i was always excluded from the rope-jumping sessions. I was too clumsy to jump double-Dutch and they didn't even like me to turn because they said i was "uneven-handed."

But i always had one best friend and she was always a girl. I had other friends to play with and hang out with, but i always had one special friend that i could really talk to. We would go to the candy store and the movies and places like that and we would sit and talk for hours about just anything. By the time i reached the sixth grade, i began to idolize and imitate the big kids who went to junior high school. I couldn't wait to grow up. The grownup world was so exciting, and when you were grown up you could do anything you wanted to. Besides, i was beginning to feel different. I was beginning to be interested in boys.

CRACKERJACKS

I coulda told you,
in the old days,
in the park,
or skating down some hill
what it was all about.

I coulda sat next to you
on some stairway
and gave you half my bubblegum,
and, in between the bubbles
and the giggles,
I coulda told you.

But we are grown up now.
And it is all so complicated
when you dig somebody.

Now, when i open up my crackerjacks,
I find no heart-shaped ring.
Only a puzzle
that i don't wanna solve.

Chapter 3

It seemed like the middle of the night. Someone was calling me. Waking me up. What did they want? Suddenly i was aware of all kinds of activity. Police, the crackling of walkie-talkies. The place was buzzing.

"Here, put this on," one of them said, handing me a bathrobe.

"What's going on?" i asked.

"You're being moved."

"Where am i being moved to?"

"You'll find out when you get there."

A wheelchair was waiting. I figured they were taking me to jail. There was a caravan of police cars outside the hospital. It looked like i was gonna be in a parade again.

The ride was pleasant. Just looking at houses and trees and people passing by in cars was good. We arrived at the prison at sunrise, in the middle of nowhere. It was an ugly, two-story brick building. They pushed me up the stairs to the second floor.

I was put in a cell with two doors. A door of bars was on the inside, and directly outside of that was a heavy metal door with a tiny peephole that i could barely see through. The cell contained a cot with a rough green blanket on it and a dirty white wooden bench with a hundred names scratched on it. Adjacent to the cell was the bathroom, with a sink, a toilet, and a shower. Hanging above the sink was the bottom of a pot or pan. It was supposed to serve as a mirror, but i could barely see myself in it. There was one window covered by three thick metal screens facing a parking lot, a field, and, in the distance, a wooded area.

I walked around the cell, to the bath, to the

window, to the door. Back and forth until i had tired myself out. I was still pretty weak. Then i lay down on the cot and wondered what this place was going to be like. Here i was, my first day in prison.

In about an hour, a guard unlocked the outside door and asked me if i wanted breakfast. I said, "Yes," and in a few minutes she came back with eggs and bread in a plastic bowl and a metal cup containing something that was supposed to be coffee.

The eggs didn't taste too bad. "Maybe prison food isn't as bad as they say it is," i remember thinking.

I heard voices and it was clear they weren't police voices. Then the radio came on. Black music. It sounded so good. I looked through the peephole and saw faces, weird and distorted because of the concave glass, but Black faces to match the Black voices i had heard.

"How y'all doin'?" i asked.

No response. Then i realized how thick the metal door was, so i shouted this time: "How y'all doin'?" A chorus of muffled "Fine"s came back. I was feeling good. Real people were just on the other side of the wall.

The guard opened the metal door and handed me some uniforms, maid's uniforms—royal blue, white buttons, collars, and cuffs.

I kept trying them on until two of them fit. Then she gave me a huge cotton slip that looked like a tent dress and a nightgown that looked exactly like the slip.

"You are entitled to a clean uniform once a week."

"Once a week?" i nearly screeched. They had to be crazy. Behind the guard, through the open door, i could see some of the women standing around. They were all, it seemed, Black. They smiled and waved at me. It was so good to see them, it was like a piece of home.

"When are you going to unlock me and let me go out there?" i asked, motioning to the other women. The guard looked surprised.

"I don't know. You'll have to ask the warden."

"Well, when can i see the warden?" i pushed.

"I don't know."

"Well, why am i being locked in here? Why can't i go out there with the other women?"

"I don't know."

"Then why can't you let me out?"

"We were told you were to remain in your room."

"Well, how long am i supposed to stay in here locked up like this?"

"I don't know."

I saw it was useless. "Would you please tell the warden or the sheriff that i would like to see him?" i requested.

The guard locked the door and was gone.

The metal door was unlocked again. An ugly, shriveled white woman stood in front of the bars. "My name is Mrs. Butterworth and I am the warden of the women's section of the workhouse." She reminded me of a dilapidated horse. "Well, JoAnne, is there something I can do for you?"

I didn't like her looks or her tone of voice, but i decided to ignore that for the moment and get to the business at hand.

"When can i be unlocked from this cell and go outside in the big room with the other women?"

"Well, I don't know, JoAnne. Why do you want to go out there?"

"Well, i don't want to stay in here all day, locked up by myself."

"Why, JoAnne, don't you like your room? It's a very nice room. We had it painted just for you."

"That's not the point," i said. "I would like to know when i will be able to be with the other women."

"Well, JoAnne, I don't know when you'll be able to come out. You see, we have to keep you in here for your own safety because there are threats on your life. You know, JoAnne," she said, lowering her voice like she was speaking confidentially, "cop killers are not very popular in correctional institutions."

"Have any of the women here made threats against me?"

"Well, I don't know, but I'm sure they have."

"I'll bet," i said to myself. "Nobody has threatened my life. They just don't want to let me outta here."

"Well, JoAnne, the important thing is for you to behave and to cooperate with us so that we'll be able to send a good report to the judge. It's important for our girls to behave like ladies."

This woman was making me sick. Did she think i was fool enough to believe that either she or the judge was gonna help me in any way? But it was the superior-sounding tinge to her voice that really ticked me off.

"Butterworth, is it?" i asked. "What's your first name?"

"Why, I never tell my girls my first name."

"I'm not one of your girls. I'm a grown woman. Why don't you tell people your first name? Are you ashamed of it?"

"No, JoAnne, I'm not ashamed of my name. It's a matter of respect. I am the warden here. My girls call me Mrs. Butterworth and I call them by their first names."

"Well, you haven't done anything for me to respect you for. I give people respect only when they earn it. Since you won't tell me your first name, then i want you to call me by my last name. You can either call me Ms. Shakur or Ms. Chesimard."

"I'm not going to call you by your last name. I'm going to continue calling you JoAnne."

"Well, that's okay by me, if you can stand me calling you Miss Bitch whenever i see you. I don't give anybody respect when they don't respect me."

"Lock the door," she told the guard and walked away.

Days passed. Evelyn called the sheriff, the warden (there were two wardens in that jail: Butterworth and a man named Cahill. Cahill had all the power, though. Butterworth was only a figurehead) and everybody else. Nothing more could be done outside of going to kourt.

I had little or no feeling in my right arm. I knew i needed physical therapy if i was ever to use it again. I had learned to write with my left hand, but that was no substitute. I needed a more specific diagnosis of exactly what had been damaged before i would know whether or not i would ever use it again, even with physical therapy.

Isolation was driving me up the walls. I needed materials to write and to draw, paint, or sketch. All my requests went unheeded. I was permitted nothing, including peanut oil and a small ball to aid movement in my arm.

When the jail doctor examined me i asked him about my arm.

"Why, we doctors aren't gods, you know. There's nothing anyone can do when someone is paralyzed."

"But they said i might get better," I protested. "Oh, yes, and the physical therapist at Roosevelt Hospital said that some peanut oil might help."

"Peanut oil?" he asked, laughing. "That's a good one. I can't write a prescription for that now, can I? My advice to you is to forget about all of that stuff. You don't need any of it. Sometimes in life we just have to accept things that are unpleasant. You still have one good arm."

I kept talking but i could see i was wasting my time. He had no intention of even trying to help me. "Well, would you at least prescribe some vitamin B?"

"All right, but you really don't need it."

Every time they called me to see the doctor after that, i went reluctantly. He would take my arm out of the sling and move it back and forth about two inches. "Oh, yes, you're getting better," he would say. I always asked about physical therapy and he always said there was nothing he could do.

Finally, Evelyn went to court. Some of the items we petitioned for were ridiculous. In addition to physical therapy and nerve tests, we asked for peanut oil, a rubber ball, a rubber grip, books, and stuff to draw or paint with. The kourt finally granted a physical therapist if we would find one and pay the bill, but i never got one. It seems that no physical therapist in Middlesex County was willing to come to the prison to treat me, and only a physical therapist from Middlesex County was permitted.

But i did get the peanut oil and the grip. And in a short time i had a whole physical therapy program worked out.

I was receiving a lot of mail from all over the country. Most of it came from people i didn't know, mostly militant Black people, either in the streets or in prison. I got some hate mail, though, and some letters from religious people who were trying to save my soul. I wasn't able to answer all of those letters because the prison permitted us to write only two letters a week, subject to inspection and censorship by the prison authorities. It was hard for me to write anyway. I was also very paranoid about letters. I could not bear the thought of the police, FBI, guards, whoever, reading my letters and getting daily insight on how i was feeling and thinking. But i would like to offer my sincerest apology to those who were kind enough to write to me over the years and who received no answer.

I spent my first month at the middlesex county workhouse writing. Evelyn had brought some newspaper clippings and it was obvious the press was trying to railroad me, to make me seem like a monster. According to them i was a common criminal, just going around shooting down cops for the hell of it. I had to make a statement. I had to talk to my people and let them know what i was about, where i was really coming from. The statement seemed to take forever to write. I wanted to make a tape of it and enlisted Evelyn's help. As my lawyer, she was dead set against it and advised me not to make the tape. But as a Black woman living in amerika, Evelyn understood why it was important and necessary. When the prosecutor found out about the tape he tried to get her thrown off the case. She was ordered by the court never to bring a tape recorder again when she visited me.

I made the tape of "To My People" on July 4, 1973, and it was broadcast on many radio stations. Here is what I said:

Black brothers, Black sisters, i want you to know that i love you and i hope that somewhere in your hearts you have love for me. My name is Assata Shakur (slave name joanne chesimard), and i am a revolutionary. A Black revolutionary. By that i mean that i have declared war on all forces that have raped our women, castrated our men, and kept our babies empty-bellied.

I have declared war on the rich who prosper on our poverty, the politicians who lie to us with smiling faces, and all the mindless, heartless robots who protect them and their property.

I am a Black revolutionary, and, as such, i am a victim of all the wrath, hatred, and slander that amerika is capable of. Like all other Black revolutionaries, amerika is trying to lynch me.

I am a Black revolutionary woman, and because of this i have been charged with and accused of every alleged crime in which a woman was believed to have participated. The alleged crimes in which only men were supposedly involved, i have been accused of planning. They have plastered pictures alleged to be me in post offices, airports, hotels, police cars, subways, banks, television, and newspapers. They have offered over fifty thousand dollars in rewards for my capture and they have issued orders to shoot on sight and shoot to kill.

I am a Black revolutionary, and, by definition, that makes me a part of the Black Liberation Army. The pigs have used their newspapers and TVs to paint the Black Liberation Army as vicious, brutal, mad-dog criminals. They have called us gangsters and gun molls and have compared us to such characters as john dillinger and ma barker. It should be clear, it must be clear to anyone who can think, see, or hear, that we are the victims. The victims and not the criminals.

It should also be clear to us by now who the real criminals are. Nixon and his crime partners have murdered hundreds of Third World brothers and sisters in Vietnam, Cambodia, Mozambique, Angola, and South Africa. As was proved by Watergate, the top law enforcement officials in this country are a lying bunch of criminals. The president, two attorney generals, the head of the fbi, the head of the cia, and half the white house staff have been implicated in the Watergate crimes.

They call us murderers, but we did not murder over two hundred fifty unarmed Black men, women, and children, or wound thousands of others in the riots they provoked during the sixties. The rulers of this country have always considered their property more important than our lives. They call us murderers, but we were not responsible for the twenty-eight brother inmates and nine hostages murdered at attica. They call us murderers, but we did not murder and wound over thirty unarmed Black students at Jackson State—or Southern State, either.

They call us murderers, but we did not murder Martin Luther King, Jr., Emmett Till, Medgar Evers, Malcolm X, George Jackson, Nat Turner, James Chaney, and countless others. We did not murder, by shooting in the back, sixteen-year-old Rita Lloyd, eleven-year-old Rickie Bodden, or ten-year-old Clifford Glover. They call us murderers, but we do not control or enforce a system of racism and oppression that systematically murders Black and Third World people. Although Black people supposedly comprise about fifteen percent of the total amerikkkan population, at least sixty percent of murder victims are Black. For every pig that is killed in the so-called line of duty, there are at least fifty Black people murdered by the police.

Black life expectancy is much lower than white and they do their best to kill us before we are even born. We are burned alive in fire-trap tenements. Our brothers and sisters OD daily from heroin and methadone. Our babies die from lead poisoning. Millions of Black people have died as a result of indecent medical care. This is murder. But they have got the gall to call us murderers.

They call us kidnappers, yet Brother Clark Squire (who is accused, along with me, of murdering a new jersey state trooper) was kidnapped on April 2, 1969, from our Black community and held on one million dollars' ransom in the New York Panther 21 conspiracy case. He was acquitted on May 13, 1971, along with all the others, of 156 counts of conspiracy by a jury that took less than two hours to deliberate. Brother Squire was innocent. Yet he was kidnapped from his community and family. Over two years of his life was stolen, but they call us kidnappers. We did not kidnap the thousands of Brothers and Sisters held captive in amerika's concentration camps. Ninety percent of the prison population in this country are Black and Third World people who can afford neither bail nor lawyers.

They call us thieves and bandits. They say we steal. But it was not we who stole millions of Black people from the continent of Africa. We were robbed of our language, of our Gods, of our culture, of our human dignity, of our labor, and of our lives. They call us thieves, yet it is not we who rip off billions of dollars every year through tax evasions, illegal price fixing, embezzlement, consumer fraud, bribes, kickbacks, and swindles. They call us bandits, yet every time most Black people pick up our paychecks we are being robbed. Every time we walk into a store in our neighborhood we are being held up. And every time we pay our rent the landlord sticks a gun into our ribs.

They call us thieves, but we did not rob and murder millions of Indians by ripping off their homeland, then call ourselves pioneers. They call us bandits, but it is not we who are robbing Africa, Asia, and Latin America of their natural resources and freedom while the people who live there are sick and starving. The rulers of this country and their flunkies have committed some of the most brutal, vicious crimes in history. They are the bandits. They are the murderers. And they should be treated as such. These maniacs are not fit to judge me, Clark, or any other Black person on trial in amerika. Black people should and, inevitably, must determine our destinies.

Every revolution in history has been accomplished by actions, although words are necessary. We must create shields that protect us and spears that penetrate our enemies. Black people must learn how to struggle by struggling. We must learn by our mistakes.

I want to apologize to you, my Black brothers and sisters, for being on the new jersey turnpike. I should have known better. The turnpike is a checkpoint where Black people are stopped, searched, harassed, and assaulted. Revolutionaries must never be in too much of a hurry or make careless decisions. He who runs when the sun is sleeping will stumble many times.

Every time a Black Freedom Fighter is murdered or captured, the pigs try to create the impression that they have quashed the movement, destroyed our forces, and put down the Black Revolution. The pigs also try to give the impression that five or ten guerrillas are responsible for every revolutionary action carried out in amerika. That is nonsense. That is absurd. Black revolutionaries do not drop from the moon. We are created by our conditions. Shaped by our oppression. We are being manufactured in droves in the ghetto streets, places like attica, san quentin, bedford hills, leavenworth, and sing sing. They are turning out thousands of us. Many jobless Black veterans and welfare mothers are joining our ranks. Brothers and sisters from all walks of life, who are tired of suffering passively, make up the BLA.

There is, and always will be, until every Black man, woman, and child is free, a Black Liberation Army. The main function of the Black Liberation Army at this time is to create good examples, to struggle for Black freedom, and to prepare for the future. We must defend ourselves and let no one disrespect us. We must gain our liberation by any means necessary.

It is our duty to fight for our freedom.
It is our duty to win.
We must love each other and support each other.
We have nothing to lose but our chains:

In the spirit of:

Ronald Carter
William Christmas
Mark Clark
Mark Essex
Frank "Heavy" Fields
Woodie Changa Olugbala Green
Fred Hampton
Lil' Bobby Hutton
George Jackson
Jonathan Jackson

James McClain
Harold Russell
Zayd Malik Shakur
Anthony Kumu Olugbala White

We must fight on.

The workhouse had a whole heap of rules, most of them stupid. No newspapers or magazines were permitted. When i asked why we couldn't read newspapers, they told me that newspapers were "inflammatory." Obviously, if a person read in the paper that his or her sister had been raped, he would wait until the rapist came to jail and then do him bodily harm.

"But," i protested, "the other inmates watch television and listen to the radio (i wasn't allowed either). They could receive the same information that way or from a visit from home."

"In that case," the warden told me, "we don't let you read newspapers because they are a fire hazard."

One of the saddest rules prohibited children from visiting their mothers in jail. I could see the children waiting outside, looking up at that ugly old building with sad, frustrated faces. Their mothers would run to the only window that faced the parking lot just to get a glimpse of their children. Yelling out of the window was a no-no, but once in a while somebody would get carried away. Sometimes their frantic screams went unheard.

Gradually, i began to know the women. They were all very kind to me and treated me like a sister. They laughed like hell when i told them that i was supposedly being protected from them. Those first days, before i had really learned to maneuver with one hand, they did whatever they could to make things easier for me. They volunteered to iron my uniforms and sneak them into the laundry to be washed more than once a week. When they told me their charges and the time they were doing, i couldn't believe it. Quite a few of them were doing time for the numbers, either six months or a year. In New York, doing time for number running was practically unheard of, and it certainly didn't get six months or a year. Everybody in the world knows that the numbers business keeps the cops fat. These women hadn't hurt anybody or stolen anything, yet they were sitting in jail, probably busted by the same cops that they paid off. Their only crime was competing with the state lottery. Most of them had already been sentenced. If the sentence was less than a year, time was served in the county jail rather than in the state penitentiary.

If i had expected to find so-called hardened criminals or big-time female gangsters or gun molls in the workhouse, i would have been sadly disappointed. The rest of the women who weren't doing time for the numbers were in for some form of petty theft, like shoplifting or passing bad checks. Most of those sisters were on welfare and all of them had been barely able to make ends meet. The courts had shown them no mercy. They brought in this sister shortly after i arrived who was eight months pregnant and had been sentenced to a month for shoplifting something that cost less than twenty dollars.

Later a middle-aged sister began coming to the workhouse on weekends. She worked during the week and served her six-month sentence for drunken driving on weekends. Knowing that white women with the same charges would never have received such a sentence, i thought it was harsh. But i didn't realize how harsh until she told me that she had been arrested for drunken driving in the driveway of her own house. She hadn't even been on a public road. She also told me that the cops had arrested her because they didn't like the way she talked to them.

In that jail it was nothing to see a woman brought in all beat up. In some cases, the only charge was "resisting arrest." A Puerto Rican sister was brought in one night. She had been so badly beaten by the police that the matron on duty didn't want to admit her. "I don't want her dying on my shift," she kept saying. It was days before this sister was able to get out of bed.

In spite of it all, those sisters kept the place jumping. They told all kinds of funny stories about their lives, things they had seen and experienced. Some had a natural knack for comedy. What amazed me was the way they told the saddest stories in the world and made everybody laugh about them.

Girl, that nigga was always in my pocketbook stealing my money. And all he did with it was blow it at the racetracks. Girl, that man spent so much money on the racetracks, he made me wish i was a horse. One day i fixed his ass, though. I was sick and tired of his mess. Betcha he won't go in nobody's pocketbook no time soon. I put a mousetrap in that sucker. Girl, you should have heard that nigga howl.

My husband and me, we used to fight like cats and dogs. And he was jealous as the day is long. Chile, we went to the bar this night and the nigga got all high, and started thinkin' i was messing around with some dude at the bar. As soon as we got outside, boy, he jumped on me like a gorilla jumps on a banana. Don't you know that man hit me so hard he knocked my teeth straight out of my mouth. "Now, hold on a minute!" i told that fool. "We can fight later. I ain't got no 'nother four hundred dollars to spend on no false teeth." Chile, we was drunk as skunks, down on our knees for 'bout an hour looking for those teeth. And when that fool found them, he said the teeth jumped up and tried to bite him. Lord, chile, that man is a fool.

I could listen to these stories only when the outside door was open. During the day they had a female "sheriff's officer" posted outside my cell. When she was there, the door usually stayed open.

The whole time i was at that jail i saw very few white women. The few who did come were there only a few hours or a day or so before they were bailed out. There was one white woman who was busted on the turnpike with fifty pounds of reefer. Everyone waited to see what her bail would be. Then we found out she had been released on her own recognizance (that is, without bond). To be released on recognizance in the state of new jersey, one of the requirements is jersey residence. The woman lived in Vermont. But nobody was really shocked. She was white.

I was going crazy in that little cell. The only time they let me out was for visits and to see the so-called doctor. I have always been an active and restless person, and being locked up in that little cage all day drove me wild. I needed to stretch my legs. I started to run around the cell. I would run in this tiny circle until i was exhausted. Two or three days after i started, the warden, Miss Bitch, accompanied by some male guards, visited me.

"We hear that you are running around your cell," she said. "You will have to stop this activity at once."

"What? Why?"

"Because you are disturbing the people downstairs."

"What people?"

"There is an office underneath you and you are disturbing the workers."

"Are you crazy? They'll just have to be disturbed. I don't run for that long anyhow. If you let me go out into the yard to exercise with the other women, i'll stop running around my cell."

"I order you to stop running around your room."

"I don't remember joining your army," i said. "When i join your army, then you can order me around."

She left in a huff and i kept on running. That was the end of that. I have to thank her, though. If she hadn't come and harassed me, i would have probably given up running around that tiny space in a few days.

The food in the workhouse was horrible. Actually, it was disgusting. The food there is worse than the food in any jail that i have been in since, and that is quite an accomplishment. I would sit and wait for lunch or dinner, hungry as hell, and they would bring me some greenish-brown iridescent chunks floating around in a watery liquid (liver stew, they called it) or some lamb fat floating around in some water which was supposed to be lamb stew. And that nasty-looking, foul-smelling stuff tasted much worse than it looked. The place was infested with flies and so was the food. The only thing edible was eggs, when they had them, and mashed potatoes. I lived off the nuts and candy i bought from the commissary and the fruit my family brought on visits.

Every single day for one whole week they brought us this nasty stuff that was supposed to be ravioli. Well, that was the last straw. We all decided to go on a food strike. I wrote a petition which everybody signed and we sent it down to the warden's office. Later, the warden agreed to discuss making the food more edible, but he refused to talk to me. He said the fact that i had referred to the food as "slop" showed i was unreasonable. The food was better for a few days, and then it reverted to the same old nasty slop.

The woman sheriff's officer who guarded me had to be the oldest "dumb" blonde alive. She played the part to a bust. She was nosy and was the world's biggest gossip. Every time she saw me she smiled and pretended to be oh so friendly. One day some workmen were drilling a big hole in the wall to install new electrical circuits. Of course, as soon as she came in, the nosy sheriff's officer began her questions.

"What are they building?"

I said, "Haven't you heard? Well, you know, they passed a special law and they're going to execute me. They're building the gas chamber now."

"Well!" she said indignantly. "Well! Nobody told me about it." And she rushed off to find out why no one had informed her.

The lights were turned off every night at ten. I was lucky because there was a night switch that i controlled in the bathroom adjacent to my cell. I would move the cot so that i was in as much light as possible and i would read way into the night. When i tired of reading, i'd turn off the light and look out the window. Outside, police patrolled the area. A lot of times there were two police on foot who seemed to be standing around near the parking lot. They carried rifles and shotguns. One night, in my usual condition of boredom, while standing at the window and feeling mischievous, i cried out a birdlike sound in the shrillest voice i could muster: "Eeeeenk, eeeenk, eeeeenk, eeeeeeeeeeeeeeeeeenk." The pigs started looking around like crazy. They jerked this way and that way as if they thought someone was behind them. Again i cried, "Eeeeeeenk, eeeeeeeeenk, eeeeeeeewa, eeeeeeeeeeeewa." This time they really jumped around. You would have thought it was World War II and the Japanese were two feet away. I waited awhile. When they calmed down, in a voice even shriller than before, i cried, "Naaaaaaeeeeee, naaaaeeeeeee, naaaaaaeeeeeeeeeeee." They pointed their guns and actually walked backward, prepared to fire at anything moving. Then, quite by accident, my metal cup fell to the floor. Well, in a second they were down on the ground, crawling, holding their rifles. When i saw these fools crawling around on the ground like that, i just couldn't take it anymore. I laughed until i was sick. Great, big, bad police, crawling around scared of their own shadows. Every once in a while i tried it again with different police and usually the results were similar, but it was never as good as that first night.

Because i had a broken clavicle, i had to wear a figure-eight brace around my shoulders. It was made of foam and cotton with a tiny belt buckle fastener in the back, about a half-inch wide. One morning, as i was eating, the guard came in my cell and took it.

"You can't have this."

"Why?"

"Because it contains metal," she replied. "You can't have anything with metal on it." Now, there i was, sitting on a metal cot, drinking out of a metal cup, eating out of a metal bowl, and this policewoman was standing in my face telling me i couldn't have my brace because of this tiny metal buckle. I raised all the hell i could, but i saw that she was, like she said, like they all say, "only following orders."

"If the prison doctor says you need it, you can have it back."

As soon as Dr. Miller came into the workhouse, i asked to see him. Without the brace, my shoulder felt weak and fragile. I could barely hold myself up straight.

"Don't worry about that old brace," Herr doctor told me. "You don't need that thing anyway."

It was all i could do not to kick him in his groin. Luckily, later that week, the bone specialist came out from the hospital to see me. He was a very good doctor and a very kind man. He told the warden in no uncertain terms that i needed my brace and without it i could be disfigured. He gave me a lot of encouragement for my hand so that i could regain full use of it. Finally, they returned the brace.

It was about that time that the miracles started. I was sure now that my hand was coming back to life. I was beginning to be able to tell it to do things and it would actually respond. Each little bit of progress was a miracle. Being able to touch my pinky with my thumb, to pick up a cup, to hold a pencil, to pinch myself were feats that took days of practice and exercise to accomplish. And then the day came when i knew i was almost there. After months of trying, i could finally snap my fingers. Whenever anyone came to see me, i would show them my new talents. I felt like a little kid saying, "Look, Mommy, see what i can do."

Finally a joint conference was arranged between Sundiata and me with Evelyn present. It took place at the workhouse. Sundiata was brought from the new brunswick jail. I've never been happier to see anyone in my life. It was difficult to talk because the guards were practically sitting in our laps. I can't whisper for nothing and Evelyn kept telling me to lower my voice. We talked about the case and decided that it was politically correct to be tried together. Just seeing Sundiata cooled me right out. I was feeling bad and i was real self-conscious about how i looked. I had broken out in a horrible rash from the prison soap and i looked like a lopsided scarecrow with bumps. There is something about Sundiata that exudes calm. From every part of his being you can sense the presence of revolutionary spirit and fervor. And his love for Black people is so intense that you can almost touch it and hold it in your hand. There's nothing put on about him. He is a real folksy kind of person. Every time i see him he looks like he belongs on a porch somewhere down South, breathing in the summer air and bouncing babies off his knee. The truth of the matter is that Sundiata is country. He would deny it to the bitter end, but he is sho nuff country. And when he laughs that giggle laugh of his, it's like a trip to Texas in the backwoods. When the conference ended, i was a different person. I felt much stronger and i didn't feel alone.

I don't know when, but somewhere along the way i started to collect the metal cups we were given to drink from. At first i think it was just my slow way of drinking that caused the cups to accumulate. I was none too popular with the guards, especially the men. Most of them hadn't said boo to me and vice versa, but they hated my guts. To them, i was a cop killer and they were cops. Something told me to be real careful. They had given me a little table to eat and write on, and at night, before i went to sleep, i pushed the table up next to the bars and stacked the cups precariously on top of it. The bars opened into the cell, and the slightest movement would send the whole stack of cups clanging to the floor. I would push the wooden bench behind the table. In that way, anyone who tried to come in would have to apply some real pressure. I went through this routine every night, feeling slightly foolish but compelled.

One night, in the middle of the night, the cups came crashing down. I immediately awoke to find four or five male guards standing in the doorway of my cell.

I screamed, "What do you want? What are you doing in my cell?" loud enough for someone to hear me. The guards stood in the doorway like they didn't know what to do. Finally one of them locked the door and said, "We heard a noise and we came to investigate. We were just checking it out." They weren't even supposed to be in the women's section. The female guard on duty that night, the slimiest one in the prison, was nowhere in sight. After that, no matter what jail i was in, i always found some way to barricade my cell. In prisons, it is not at all uncommon to find a prisoner hanged or burned to death in his cell. No matter how suspicious the circumstances, these deaths are always ruled "suicides." They are usually Black inmates, considered to be a "threat to the orderly running of the prison." They are usually among the most politically aware and socially conscious inmates in the prison.

When Eva came to the workhouse it was something of an event. Usually she occupied the cell i was in. (The rest of the women were housed in two open dormitories.) The guards didn't know what to do with her. She had been in that jail many times before and she was known as a hell raiser. Everybody said she was crazy.

My first encounter with Eva was when she came over to the bars and sat down outside my cell and told me she could astro-travel. She called it something like astro-space projection.

"I can go anywhere I want to, whenever I want to," she told me. "I've just come from Jupiter."

"How was it?" i asked her.

"Oh, it was fine. They had these cute little people. They were purple with crocodile skin and blue hair. You can go anywhere you want to," she told me. "You just have to project yourself."

"Can you show me how to project myself the hell out of here?"

"Oh, that's easy," she said, "I do that all the time. As a matter of fact, I'm not here now."

"No," i said, "that's not good enough. I want to project my mind *and* my body out of here."

"You'll be in jail wherever you go," Eva said.

"You have a point there," i told her, 'but i'd rather be in a minimum security prison or on the streets than in the maximum security prison in here. The only difference between here and the streets is that one is maximum security and the other is minimum security. The police patrol our communities just like the guards patrol here. I don't have the faintest idea how it feels to be free."

Eva told me that she knew how i felt. She had to know. Any Black person in amerika, if they are honest with themselves, have got to come to the conclusion that they don't know what it feels like to be free. We aren't free politically, economically, or socially. We have very little power over what happens in our lives. In fact, a Black person in amerika isn't even free to walk down the street. Walk down the wrong street, in the wrong neighborhood at night, and you know what happens.

Eva and i got on famously. A lot of times i didn't understand what in the world she was talking about. But at times she made so much sense i wondered if it was really the world that was crazy. She taught me a lot about prison, and she was forever telling some funny story about her life.

Eva was a huge sister; she weighed about 300 pounds. She had very dark skin and her hair was cut short next to her scalp. People who have accepted white, European standards of beauty would find her unattractive. But to me there was something beautiful about her and i loved to look at her. She is one of the few people that i have met in life who have the courage to be almost totally honest.

Altogether, Eva had spent about ten years in the clinton correctional facility for women in new jersey. She had been there in the old days when the women worked out on the farm. She told me how the women were treated, that state troopers would be called in for the slightest disturbance. She was there during a riot at clinton and had seen state troopers beat the women mercilessly; once they had beaten a pregnant woman so badly she lost her baby.

Around this time i started taking my little walks. Staying cooped up in that cage all day was driving me up the wall. So when the guards brought my food, i would walk past them into what was called the day room, where the women ate and watched TV. I would walk first to one dorm, then to the other, and then return to my cell. There was no place i could run to since there were two or three locked doors between me and the outside. Most of the guards would nag me to come back into my cell and, after a short time, i would. But none of them got too crazy about it until one day a guard yelled at me, "Get back here! Did you hear me? Get back here!"

If there's one thing i can't stand it's being ordered around, and if there's another thing that makes me go wild it's for a white person to talk to me in that tone of voice. "You make me come here," i told her. "You so big and bad, i want to see you make me come back in there." She made a move like she was going to grab me. "You put your hands on me and it's gonna be you and me. You lay a hand on me and i'm gonna splatter your brains all over these walls." It's a good thing she didn't try me, though, because she outweighed me by at least fifty pounds and i was still pretty much the one-armed bandit. But i would have given her a hell of a fight. I was mad and frustrated and i had already stored up about two or three months of anger. Anyway, i finally went back into the cell, when i was ready. But her attitude made me defiant. Whenever she opened my cell for anything, i would push past her and walk around for a minute. She would stand in the doorway like she was a door or something and i would rear back and butt her out of the way. She was as big as a house, but she didn't have one bit of strength. Finally, she called the male guards. I was in one of the dorms talking to the women, wondering why she wasn't bothering me, when about ten male guards came into the room.

"Who is JoAnne Chesimard?" the head guard asked. Nobody said anything. "Which one of you is JoAnne Chesimard?" They looked like they were ready to leap on somebody. Again no one responded. "All right, I'm gonna ask you again, which one of you is JoAnne Chesimard?"

"I'm JoAnne Chesimard," Eva said. Well, when the guards took one look at Eva and saw how big she was, their tone changed immediately.

"Miss Chesimard, would you please return to your cell?"

One of the guards came from the back and tapped the sergeant on the shoulder.

"I know her," he said. "She's not Chesimard."

"I am who you are looking for, " i said. I didn't want Eva to get too involved in my madness. "I'll see you sisters later. I've had enough excitement for the moment." I walked past them and went to my cell and opened a book.

The next day this same guard managed to tick me off again.

"I don't want anymore trouble out of you," she said. "I don't want to have to call the men again."

"You can call the national guard, the militia, the FBI, and anybody else for all i care. You can call your mother if you want to," i told her. As soon as she opened the door for lunch, i pushed right past her. I took my tray, sat down with the other women and started eating my lunch. I didn't know what was going to happen but i wanted to see what they were gonna do. I had about three mouthfuls of food left on my plate when the goon squad came in.

"All right, get up and get in your cell."

"As soon as i finish what i have on my plate."

"Now!" they ordered.

"I only have two spoonfuls left."

"Now!" They beckoned to the female guard. "Remove the prisoner to her cell." She came near me with her hands stretched out.

"Don't you put your hands on me," i told her. "I'll walk to my cell."

"Remove the prisoner to her cell," they ordered. She went to grab my arm and all at once the room was in motion. Chairs, tables, cups, trays were flying in the air. Everybody was either running to get out of the way or fighting. The female guard made a wild dash for the door. The male guards jumped on me. I was hitting, kicking, scratching, punching, biting, and i don't know what all else. They finally managed to get me in my cell and the other women locked in their dormitories. None of the women was seriously injured. I had a few nicks and scratches, but otherwise i was fine. And i felt fine. Some of that anger pent up inside me had been released. One of the guards was wounded. Somehow his face had got cut. He was the same little runt who had sat across from me in the hospital, pointing a shotgun at me and switching the safety on and off, talking about how he liked to kill animals. Nobody knows how he was cut or who cut him. But everybody knows that the hunter got hunted.

Later that day they brought a photographer to photograph the evidence. The local newspaper later reported a "riot" at the workhouse. Some police and the sheriff came around and searched the jail. They said they were looking for the weapon that had cut the guard. They didn't find anything. That night they came and got Eva. They took her to the Vroom Building, the new jersey "hospital" for the criminally insane. She spent about three weeks there before she came back. The night she left i felt sad and guilty. Here i had got her caught up in my madness. I was sitting and thinking about her. So i sat down and wrote this poem:

Rhinocerous woman
Who nobody wants
and everybody used.

They say you're crazy
cause you not crazy enough
to kneel when told to kneel.

Hey, big woman—
with scars on the head
and scars on the heart
that never seem to heal—
I saw your light
And it was shining.

You gave them love.
They gave you shit.
You gave them you.
They gave you hollywood.
They purr at you
cause you know how to roar
and back it up with realness.

Rhinocerous woman.
Big momma in a little world.
You closed your eyes
and neon spun inside your head
cause it was dark outside.

You read your bible
but god never came.

Your daddy woulda loved you
but what would the neighbors say.

They hate you momma
cause you expose their madness.
And their cruelty.
They can see in your eyes
a thousand nightmares
that they have made come true.

Black woman. Baad woman.
Wear your bigness on your chest like a badge
cause you done earned it.

Strong woman. Amazon.
Wear your scars like jewelry
cause they were bought with blood.

They call you mad.
And almost had you
believing that shit.

They called you ugly.
And you hid yourself

behind yourself
and wallowed in their shame.

Rhinocerous Woman—
This world is blind
and slight of mind
and cannot see
How beautiful you are.

I saw your light.
And it was shining.

Most of the women benefited from the "riot," though. Over the next few days almost everybody was released or sent to some kind of program. The jail was practically empty. It's strange how things work. When it suits the government's interest, they put people in jail for rioting. And when it suits their interests, they let them out of jail for the same thing. Afterward, the outer door to my cage remained shut at all times. This was no great deprivation since it had remained closed most of the time before anyway.

One day they brought me a big bushel of stringbeans. (They grew a lot of their food at the workhouse. The men worked in the field.) "Here, we want you to snap these stringbeans."

"How much are you gonna pay me?" i asked.

"We don't pay no inmate nothin', but if you snap these beans we'll let your door stay open while you snap them."

"I don't work for nothing. I ain't gonna be no slave for nobody. Don't you know that slavery was outlawed?"

"No," the guard said, "you're wrong. Slavery was outlawed with the exception of prisons. Slavery is legal in prisons."

I looked it up and sure enough, she was right. The Thirteenth Amendment to the Constitution says:

> Neither slavery nor involuntary servitude, except as a punishment for crime whereof the party shall have been duly convicted, shall exist within the United States, or any place subject to their jurisdiction.

Well, that explained a lot of things. That explained why jails and prisons all over the country are filled to the brim with Black and Third World people, why so many Black people can't find a job on the streets and are forced to survive the best way they know how. Once you're in prison, there are plenty of jobs, and, if you don't want to work, they beat you up and throw you in the hole. If every state had to pay workers to do the jobs prisoners are forced to do, the salaries would amount to billions. License plates alone would amount to millions. When Jimmy Carter was governor of Georgia, he brought a Black woman from prison to clean the state house and babysit for Amy. Prisons are a profitable business. They are a way of legally perpetuating slavery. In every state more and more prisons are being built and even more are on the drawing board. Who are they for? They certainly aren't planning to put white people in them. Prisons are part of this government's genocidal war against Black and Third World people.

On July 19, 1973, i was taken to New York to be arraigned on a Queens bank robbery indictment in Brooklyn federal court. The trip was like a surrealistic cartoon. There must have been at least twelve cars in the procession, and a new jersey state trooper's car was stationed at every exit on the turnpike. All the cars had lights on and sirens going. A helicopter trailed us. And the pigs in the car i was in were comical. At every point they said something like "At least we got to the turnpike." "At least we got to the bridge." "At least we got to New York." "At least we made it to the court."

Whenever they passed a police car they waved and sometimes raised their fists. When the jersey police were replaced by New York police at the bridge to Staten Island, they shook hands and gave each other the power sign. They even called each other "brother." "This is my brother officer, so and so." They acted like they were on some dangerous mission inside Russia. They were actually afraid. White people's fear of Black people with guns will never cease to amaze me. Probably it's because they think about what they would do were they in our place. Especially the police, who have done so much dirt to Black people—their guilty conscience tells them to be afraid. When Black people seriously organize and take up arms to fight for our liberation, there will be a lot of white people who will drop dead from no other reason than their own guilt and fear.

In September, i was moved from the workhouse and entombed in the basement of the middlesex county jail, allegedly because of the jail's proximity to the middlesex county courthouse where the new jersey trial was scheduled to begin on October 1. I was the first, and last, woman ever imprisoned there. It has always been a men's jail.

When i arrived i was given a dirty, scratchy horse blanket and one sheet. Thinking they had made a mistake, i asked for another sheet. "That's all you get," they told me.

"I can't sleep with that filthy thing over me. I need another sheet."

"Sorry."

"Why am i allowed only one sheet?"

"That's all the men get. We only give one because they might hang themselves."

"They can hang themselves as easily with one sheet as they can with two," i reasoned.

"Sorry."

For me to sleep on that filthy thing with one sheet was out of the question. I hooped, hollered, demanded they call my lawyer, and told the guard that the next time she came into my cage i was going to wrap the sheet around her neck. Finally, she gave me another sheet.

If i wrote a hundred pages describing the basement of the middlesex county jail, it would be impossible for you to visualize it. It was a big, grayish, pukey-greenish cell. The ceiling was covered with all kinds of pipes, some small, some huge, some dry, some leaky. There was no natural light, and the jailers refused to open the small windows located near the ceiling. The average temperature was 95 degrees. It was infested with ants and centipedes. I had never seen a centipede before and they scared me to death. They were huge, albino monsters and they crawled all over me.*

Female guards were stationed at the door of my cell twenty-four hours a day. Their job was to sit there and look in the cell at me. They could see every move i made. The first day i moved the bed

*On December 11, 1978, attorney Lennox Hinds, on behalf of the National Conference of Black Lawyers, the National Alliance Against Racism, and the Commission for Racial Justice of the United Church of Christ, sent a petition to the United Nations Commission on Human Rights alleging a "consistent pattern of gross . . . violations of human rights and fundamental freedoms of certain classes of prisoners in the United States because of their race, economic status, and political beliefs." In response to the petition, seven international jurists visited a number of prisoners on August 3–20, 1979, and reported their findings. They listed four categories of prisoners, the first of which were political prisoners, defined as "a class of victims of FBI misconduct through the COINTELPRO strategy and other forms of illegal governmental conduct who as political activists have been selectively targeted for provocation, false arrests, entrapment, fabrication of evidence, and spurious criminal prosecutions. This class is exemplified by at least: The Wilmington Ten, the Charlotte Three, Assata Shakur, Sundiata Acoli, Imari Obadele and other Republic of New Africa defendants, David Rice, Ed Poindexter, Elmer 'Geronimo' Pratt, Richard Marshall, Russell Means, Ted Means and other American Indian Movement defendants."

They considered my case in the section of their report dealing with solitary confinement: "One of the worst cases is that of ASSATA SHAKUR, who spent over twenty months in solitary confinement in two separate men's prisons subject to conditions totally unbefitting any prisoner. Many more months were spent in solitary confinement in mixed or all-women's prisons. Presently, after protracted litigation, she is confined at Clinton Correctional Facility for Women in maximum security. She has never on any occasion been punished for any infraction of prison rules which might in any way justify such cruel or unusual treatment."

against the wall, away from the guard's surveillance so that i could have a little privacy while i was sleeping. The guards ordered me to move the bed into the middle of the floor. I refused. The next day workmen nailed the bed to the floor in the center of the cell. They even peeked through the window in the bathroom when i was on the toilet or taking a shower. When i covered the peephole with a towel or a uniform, they ordered me to remove it and threatened to take away all towels and uniforms if i continued covering the window. I didn't refuse, i simply ignored them. After a while they gave up. A month later one of the sergeants told me that i was permitted to cover the window when i used the bathroom. But only for three minutes.

There were twelve four-foot-long fluorescent light bulbs in the cage that were blinding. When i got ready to go to sleep the first night, i asked the guard to turn off the lights. She refused. "I can't see you if the light isn't on."

"How in the world can you miss me? You can see everything in the cell."

"Sorry."

They kept me under those blinding lights for days. I felt like i was going blind. I was seeing everything in doubles and triples. When Evelyn, my lawyer, came to see me, i complained. Finally, after Evelyn accused them of torture, they turned the lights off at eleven. But every ten or fifteen minutes they would shine a huge floodlight into the cell.

Then the trial started. First, motions were argued. Practically all of our motions were denied. All the prosecution's were granted. Then jury selection began before Judge John E. Bachman.

When they brought in the first jury panel i thought i was gonna have a heart attack. There were only a few Blacks speckled here and there, and the panel looked more like a lynch mob than a jury. Most of the jurors openly glared at us, as if they would kill us if they could. Half said they thought we were guilty. The other half, although they didn't say it right out, answered questions like they believed more or less that we probably were guilty. I was convinced some of them deliberately lied just to get on the jury and convict us. Most of the few Black people excused themselves on the grounds of hardship. They had children, families, jobs and simply could not afford to be on a lengthy jury trial. If ever there was a case of the blues, i had it.

"Do something," i kept telling the lawyers. "Do something!"

"What can we do?" the lawyers would answer. "We're doing the best we can."

It was true, but i just could not accept it. This was my life they were talking about. I must have bugged the lawyers to death.

"Object to this, object to that," i would tell them.

"Our objection is already on the record."

"Well, object again anyway." I was outraged, trapped and helpless. Whenever a juror said something that revealed out-and-out prejudice, the judge would try to clean it up. Poor Ray Brown, one of the defense lawyers, caught most of my fire.

"I want you to object."

"On what basis?" he would ask.

"Don't you see it? The judge is asking leading questions."

"But the judge is legally allowed to ask leading questions during jury selection."

"Well, object anyway." I knew nothing about law then. I had never even seen a trial. I just couldn't understand how the judge could be so blatantly prejudiced in favor of the prosecution and there was nothing we could do about it.

"Why can't y'all be like Perry Mason?" i asked the lawyers jokingly.

"Did you ever see Perry Mason defend a Black defendant?" Ray Brown answered.

Sundiata was a lifesaver. He would try to calm me down and would explain what to expect. Logically, i accepted what he said, but i was still frantic.

"We just can't let ourselves be railroaded," i'd say, coming up with one wild idea after another. Sundiata would patiently explain why none of my fantastic ideas would work. After a while of participating in my own legal lynching, i became convinced that Sundiata and i should fire the lawyers and defend ourselves. In that way we wouldn't be tied to those stupid rules and we could say anything we wanted to.

"That's not true," Sundiata told me. "Even if you defend yourself, you're still bound by their rules."

"How am i supposed to know those rules? I'm not a lawyer. And i still have a constitutional right to defend myself."

"True, but you still have to play according to their rules or they can bind and gag you. Look at what they did to Bobby Seale."

Every time i looked up at the jury box, i'd argue the point again. But i also knew that i didn't know one thing about the law, and it was hard to picture myself actually defending myself. Evelyn was always repeating the old cliché that a person who defends himself has a fool for a lawyer.

As we came closer and closer to completing the selection of

the jury, i became more and more upset. Then, one day, a kid who couldn't have been more than twenty was being examined as a potential juror. He spilled the beans. The judge asked him if he had an opinion of the case and he said, "They say she's guilty." The judge questioned him further and he blurted it all out. The prospective jurors in the jury room were talking about the case, although they had been ordered not to discuss it. The judge asked what they were saying.

"They say she's guilty."

"Only Mrs. Chesimard?" the judge asked.

"They're saying they're Black, they're guilty."

At that moment the lawyers were all on their feet, talking a mile a minute. They demanded a complete investigation of what was going on in the jury room. They wanted the juror asked more questions. They wanted the jurors to whom he talked questioned.

The judge immediately realized the boy had opened a can of worms. He did everything he could to avoid opening the can any further, but it had gotten out of his control. He finally agreed to conduct an impartial investigation. This time, when he questioned the jurors, he was very careful to downplay the gravity of what was going on in the jury room. But the other jurors substantiated what the boy had said. Our lawyers filed a motion asking that the jury be selected from another county because we couldn't get a fair trial in Middlesex. The assignment judge, not Judge Bachman, was to decide the motion. Meanwhile, the trial was stopped.

Evelyn told me the decision. The assignment judge had determined that it was in fact true that we couldn't get a fair trial in Middlesex County. The jury was to be picked from Morris County. "Where's that?" i asked Evelyn. She said she hadn't the faintest idea. Then Ray Brown came in.

"Where in the world is Morris County?" i asked him.

"Well," he said, "I'll tell you." Morris County was almost completely white with very few Black people and even fewer Hispanics and Asians.

"What does that mean? Are there ten percent Black people? Five percent? Or what?"

"A whole lot fewer."

"A jury of your peers," Evelyn said bitterly.

"What can we do?" i asked.

"We'll just have to wait and see."

"Can't we get the trial moved somewhere else where there are more Black people?"

"We can try, but don't get your hopes up too high."

I was coming back to earth, and fast.

The trial had been postponed for about a month, until January, because they needed time to secure the jail in Morristown, in Morris County.

"Maybe," i thought, "the lawyers will come up with something by then." I really didn't expect too much, but it seemed like such an obvious trick, such an obvious ploy, to ensure that we didn't receive a fair trial by a jury of our peers that i thought maybe something could be done about it. I was naive in those days. I knew it in theory, but i had not seen enough to accept the fact that there was absolutely no justice whatsoever for Black people in amerika. I still had some hope left. But they had taken something that was supposed to help us and turned it against us. They had used the law to abuse the law.

"Now, all we have to do," i reasoned, "is get the facts and figures and prove that they are trying to deny us a fair trial." How little did i know!

Chapter 4

Junior high school had its advantages and its disadvantages. It was more impersonal and much more confusing than elementary school, but it gave me the chance to move around and change classes, which i liked. Generally my subjects bored me, with the exception of English, history, and a newfound love of ceramics. Parsons Junior High School in Queens was mostly white. A lot of the Black kids had been put into remedial or what we called "dumb" classes. It never ceased to amaze me that the kids who were so smart in the street were always in the dumb classes.

In junior high everybody was going with someone. When girls got together to talk, the subject was always boys: who was cute, who was going with whom, who was fresh, etc., etc. A cute boy was tall, slim but well built, and usually had light skin. A boy was considered super-fine if, in addition to light skin, he had funny-colored eyes. Hazel and green eyes were the best. If a boy was popular or good at sports he usually got a play, but in general the boys we talked about were tall, not too dark, and handsome.

One of my earliest admirers was this boy named Joe. He was new in our neighborhood, from down South or somewhere, because everyone said he was country. He was real dark and had a long body with short little legs. He liked me, and, in the beginning, i think i kinda liked him too. Then everyone started teasing me, saying he was my boyfriend and saying he looked like a black frog because his legs were so short. At that age, i was worried to death about what everyone thought of me. I wanted desperately to be one of the pack and i didn't want anybody to make fun of me. So whenever anybody said i liked Joe, i would deny it to the bitter end and talk about him worse than everybody else. But Joe was very sweet to me. Every time he saw me he would smile and say something nice. On Valentine's Day he gave me a beautiful big valentine and some candy. One day, in the spring, i heard somebody calling my name outside my bedroom window. It was Joe. Quickly, he put a flower on the sill and ran away. Every day after that he did the same thing. When i would see him on the street, i would smile. I was really touched by the flowers. Then one day my mother saw him at the window putting a flower on the sill.

"You tell that boy to stay away from that window," she said. "Now he's putting flowers in the window, the next thing you know he'll be trying to climb in." But she still thought it was kinda cute. The next thing i knew she was telling all her friends about it. While i was embarrassed, it also made me think i was cute. No boy had every paid me that much attention before and i loved it.

One day i was coming from the store and i saw Joe. He started walking beside me. He was kinda shy and he had never said anything to me except "You look nice" or "You look pretty." This day we tried to make conversation as we went along. Then, all of a sudden, he said, "Will you go with me? I want you to be my girl." Somehow i was shocked. Did he really think i would go with him and ruin my reputation forever?

"No," i answered.

"No," he repeated. "Why not?"

I didn't know what to say. My tongue became heavy and twisted, I started to stutter. Nothing came out of my mouth. "Why not?" he asked again. I stammered and stuttered and then, with icy bluntness, i said, "Because you're too black and ugly." I will never forget the look on his face. He looked at me with such cold hatred that i was stunned. I was instantly sorry for what i had said, but there was no taking it back. He looked at me as if he despised me more than anyone else on the face of the earth. I felt so ugly and dirty and depraved. I was shaken to the bone. For weeks, maybe months, afterward, i was haunted by what happened that day, by the snakes that had crawled out of my mouth. The sneering hatred on his face every time i saw him after that made me know there was nothing i could do to make it up to him. There was nothing i could do but change myself. Not for him, but for me. And i did change. After that i never said "Black" and "ugly" in the same sentence and never thought it. Of course, i couldn't undo all the years of self-hatred and brainwashing in that short time, but it was a beginning. And although i still cared too much about what people thought about me, i always tried hard after that to stand on my own two feet, to stand by what i felt and thought and not just be a robot. I didn't always succeed, but i always tried like hell.

Mostly, when i was young, the news didn't seem real. In fact, my vision of the world was like a comic strip: In China they ate fortune cookies and the men wore braids; in Africa they lived in huts, wore bones in their noses, and were cannibals; in South Amerika they wore big hats, slept in the middle of the day, drank a lot of rum, and danced the cha-cha. The only place, besides the United States, that i could talk about with anything resembling realism was Europe. And my perception of Europe was almost as unreal. The first president i remember was Eisenhower and even he didn't seem real. My mother said that all he did was play golf. When he gave a speech on TV, we turned the channel, and, if he was on all the stations, we turned the TV off.

Only the news concerning Black people made any impact at all on me. And it seemed that each year the news got worse. The first of the really bad news that i remember was Montgomery, Alabama. That was when i first heard of Martin Luther King. Rosa Parks had been arrested for refusing to give her seat to a white woman. The Black people boycotted the buses. It was a nasty struggle. Black people were harassed and attacked and, if i remember correctly, Martin Luther King's house was bombed. Then came Little Rock. I can still remember those ugly, terrifying white mobs attacking those little children who were close to my own age. When the news about Little Rock came on, you could hear a pin drop at my house. We would all sit there horrified. Sometimes, afterward, somebody would say something, but usually we would just sit there lost in our own thoughts. I guess there was nothing to say. And each year i would sit in front of that box, watching my people being attacked by white mobs, being bitten by dogs, beaten and water-hosed by police, arrested and murdered. Then the news seemed too real.

The older i got, the more i seemed to grow into myself. My mother and stepfather were having all kinds of problems. They were fussing and fighting like cats and dogs. They were like a whole lot of other Black people in that respect. They were catching hell every day on their jobs, in society, and they took their frustrations out on each other. To make matters worse, she was a teacher and he worked in the post office: she had been to college and he hadn't. As far as i'm concerned, if a Black man and woman make a marriage work in amerika, they've accomplished a miracle. Because everything is against them. Just being poor is one of their biggest obstacles. Most of the arguments are about money. It's hard as hell to be loving and caring when you can't pay the bills and you don't know where the next dollar is coming from. And the way that we're brought up to think adds insult to injury. It's changing a little bit now, but when i was growing up, every white man on television was able to support his family with no particular strain. There was no need for his wife to work. Her job was to stay home and take care of the kids. Black people accepted those role models for themselves even though they had very little to do with the reality of their own existence and survival.

While my parents were going through their changes, i was going through mine. I was at the age where i questioned everything. The world was beginning to have more and more impact on me. I was curious about, and wanted to experience, everything. On weekends, whenever i could, i would take off. I went to the movies or to the library, but my favorite activity was riding subways and buses. I would hop on any subway or bus, ride until i got tired, then get off at any stop and walk around. Sometimes i talked to people or played handball with kids my age. Other times i just walked and looked. I went into all kinds of neighborhoods—white, Black, Puerto Rican, Chinatown too. But Harlem was my favorite place. I was fascinated by the street life. I was always trying to figure out what was going on. Everything was so colorful and busy. Men standing on the corner drinking, boys playing basketball, hustlers buzzing up and down the streets huddling and making deals. It was the land of dream books, kitchenettes, and Johnnie Walker Red. I loved the stores. From the market on Park Avenue to the greasy fish joints, to the candy stores that sold penny candy and penny cigarettes and god knows what else. I would walk and look and think. The world for me then was a big question mark, and the biggest question of all was where i fit in.

I was always late getting home and in trouble. It was like i had some kind of disease. I could never make it home on time. I would leave with the best intentions, but as soon as i got out in the street, it was as if i was in a trance. I would forget all about the time until it was too late. And half the time when i realized that it was getting dark, i didn't even know where i was, much less how to get home. My mother would talk to me, slap me, shake me, punish me, but nothing worked. I was a lost cause. I was running away from home and i didn't even know it. And one thing always led to another. I was turning into a fantastic liar. As soon as i got near home i began making up lies. When i look back at it now, i know my mother must have wanted to choke me when she heard those farfetched creations, but at the time i thought they were brilliant. As the problems in my family intensified, i ran away consciously instead of unconsciously.

The first time i ran away, i went to Evelyn's house. She wasn't home so i fell asleep on the stairway. When she came home, she thought i was some kind of drunken bum, so she walked by me and went to her apartment. I came back the next day and she talked to me, played shrink and family counselor, and sent me home. It worked for a while, but things were a mess. My mother and i couldn't see eye to eye about anything, and i was just as stubborn and self-willed as she was. And even when i tried to do right, it just seemed like i couldn't do anything that made her happy. And when my mother and stepfather were at each other's throats, it drove me wild. I would simply get my coat and walk out. Some days i just didn't come back.

At times, running away was fun and exciting. At other times it was miserable, cold, and lonely. The part i dug about it, though, was surviving. Being out there, face to face with the raunchiest side of life was like living on a roller-coaster, everything hurling itself at you at breakneck speed. It was one hell of an education, and, when i think about it, i was one lucky chile. So many things could have happened to me, and almost did.

The first time i ran away i had just the clothes on my back and very little money. I rode the subway and slept in hallways until i just couldn't take it anymore. Then i started talking to people. One of the first people i met was this boy named David. I told him that my mother was in the hospital and that i didn't have any other family in New York and i was scared to stay home alone. He took me home to his mother's house and we told his mother the same story. She said it would be okay for me to spend the night. They lived in the Farragut Projects in Brooklyn. David took me out and introduced me to all his friends. We got along fine until nighttime. Then it was war—an all-night wrestling match. When he wasn't attacking me, he was begging and pleading and thinking up a thousand arguments why i should give him some. I told him i was afraid of getting pregnant. He went and got this big jar of Vaseline and told me that, if you used Vaseline, you couldn't get pregnant. I was dumb, but not that dumb. I told him to go to hell, and the wrestling match continued. After a day or two at David's, i was ready to move on. Besides, his mother was getting suspicious.

My next new friend was a girl. I couldn't take any more Davids. Tina lived in the Fort Greene section of Brooklyn with her mother and her brother in a brownstone house. It was a rickety old house and half of it looked like it was condemned. There was nothing whatsoever in that house that was orderly. There were rooms with all kinds of junk in them, stacked almost to the ceiling: tables, chairs, record players, old radios. I told the same old story to Tina's mother and she was sweet as pie. I could stay there just as long as i wanted, she said. In fact, she said, she "just loved to have young people around her." And she wasn't lying either. All day long there was a procession of people in and out of that house, and most of them were young. When Tina's mother saw that i didn't have any clothes, she said, "We'll just have to take you shopping." I remember thinking how nice she was, to be willing to spend money on me, a stranger. The next morning we went down to Fulton Street.

"All right," she told me, "now I want you to go with Tina into A&S and pick out what you want; I'll be here at the soda place. Just remember where everything is."

Off we went, Tina and I. I was happy as a jaybird; my clothes were kind of on the funky side. When we got inside the store, i started to pick up things and got ready to try them on.

"Be cool," said Tina. "Don't you know what size you wear?"

"Yeah," i said. "Why?"

"Let's just get the stuff and get out of here. If you like something, just say so. Don't go picking it up and putting it on and carrying on."

"O.K.," i said, thinking that she was strange. I liked a plaid kilt with a big safety pin and a blouse and sweater to match.

"This will go with it, too," Tina said, pointing to a white blouse. "Now you just do what i tell you. Step in this."

"Step in what?" i said, looking down.

"Be cool, fool!" Tina whispered. "Just keep looking ahead and help me pull this thing up." She had already got half the skirt up around my thighs. Finally we got the skirt up and fastened under my own skirt. "O.K., let's get out of here," Tina said. "Wait a minute. Roll that skirt up, it's hanging down, and don't look down!" I was scared out of my wits, but i started to roll.

"Not *your* skirt, fool," Tina whispered, "the one underneath."

Well, i was walking and rolling and trying to look cool and, if anyone had seen me, i know i musta looked like a slapstick comedy. But somehow we made it out of there. I expected the police to come swooping down on us at any moment. Tina's mother was still sitting in the same place, sipping on a soda.

"How'd it go?" she asked Tina.

"She's O.K.," Tina said. "She don't know nothin', but she was cool." I felt like fainting. Everybody else's mother i knew would knock you down if they even thought you were stealing. This was surely something new. I just kept staring at Tina's mother. She must've seen me staring at her, too, because she told me, "That's right, i steal and my kids steal, too. They tryin' to take my house from me. Tryin' to take everythin' i got. I got to survive by the best way i know how. But it ain't really stealing; it's just a discount. You need a discount, high as these stores is. We call it the 'five-finger discount.' " She started laughing.

When we got to the house, she said, "All right, let's see all the pretty clothes you got." Tina took the blouses and sweater from somewhere and i took the skirt from under my skirt. "That's all you got?"

"Yeah," said Tina. "She don't know how to do nothin', an' we was takin' too long."

"Y'all didn't get no underwear?" Tina's mother asked.

"No."

"Well, here," she said, giving us some money. "Go to the five and dime and buy some. And I don't want y'all taking nothin', ya hear? I didn't raise no nickel-and-dime-store kids, understan'?"

"Yes." And we were gone.

"We're gon teach you how to deal," Tina said on the way from the store. I just looked at her. My mind was spinning. Then i started to feel glad about it. We had gotten over. We had gotten over tough. The idea of five-finger discounts was beginning to appeal to me. And it was easy as hell.

That night i dressed up in my new clothes and went with Tina and her brother to hang out. He was on the quiet side, and evil-looking, but he turned out to be nice. We were going to a party at the Fort Greene Projects. We stopped and bought some french fries and Thunderbird. At the party, Tina introduced me to Tyrone. It was love at first sight. I thought he was the cutest boy i'd ever seen. Tyrone was the warlord of the Fort Greene Chaplins, and i thought it was just so romantic, like *West Side Story*. We sat in the hallway, drinking wine and smoking cigarettes. I had smoked before, but i had never drunk any wine. The music was playing and the lights were down low and i was feeling goooooooddd. They were playing those old slow sides like "Wind," "Gloria," "In the Still of the Night," "Sunday Kind of Love." We went inside and started to dance. I was in love and dancing on clouds, whirling around the dance floor. I was whirling and spinning, and all of a sudden i was outside, holding onto some bench for dear life, drunk as a skunk and sick as a dog. When i was finally able to stand, Tyrone walked me to Tina's house. We held hands all the way and he made a big deal out of kissing me good night, although i'll never understand how he could stand my vomit-tasting mouth.

I woke up the next morning feeling like elephants had been doing the Watusi on my forehead and like i was walking on my eyelids. Tina's mother wanted me to go someplace with her. I got up, washed, and got dressed. "What kind of jewelry do you like?" she asked me.

"I don't know," i said. "I guess i like rubies because they are my birthstone."

"Oh, no! You look like a girl that's made strictly for diamonds."

"Really?" i asked, flattered.

"Oh yeah, diamonds are a girl's best friend. And I'm gonna show you how to get some." She spent the morning and most of the afternoon showing me how to do just that. "You have nothin' to worry about," she kept telling me. "Even if they catch you, they can't do nothin' to you, you're a kid." I was supposed to go in a store and talk very proper. I was to ask the price of everything and tell the clerk that my father gave me $80 to spend, but that i had some money of my own. Tina and her brother would come in and create a diversion and, while everyone was looking at them, i was to put the biggest earrings i could get in my mouth under my tongue. I was to say something to the salesman and walk calmly out of the store. There were a few more parts to the plan, but i don't remember them. She had me practice talking with things under my tongue.

When we got to the store, i thought i was going to die of fright. I acted like i didn't know Tina and her brother and went in as planned. The store was pretty crowded and i went into my act. I was so scared, i felt like i was having hot flashes. At first the salesman acted like he didn't want to show me anything, but when i told him about the $80 and my extra money, he hurried up and pulled out trays. I held them up, saying, "Do you think she'll like these? Do you think she'll like these better?" Then, all of a sudden, Tina and her brother came running into the store. They were laughing real loud and chasing and grabbing each other. I almost forgot what i was supposed to be doing because I was so busy watching them. Then i remembered and, when i saw that no one was watching, i picked up the biggest earrings i saw and put them into my mouth. "I don't see anything Mommy would really like," i said. "Maybe i'll come back later." I started walking to the door. I just knew that that man was going to call me back.

"Miss," someone called. I felt like dropping through the floor. I looked out of the corner of my eye and saw that it was another salesman calling someone else. I walked out of the store, turned a corner, and ran. I was halfway to Tina's house before they caught up with me. The earrings were still in my mouth.

"Did you get over?" Tina asked me. I looked at her almost as if i didn't know her. "Did you cop or not?" she asked again, impatiently. Finally, i spit the earrings out into my hand.

"Shit," said Tina's mother, "them's pretty numbers there, I like them myself." As it turned out, the earrings were for pierced ears and my ears weren't pierced. "Sell them to me," Tina's mother said. "I'll give you $20 for them."

"It's a deal," i told her. I was glad as hell to get $20. I didn't care about no diamond earrings and i needed some money to get away and try to find a job. I was convinced that i wasn't cut out to be no thief.

That night we went out to celebrate. Tina's mother had given me $20 plus $2 extra for good work and she had also given me a pretty, gold-colored dress and nice black shoes. I was dressed up clean as the board of health and we all had some money in our pockets and were ready to "do it." We looked for Tyrone but he wasn't home. We walked all around the projects until we found him. He was at the house of these twins Jessie and James, or something like that. They all went downstairs for some kinda meeting. Everybody said they were gonna fight. They were at war with another gang, the Bishops, and one of their members had got messed up by the Bishops. Finally, the meeting was over and Tyrone came and hung out with us. But it wasn't the same. He spent the whole night talking about what he was gonna do to the Bishops. And if he wasn't talking about that, he was talking about the fights he'd had before, gang fights, school fights, fight fights, etc. It seemed like his whole life was fighting.

"Why?" i kept thinking. "Why was he so into fighting?" The question was on the tip of my tongue, but i just couldn't bring myself to ask it. I tried to imagine the future, Mrs. Tyrone whateverhisnamewas, and the children. Me, packing his lunch as he went off to fight the Bishops. Somehow, the picture didn't work. I was tired of this adventure. I was ready to go home. Whatever the consequences!

Chapter 5

ll right, Chesimard, pack your things. You're being moved."

"Moved? Where?"

"You'll find out when you get there."

"Then i'd like to call my lawyer."

"You can call your lawyer when you get where you're going."

I kept trying to find out where they were taking me. The continuation of the jersey trial, after the change of venue to Morristown, was still a month away. Maybe they were just moving me ahead of time. Maybe they were taking me back to the workhouse. I wasn't too worried, though. Anywhere was better than that basement in the middlesex county jail. The sheriff came down with a piece of paper in his hand.

"Where am i going?" i asked him.

"I have a federal order to produce you," he said, waving the paper around. "You are being turned over to the custody of the federal goverment."

"What for?"

"I don't know. You'll have to ask the feds."

My abrupt transfer from one jail to another, without either notice to my lawyers or explanation to me, was a scenario that would be repeated over and over again during the next few years.

After our motion for a change of venue from Middlesex County was granted in October 1973, i was returned to the basement of the middlesex county jail, where i believed i would remain until the trial resumed in Morris County on January 4, 1974. Evelyn immediately swung into action, contacting the national Jury Project to explore the level of racism in Morris County and preparing a number of motions she anticipated would have to be made before the morris county kourt. In addition, she was working on the continuous motion to remove me from solitary confinement in the middlesex county jail that was then before the new jersey federal district kourt. The underlying argument of the motion—that this kind of confinement destroyed my ability to adequately participate in preparation for my trial—had to be supported by psychological data and the opinions of experts. Evelyn was trying to find psychologists and sociologists willing to provide their professional assessments in support of the motion. She was also trying to locate a forensic pathologist, a ballistics expert, a forensic chemist, and other specialists we needed for the trial, and trying to raise money to pay them.

I was aware that there were two indictments outstanding against me for alleged bank robberies. Evelyn had been told that trials for these charges would follow the trial in jersey. One of the indictments was for a Bronx bank robbery that occurred in September 1972. I had been indicted for this crime along with Kamau, Avon White, and others in the federal kourt, southern district of New York, located in Foley Square in lower Manhattan.

I knew that Evelyn had made a motion before the southern district judge, gagliardi, to have that trial postponed until after the termination of the jersey trial. Having learned that the motion had been granted, i didn't connect the move to New York with the bank robbery trial. I was wrong.

The trip was the usual high-security endless procession of cars. And, as usual, i enjoyed the ride. Just the walk from the door of the jail to the car did me good—it had been so long since i had seen daylight or breathed fresh air. I looked at the trees and the grass and the sky as if i had never seen them before. It was a gloriously beautiful day.

When the feds told me they were taking me to New York to go to trial, i didn't know what in the world was going on, but i was sure Evelyn would straighten things out. There was no way in hell i could go to trial in federal kourt. Not unless they gave us time to prepare for it and canceled the jersey trial. There was no way that Evelyn could deal with both trials at the same time. She was working so hard i couldn't keep track of all that she was doing.

I knew we had arrived somewhere in Queens, but i didn't know where. There was no courthouse in the direction we had gone. The car came to a bridge where pigs were stationed, pointing rifles and shotguns. On the other side of the bridge were more police.

"Where are we? Where is this place?"

"You are now on Rikers Island. This will be your new home for a while," the marshal told me.

"It'll never be my home."

I looked around while they waited for clearance to pass through the gate. There were huge, ugly buildings in front of us, not old or dilapidated as i had imagined when i pictured Rikers Island, but institutional-looking nevertheless.

"Are all these buildings jails?" i asked.

"Yep," said the marshal. "They're all jails. There are a lot of criminals in the world."

"Everybody in jail isn't a criminal," i told him. "And they've got a lot of criminals locking people up. They've got a gang of criminals in the White House."

The marshal just grunted. The car turned into a modern brick building. There were no old-fashioned bars, just jalousied window-bar combinations. I was brought into a large receiving room and locked into one of the small rooms that lined the sides, empty except for some benches and a dirty bathroom. After a long wait, i was taken out to be printed and photographed. I was returned to the room, then called out again to fill out forms. I immediately got into a hassle about the forms: i had left the line for "address" blank.

"Where do you live?"

"I don't live anywhere. I'm in jail. And i've been in jail for six months."

"Well, where did you live before that?"

"I don't remember." And it wasn't a lie. I remembered the place, but i couldn't even begin to tell anyone the address. While i was underground i made it a habit never to remember addresses. I used landmarks to remember a place, and i never had trouble locating any place i had been to once, but even if i visited it a hundred times, i never looked at the address.

"Well, where does your mother live?"

"Why?"

"We need an address."

"I haven't lived with my mother in years."

"Well, give me the address anyway."

"I don't know if my mother would want you to have her address. I'll have to ask her."

The guard insisted, but that line was left blank. The guard was a Black woman with an Afro. And there was another one, next to her, with a lopsided wig on. She was Black, too. In fact, most of the guards i had seen so far were Black. I was quickly to find out that the overwhelming majority of guards in the female jail at Rikers are Black. But when they opened their mouths and expressed their opinions, you wondered. But that's another story.

After i had been waiting for what seemed like hours, they brought in a whole bunch of women. It was wonderful. They were real, live people, talking and laughing. It had been so long since i had even heard a conversation. I just sat there staring at them. I know i must have looked like i was crazy, staring like i was, but i just couldn't help it. I was overwhelmed. I could barely talk, though. When someone asked my name i stammered and stuttered. My voice was so low everyone constantly asked me to repeat myself. That was one of the things that always happened to me after long periods of solitary confinement: i would forget how to talk.

The next phase was the strip and search. There were two groups of women: those who were returning from kourt and those who, like me, were new admissions. We were directed to stand in little booths and take off all our clothes. Then we were told to turn around, squat, run our fingers through our hair, lift up our feet and open our mouths. This was for everybody. The next step was only for the new admissions. They put us in shower stalls without curtains, we were told to take a shower, and then were given this stuff which they told us to put it in our hair and on our pubic hairs and wash with it.

"What is this for?" i asked.

"It's for lice and crabs," the guard said. It was humiliating. The last stage was the "search." Every woman who came into the building had to go through this process, even if she had been nowhere but to kourt. Joan Bird and Afeni Shakur had told me about it after they had been bailed out in the Panther 21 trial. When they had told me, i was horrified.

"You mean they really put their hands inside you, to search you?" i had asked.

"Uh-huh," they had answered. Every woman who has ever been on the rock, or in the old house of detention, can tell you about it. The women call it "getting the finger" or, more vulgarly, "getting finger-fucked."

"What happens if you refuse?" i had asked Afeni.

"They lock you in the hole and they don't let you out until you consent to be searched internally."

I thought about refusing, but i sure as hell didn't want to be in the hole. I had had enough of solitary. The "internal search" was as humiliating and disgusting as it sounded. You sit on the edge of this table and the nurse holds your legs open and sticks a finger in your vagina and moves it around. She has a plastic glove on. Some of them try to put one finger in your vagina and another one up your rectum at the same time. Anyway, i had an instant, mile-long attitude. I wanted to punch that nurse clear to oblivion. Afterward, the guards had the nerve to tell me that a mistake had been made and a doctor would have to make a complete examination. I was just too disgusted. He was a filthy-looking man who looked more like a Bowery bum than a doctor. He coughed all over me without even covering his mouth, and his fingernails looked like he had spent the last five years in a coal mine. The only good thing about him was that he was quick. He rattled diseases off like he was an auctioneer and asked me if i had had them. Then he gave me a one-minute examination, took my blood, and that was it.

I was kept in the receiving room until long after everyone had left. Then a pleasant enough guard, with a scar on her nose and mouth, took me to my cell. We went down a corridor that seemed to be a mile long to a hallway where a guard sat inside a glass cage. Buttons and knobs and lights decorated the cage. It looked like the inside of some kind of spaceship.

"Open up five," the guard who had brought me said.

There was a thumping sound and then a humming sound and then nothing.

"You can go to your room now."

"Go where?" i asked.

"Just walk down the hall and the door will be open. You'll see it."

The hallway was long. When i got to the cell, the light came on. When i went in, the door slid shut behind me. It was something out of a science-fiction movie. The long halls, the sliding door, the control panel. "Space jail," i said to myself. Inside, there was a cot, a dirty sink, a seatless toilet, and a roll of toilet paper. I was tired and wanted to go to sleep.

"I'm turning the light out now," a voice said over the microphone.

The light went out, but a yellow light stayed on.

"Turn the little light off, please," i called to the guard.

Again, a voice came on over a microphone. "The light must stay on. It is there for your own protection."

The light stayed on and i went to sleep.

Morning! The doors slid open.

"Breakfast, ladies!" came over the microphone. It was early, but i was anxious to get dressed and look around. The first thing that hit me was the smell. I don't care what jail i've been in, they all stink. They have a smell unlike any smell on earth. Like blood and sweat and feet and open sores and, if misery has a smell, like misery. The walls of the cell were covered with obscenities and love declarations. "Apache loves Carmen;" "Linda and Lil bit;" "India and Rosa—true love, always." From the window i could see a small paved yard with grass growing between the cracks in the pavement and then another long building.

A few women were in the dayroom, but most stayed in their cells, which were barren except for the toothpaste writing that covered the walls. In prison, toothpaste serves many functions, one of which is glue to hang up pictures. A few of the cells were "fixed up" with pictures from magazines hung on the walls and a knitted or crocheted afghan on the bed. Clothes, in cardboard boxes, were on the floor. The women looked evil and ashen. They glanced at me with only vague interest and went about their business. They were all Black or Hispanic.

I took a shower and spent the rest of the morning walking back and forth. Some of the women were bloated, with swollen hands and feet. A few had a real strange look about them. One sat in a chair, her eyes crusted with sleep, giggling quietly to herself. A group of women sat at a table playing spades. They asked me if i wanted to play, and since i had never heard of the game, volunteered to teach me. It turned out to be like whist, only spades are always trumps. Then it was lock-in time again, the second one for the day. The first had come after breakfast.

There were two women on either side of me who had been locked in their cells all day. "Don't you want to come out?" i asked, stupidly. They broke up laughing.

"No," one said, "I like it here." When she stopped laughing, she told me she was "locked." That meant she was locked into her cell until she was seen by the Board.

"What's the Board?" i asked.

"It's the Disciplinary Board. When you get an infraction, they lock you up until you see the Board."

"Then they let you out?"

"Sometimes, but we're going to PSA."

"What's that?"

"It's the hole, the bing. This is 2 Main, where you go before they take you to the Board; then, after that, if they think you haven't done enough time down here, they send you to PSA." (PSA stands for punitive segregation area: solitary.)

"You mean you don't stay in this part all the time?"

"No. We're on the sentence side. We only had to come here

because we stole the medication. We stole almost everything on the medication truck and drank it. Coke almost OD'd. That's why we're down here. This part is for people who have infractions or for crazy people."

"Crazy people?"

"Yeah!" the one named Coke answered. "They've got some real bugs down here. How come you here?"

"I don't know. I got here yesterday and this is where they put me."

"You got a homicide?"

"A homicide?"

"Yeah, a homicide. You here for murder?"

"I have a homicide case in new jersey, but i'm here for a bank robbery trial."

"That's probably why they got you down here," they speculated. "They probably gonna move you soon." They asked a million questions.

"Who did you kill?"

"I didn't kill anybody."

"Well, who did they say you killed?"

"A cop, a new jersey state trooper."

"Oh, shit. You gon have a hard way to go. You didn't really do it?"

"No."

"You got a bank robbery, too. Did you rob the bank? How much money did you get?"

"I didn't get any money because i didn't rob the bank."

"Yeah? Then your boyfriend did it and put the blame on you?"

"No, i don't have a boyfriend."

"Oh, so you like girls funny?" They laughed. "You're kinda cute. Ya wanna go with me?" one of them joked. "You ever do time before?"

"No, never."

"You got any other cases?"

"Yeah, i have another bank robbery."

"Did you do that one?"

"No!"

"Well, damn, they got you all hooked up!" the one called Delores said. "How come they tryin' to frame you up like that?"

"Because i'm a revolutionary. They say that i'm in the Black Liberation Army."

"Oh, oh, I know you. You that girl I read about in the papers. Yeah, what's your name?"

"Assata, Assata Shakur, but my slave name is JoAnne Chesimard."

"Yeah, you the one. I never thought I'd meet you. How you doin'?"

"Yeah," Coke said, "I saw your picture on TV, but you look different now."

"How?" i asked.

"When I saw your picture I thought you was much bigger. And much blacker, too."

"Really?" I laughed. It was a statement i heard over and over. Everybody told me they thought i was bigger, blacker, and uglier. When i asked people what they thought i looked like, they would describe someone about six feet tall, two hundred pounds, and very dark and wild-looking.

"Bad as them papers said you was, I just knew you had to look bad. And here you are, just a little ole thing."

I asked them what they were in prison for. In the course of those next few days i was to learn a whole new vocabulary. *Jostling* was pickpocketing; *boosting* was shoplifting; *juggling paper* was writing bad checks and *dragging* or *playing drag* was conning.

Later that evening a woman who had just come from kourt told me that Phyllis wanted me to come to the gym at 8:30. I was overjoyed. I had heard that Simba was on the rock, but i thought they might move her to make sure we had no chance to be together. The gym was large. Women were playing handball and basketball, dancing, sitting on the bleachers, and talking. Finally, behind a clump of women, i saw Simba. We embraced and both just sat there, trying to get out all the words that were in our hearts. So much had happened since we had seen each other. We had been close when we were both members of the Black Panther Party. For a while we had lived together. She was always a real earthy sister with a heart of gold. She told me about her case, about the other comrades she was in touch with, and, then, that she was pregnant. Homey was her nickname for her lover, the baby's father, Kakuyan Olugbala. He was a beautiful revolutionary brother, and he was murdered by the New York police. Kakuyan and i had gotten to know each other pretty well while we were both at the Harlem branch of the Black Panther Party. He was one of the brothers who, in the days of the Panther Party's lumpen ideology, would be called lumpen. He was raised in Harlem around 116th Street and 8th Avenue, a relaxed, easy kind of person, but a fighter to the heart. He loved weapons and was a genius with them.

I was glad about her pregnancy and sad at the same time: she was facing twenty-five years. Although i tried to be cheerful, i guess she could see the concerned expression on my face.

"Don't worry," she told me. "These people can lock us up, but they can't stop life, just like they can't stop freedom. This baby was meant to be born, to carry on. They murdered Homey, and so this baby, like all our children, is going to be our hope for the future." I would think about her words many times later.

It's early in the morning. It feels like a quarter to zero and i want to sleep. I hear my name vaguely over the microphone. Something about kourt. They are calling me for kourt. Hurriedly i roll out of bed, shower, dress, comb my hair, and i'm ready to go. They bring breakfast on the food truck. I can't even stand the look of food, much less eat anything.

"All right, court ladies, time to go to the receiving room," the microphone wails. It's too early in the morning for that thing. I want to tear it out of the ceiling. I stumble down to the receiving room, still not fully awake. It's 7:20 A.M. I sit in the receiving room for three hours. Finally, the marshals come. Now they want me to hurry. One of them chains me up. First he shackles my feet; then he puts a chain around my waist, fastens the handcuffs to the chain, and handcuffs on my hands. I can barely walk. Or shuffle.

Kourt, dull, gray, dull green. They are putting me into the bull pen. I don't know why they call it a bull pen, though i have often speculated.

"Attorney visit," one of the marshals calls as he opens the bars to let me out.

We go to the end of the hall. Evelyn is puffing and huffing. She always puffs and huffs when she's angry. In a few minutes, i know that she will begin pacing and tapping her feet.

"They're trying to force us to go to trial right away," she tells me. "You know I've been busy, drawing up motions for federal court."

"What do you mean, federal kourt? Aren't we in federal kourt?"

"Yes, but if the judge denies our motion for postponement, I want to be ready to go straight into the circuit court."

"What's the circuit kourt?" It was all Greek to me.

"That's where we appeal if the judge issues an unfavorable opinion."

We go on talking. Evelyn is trying to explain to me and i am trying to explain to her that we can't possibly go to trial. "There's no way in the world you can be ready to go to trial right now." I am ranting.

"I know, I know," Evelyn replies.

I rant and rave indignantly while Evelyn tries to explain the law to me. They call us to court. The judge is gagliardi. He looks just like what he is: a racist dog craka. Kamau comes into the courtroom. I am delighted to see him. He has aged. He's grinning, but under the grin his face is hungry. I wonder what he's thinking. Bob Bloom, Kamau's lawyer, is up on his feet talking. He is asking for a postponement. Everything he says is logical and makes sense. Evelyn gets up and starts to rap. She is talking pure unmitigated truth and logic. The judge looks at the ceiling. I predict the outcome of the hearing and keep turning around to look at the audience. Friendly, familiar faces smiling at me. I don't want them to ever stop. The judge denies our motion for a postponement. The judge denies all our motions. I want to scream, "Dirty dog, slimy pig, you're not a judge. You're just another prosecutor."

I look at the prosecutor. He's smug. His face is unreal—like a poster. He looks like a 1940 war poster. John Q. Public. I keep staring at him. Nobody could look that corny. He's like a ghost from the past. I'm convinced he doesn't know it's 1973. The lawyers ask for a joint meeting and the judge says yes, but make it short. The lawyers outline the strategy of the appeals.

"What are our chances on this appeal?" i ask.

"There's a chance," Evelyn says. "Slim, maybe, but a chance. If the courts are interested in justice, well, of course, they'll support our position." We all know how big an "if" it is.

The next time we went to kourt five days later it had snowed. The trees were bare and covered with ice and, though i don't like winter, it was a beautiful sight. As soon as i arrived in the kourthouse, Evelyn was there to tell me that the circuit court had denied all of our appeals, and gagliardi was talking about going to trial that day.

"I just want you to understand that there is no way that I can adequately defend you on this short notice. I haven't had time to prepare pretrial motions, I have received no discovery material, and I haven't even had time to think about an appropriate defense because I haven't been able to find out the basic facts of the case. I just want you to know that."

"I know," i told her, "and i know you're doing the best that you can."

"At any rate," Evelyn said, "if worse comes to worst, you'll have a solid issue for appeal."

It was a depressing picture. We clearly were being railroaded. We went before the judge. Again, he was arrogant and belligerent, determined to force us to go to trial right away. Again, she asked the judge for a postponement, but her arguments fell on deaf ears. He ruled that we could have a joint conference later, but the trial would begin immediately.

As we left the courtroom, Akilah was standing in the hallway with Ksissay, Kamau's two-year-old daughter. As he walked near her, she held out her arms to him. Kamau took about two steps toward her and the marshals jumped him and began beating him. I jumped on the marshals and tried to pull them off. In an instant there was one hell of a fight in the hallway. Finally, the marshals drew their guns and forced us to lie down on the floor with our arms spread apart. We lay there while they stomped our backs and kicked us as they handcuffed our hands behind our backs. Akilah ran to tell everybody what was going on as Ksissay screamed hysterically. I will never forget the haunting scream of that child as she watched her father being brutally beaten.

After the fight, the marshals were vicious and vindictive. They did everything they could to provoke and harass us. Newspapers reported that we had attacked the marshals.

Kamau and i decided that we weren't just going to let ourselves be railroaded quietly. This so-called trial was such a blatant miscarriage of justice that we weren't even going to participate in it. And we didn't want Evelyn and Bob Bloom to participate in it either.

"Just sit there and don't say anything," we told them. "We'll do the talking." And do the talking we did.

At the next kourt session, gagliardi asked the lawyers if they were prepared to begin picking the jury. Both of them made statements to the effect that since it was impossible for them to represent us adequately, we had requested that they remain "mute."

"All right, then, we'll proceed with you or without you," the judge roared. "Bring in the panel."

As soon as the jury panel entered the kourtroom, Kamau and i began to tell them what was going on. We told the jury that he had been appointed by Nixon and that he was persecuting us because of our political beliefs, that he was the same judge who had just given Mitchell and Stans, the Watergate defendants, who did not have one fraction of the valid reasons for an adjournment that we had, an extended postponement. After a while, the judge ordered us removed from the courtroom. Jury selection continued with only the judge and the prosecutor participating. Every so often the judge would send the marshals back to ask us if we were going to "behave."

"Of course," we would tell the marshals.

Once returned to the courtroom, we "behaved." Again we told

the jury what was happening and that the judge was trying to railroad us. As soon as we began to talk, the judge ordered us from the kourt. Whenever we were about to be thrown out, the marshals vied for positions closest to us and for the opportunity to grab us, twist our hands behind our backs, and get their licks in. To avoid being manhandled, as soon as the judge said, "Remove the defendant from the courtroom," i would say, "The defendant will remove herself." Most of the time it worked, but one day the marshals were so gung ho they jumped on me and started brutalizing me in open kourt. Evelyn jumped up like she was ready to fight and stood between me and them, holding them away with an outstretched arm.

She complained to the judge. My arm and hand had not yet fully recovered and i was still partially paralyzed. Evelyn's remarks made the marshals more vicious. They became so brutal that all of the spectators began to cry out. As the marshals carried me out of the kourtroom, the spectators chanted, "Railroad, railroad." The judge ordered them removed. As i was being taken downstairs, i could hear the commotion. People were chanting and yelling and screaming. The marshals, i later found out, had beaten some of them. I sat in the bull pen, lost in my thoughts, when they brought a white woman and man down the hallway and put the woman in the cell with me. I looked at her without much interest.

"Assata," she said, "I'm go glad to have finally met you. But I never thought it would be this way."

I looked at her blankly.

"My name is Natalie Rosenstein. I was upstairs. I was one of the spectators in the courtroom when they started pushing and shoving and beating people."

"What?" i said. "You're kidding!"

"No. We didn't move fast enough, so they arrested us," she said, referring to herself and the white man.

"What did they charge you with?"

"Obstructing justice."

After that, Kamau and i were banned from the kourtroom. We were put into a freezing room next to the kourtroom where a loudspeaker had been installed so we could listen to the trial. In the beginning, they slammed the door shut. At first, we wanted the door open because it was so cold and the warmth from the rest of the building helped. Then we began to enjoy the privacy. It was good to be able to talk to each other without someone looking down our throats. Because we knew that sooner or later they would open the door and stare at us, we would open it.

"Let some heat in. It's freezing in here."

"The door stays closed." After a while, they locked it.

One of the first things that Kamau and i had discussed was Islam. He had been a Muslim for some time and was deep into it. He was seriously trying to convince me to convert and become a practicing, active Muslim. I had always said that if i had any religion, it was Islam, but i had never practiced it. Because of Elijah Muhammad and Malcolm X, the Muslim influence over our struggle has been very strong, but it had always been difficult for me to accept the idea of an all-powerful, all-seeing, all-knowing god. And, i reasoned, how could i be expected to love and worship a god whose "master plan" included the enslavement, torture, and murder of Black people?

Kamau argued that Islam was a just religion, opposed to oppression. "Oppression is worse than slaughter," he quoted from the Holy Koran. "A true Muslim is a true revolutionary. There is no contradiction between being a Muslim and being a revolutionary." I didn't know much about it, but i agreed to seriously check it out. Muslim services were held regularly on Rikers Island, and Simba and i began to attend.

Talking to Kamau was so good for me. Solitary had affected me really badly. I had closed up inside myself and had forgotten how to relate in an open way with people. We spent whole days laughing and talking and listening to the kourtroom madness in between. Each day we grew closer until, one day, it was clear to both of us that our relationship was changing. It was growing physical. We began to touch and to hold each other and each of us was like an oasis to the other. For a few days the question of sex was there. Then, one day, we talked about it. Surely, it was possible. But, i thought, the consequences! Pregnancy was certainly a possibility. I was facing life in prison. Kamau would also be in prison for a long time. The child would have no mother and no father.

Kamau said, "If you become pregnant and you have a child, the child will be taken care of. Our people will not let the child grow up like a weed." I thought about it. That was true, but the child would suffer. "All our children suffer," Kamau said. "We can't guarantee our children a future in a world like this. Struggling is the only guarantee our children will ever have for a future. You may never have another chance to have a child."

"I have to think," i told him. My mind was screaming. Who would take care of my baby? I thought about what Simba had said about our children being our hope for the future. I had never wanted a child. Since i was a teenager i had always said that the world was too horrible to bring another human being into. And a Black child. We see our children frustrated at best. Noses pressed against windows, looking in. And, at worst, we see them die from drugs or oppression, shot down by police, or wasted away in jail. My head was swimming. What had my mother and grandmother and great-grandmother thought when they brought their babies into this world? What had my ancestors thought when they brought their babies into this world, only to see them flogged and raped, bought and sold. I thought and thought. How many Black children are separated from their parents? How many grow up with their grandmothers and grandfathers? Didn't i stay with my grandparents until my mother had finished school and was on her feet? I remembered all the discussions i had had. "I'm a revolutionary," i had said. "I don't have time to sit at home and make no babies."

"Do you think that you're a machine?" a brother had asked me. "Do you think you were put on this earth to fight and nothing else?"

I thought about what Zayd had always told me. "While you're alive, girl, you betta live."

"I am about life," i said to myself. "I'm gonna live as hard as i can and as full as i can until i die. And i'm not letting these parasites, these oppressors, these greedy racist swine make me kill my children in my mind, before they are even born. I'm going to live and i'm going to love Kamau, and, if a child comes from that union, i'm going to rejoice. Because our children are our futures and i believe in the future and in the strength and rightness of our struggle." I was ready for whatever happened. I relaxed and let nature take its course.

When something important was happening in the kourtroom, we listened. But, usually, whatever was happening droned on in boring chatter that amounted to nothing. Lawyers have the habit of turning ten words into a hundred and saying nothing more in the process. The trial was like something out of some playwright's imagination. We called it the "vaudeville show." Evelyn and Bob, after registering their daily protests, sat mute. The judge raved and ranted. The pigs barked like vicious dogs. The "witnesses" lied like crazy. The jurors (who had been picked solely by the prosecution) looked and listened expressionlessly. There were a couple of Black jurors, and although we held little hope we would be acquitted, we placed the microscopic hope we did have in the Black jurors. Even though we had presented no defense, had not participated in the trial, we thought that there was a slim chance they might not go along with the program. Black people are generally not as brainwashed as white people when it comes to the so-called system of justice.

The whole kourt process began to take its toll on me. Half the time i wasn't eating because they usually served pork for lunch and, sometimes, they had pork for dinner. Breakfast was out of the question. I could never figure out what they gave us. I called it "monster stew." I was always freezing and i didn't have a coat. My mother had brought me one, but i had given it to Simba. She was pregnant and needed it more than i did. One night, when i returned from kourt, i began to feel awful, like a knife was stabbing me in my side. I could hardly breathe. I went to the prison doctor and the diagnosis was plueurisy. When the judge learned i was sick and unable to come to kourt, he had a fit. He acted like i had gotten sick just to delay the trial. The next time i saw the prison doctor, he was nervous and shook up.

"They keep calling me about you," he said. "They want you back in court right away. They want to know how fast I can have you back in the courtroom."

"Who keeps calling you?" i asked.

"Everybody. People. I've got to get you back in court as soon as possible."

And that's exactly what he did.

Every day they brought us into the kourtroom. And, every day, as soon as the jury came in, we began to tell them what was happening, that we were being forced to trial without being given time to prepare a defense. And every day, the judge ordered us removed from the kourtroom and cited us for contempt. It was comical.

"What are you going to do?" i would ask him, after i had been cited for contempt for the hundredth time. "Put me in jail? Lock me up?"

One day, when the judge had been particularly crazy and the marshals had been particularly brutal, Evelyn just couldn't take it anymore.

"I'm not going to sit here and watch this spectacle," she said. "If you won't permit me to defend my client, there is no purpose in my being here." And with that, she got up and started to leave.

"Get back in here," the judge yelled. "I order you to get back here and sit down."

Evelyn kept walking.

"If you don't come back and sit down, I'm citing you for contempt."

Evelyn walked out of the kourtroom. The judge cited her for

contempt. (In 1975, after all appeals, including the supreme kourt of the united states, were denied, she served the ten-day sentence in maximum security at the westchester county jail for women.)

The trial soon ended and we waited patiently for the verdict. Evelyn and Bob gave us lectures. "Expect nothing but the worst. There's a chance, but it's slim." Kamau and i waited for the conviction. One day of jury deliberation passed. Two days passed. The jury seemed to be taking forever. We wondered what was taking them so long. It was an open-and-shut case. We had cross-examined no witnesses, presented no defense. Kamau and i spent the time tenderly, savoring our last few moments together.

The next morning Evelyn and Bob came in, grinning. "It's a hung jury," they giggled. "gagliardi is fit to be tied. They're going to call us into court in a few minutes. We just thought we'd come in and give you the good news." Ten minutes later we were in the kourtroom. The judge was grimly thanking and dismissing the jury. The marshals looked like they wanted to fight. The prosecutor looked like he wanted to cry. We found out later that a lone Black juror had refused to convict us. He had heard us. The look on gagliardi's face gave me great pleasure. I looked at him and gave him my most meaningful smile. His face turned red and he looked away.

Afterward, we met with the lawyers. We were still giddy and in a state of shock. "What does this mean? Are they going to try us again?"

"They're going to try you again, and right away," Evelyn told us. "The new trial will begin on Monday."

Kamau and i looked at each other. We were sick of this case but were ecstatic that we were going to have more time together.

"Are we going to have the same judge?"

"No," Bob said. "They've got to assign a new judge."

Evelyn was caught up in our gleeful mood, but, as usual, she was business first. "We've got to come up with a trial strategy." Sitting in that courtroom day after day and watching that fiasco enabled us to do one thing. We were able to see and analyze their case. "I feel that now we are ready to go to trial."

"They don't have a case," Bob said. "I don't even know how they got an indictment."

"We know," Kamau and i said.

"Their case is utterly absurd," Evelyn said.

"We know," Kamau and i droned again.

"Their witnesses are as phony as three-dollar bills," Evelyn said.

"We know."

"They don't have one piece of physical evidence," Evelyn ranted. "No photographs, no fingerprints, no witnesses, no nothing."

"We know," Kamau and i chanted in unison.

"They couldn't possibly have any evidence," i said. "We weren't there."

"Well, I know that," Evelyn said indignantly. "That's not the point."

Bob and Kamau looked perplexed. Evelyn and i just looked at each other and smiled knowingly. We had found out in new jersey how "evidence" could appear out of nowhere and other evidence disappear.

Evelyn and i have a very close relationship. We love each other intensely and we get along wonderfully. Usually! But when we argue or disagree, it's awful. We are both outraged that the other one doesn't agree or see our point and we feel betrayed and furious. And neither of us has the mildest temper in the world. Add to that the tremendous pressure we were both under, and you have the recipe for fireworks.

During one of our strategy meetings, Evelyn and i locked horns. Try as we might, we couldn't reach any kind of agreement. After a while, we weren't even communicating. It became a matter of who had the last word and the final decision.

"I'm the lawyer," she yelled. "I know what I'm doing! If you aren't going to listen to me, then what's the point of having me defend you?"

"I'm the client," i yelled back. "I'm the one who's gonna do the twenty-five years in prison if you're wrong."

"What you're saying is that you don't trust me or my judgment." Evelyn said. Our argument went from bad to worse. After a while we were saying all kinds of things we didn't mean to each other.

"I don't need this shit," Evelyn stormed. "What the hell do I need to defend you for? You haven't got an ounce of sense."

"You don't have to defend me if your don't want to," i responded. "Don't do me any favors."

"You need all the favors you can get," Evelyn countered.

"Well, i don't need them from you. I can defend my damn self as well as you can."

"I'd like to see you try it. I don't need this mess."

"I will. I don't need you either."

"Well, go ahead and defend your stupid self then." Evelyn screamed.

"I will."

After the argument i was tired and blank. All the tension had been drained out of my body. I was still mad, but i was sorry, too. Evelyn was probably right, and i was probably crazy. It's so hard working with someone who is so close to you. It's like having your mother or your wife or husband as your lawyer. It's real hard to be objective. Personal stuff sometimes gets in the way. I didn't know whether i was being a sane adult or a rebellious child.

The next time we came to kourt, i could see right away that Evelyn was still angry with me. I fully intended to try and make up, but her cold manner made me draw back and get mad all over again.

"Is your decision still the same?" she asked coldly.

"Yes," i responded icily.

"Judge," she told the new judge, "I wish to be relieved from the case. Ms. Shakur wishes to retain another lawyer."

"Is this true?" the judge asked me.

"Yes. I want to defend myself." A little while later she was off the case.

As i sat in the bull pen feeling stupid and stubborn, the guard brought in a public defender. Gagliardi had assigned him because he didn't like the way Evelyn was behaving. I told him i didn't want him to represent me, that i was representing myself, the judge had assigned him to my case.

"What did you do before you were a public defender?"

He told me that "once upon a time" he had been a prosecutor. That was the end of the conversation. I would rather have had an alligator for a lawyer. I don't even remember his name, but he sat through both trials as my supposed lawyer, even though i refused to even speak to him.

Since i was now defending myself, i was entitled to a lawyer as an adviser. Everyone suggested lawyers, but most of them were white leftists. I wanted, if at all possible, a Black woman. Not just any Black woman lawyer, but someone who was in tune with the politics of the Black Liberation struggle.

One of the names given me was Flo (Florence) Kennedy. She was a Black lawyer who was very active in the women's movement, well known on the speaking circuit from coast to coast and more renowned as a feminist and political activist than as a lawyer. She fit the bill perfectly. She was just what i wanted.

Some argued against her.

"But, Assata," they said, "she's not a trial lawyer. Flo is not a criminal lawyer. You need both, someone who can give you sound advice." I was unmoved by their arguments. "She's wild; she's flamboyant and eccentric; she might scare the jury."

"She can't be any wilder than this case is," i countered. "Besides, i don't need a crimnal lawyer because this isn't a criminal case. I need a political lawyer."

I was in a wild mood and i was determined to handle the case the way i saw fit. I wasn't expecting any such thing as justice! This case was like something out of *The Twilight Zone* and i was convinced that it couldn't be treated like a normal, run-of-the-mill criminal trial. I was determined to use this case to expose the deceit and crookedness of the government. A meeting between Flo and me was arranged. Flo warned me over and over about her lack of trial experience.

"You know, darling, that I haven't been inside a courtroom to try a case in years."

"I don't care," i said. "You've been out in the world; you know what reality is and that's enough."

Flo agreed to be my legal adviser. And i was ready to go to trial.

Chapter 6

My mother and stepfather broke up and my mother, my sister, and i moved to a new apartment in a housing complex in South Jamaica near New York Boulevard and Foch. One side was the projects and the other side was the co-op where we lived, but they looked about the same to me. Compared to Jamaica, Parsons Gardens, where we had lived, was a little black dot. South Jamaica, Jamaica, Hollis, Bricktown, St. Albans, Springfield Gardens, South Ozone, etc., were all joined together to make up a Black city. You could live your whole life in Jamaica and the only time you'd see a white face was when you shopped on Jamaica Avenue or when the insurance man came around. At one time, Jamaica was all white. Black people had moved out to the Island to escape the ghettos of Harlem and Brooklyn. They bought old houses at exorbitant prices, only to find that, within a few years, their "nice" neighborhoods had turned into the crime-ridden, drug-ridden, poverty-stricken places they had run from.

I loved Jamaica, and i was just starting to get into the beat of it and to know my way around when my mother and i had one of our terrible arguments. I don't even remember what the argument was about, but i was hardheaded, stubborn, and under the impression that a grave injustice had been done to me. The next day i got up, packed my clothes, and headed straight for the Village. Greenwich Village was where artists and musicians and all kinds of weird people were supposed to live. I was fascinated by the idea of beatniks and bohemians, even though i had never met any. I figured that if i belonged anyplace, it must be the Village.

I walked around with my suitcase until i was exhausted. I remember thinking that people here didn't look that different from anybody else. I found a place to check my suitcase and spent the rest of the day going around door to door asking people if they had any jobs available. Most didn't even look up at me, they just gave a flat no. At the end of the day, i was tired, disgusted, and hungry. I had nowhere to live and not the slightest idea what i was going to do next. I went back for my suitcase, but the place was closed. After that, i just walked aimlessly until i reached a little park. I sat down on a bench, tired as hell and unable to take another step. After a while, a little white guy with bumps on his face sat down next to me and started talking. I didn't understand half the things he said, but he seemed nice enough. When he asked me if i wanted to go to a restaurant across the street with him, i gladly accepted. I was starving. It was an Italian restaurant and the scent in the air was heavenly. I ordered enough to feed a mule. The guy talked about all these people i didn't know and about his job. He kept saying people on his job were conspiring to get him fired.

"I worked there for eight years and they didn't even give me any notice." He told me over and over that the company he had worked for had stolen two of his inventions and patented them and that when he tried to get paid for them and to get credit for his ideas, the company tried to get rid of him.

"What did they do?" i asked.

"They did everything. They stole my files and my papers and then spread rumors about me." He said he was some kind of engineer. "I should never have trusted them," he kept saying. "You can't trust anybody."

When the food came i ate like i had spent a lifetime starving. "Doesn't this food taste funny to you?" the guy asked. I tasted some more and it was good.

"There's nothing wrong with mine," i told him.

"There's something wrong with this food," he said loudly. "What did they do to my food?"

The waiter came and tried to calm the guy down. "I don't understand," the waiter said, "but if you'd like, I'll bring you another plate." Although the guy said it was better, he still thought it tasted a little funny. To change the subject, i told him a sad story about my mother being in the hospital and that i had nowhere to stay.

"Oh, you can stay at my place," he said. Then, seeing how i was looking at him, he added, "I have an extra bed."

"No funny business?"

"No funny business," he promised. He paid the check and we left.

His apartment was a tiny one-bedroom unit with a dirty kitchen and a green moldy-looking rug. The living room was neat and sterile. There was a plain brown couch that turned into a bed. I asked him for something to sleep in and plopped down into the bed. He kept talking, but i closed my eyes and pretended to sleep. After a while he went into his bedroom and shut off the light. I woke up during the night to go to the bathroom, stumbling around disoriented until i finally found it. When i came out of the bathroom, i went into the kitchen for some water. While i was there the guy came in. His face was all puffed up and red.

"What are you looking for?"

"Some water."

"Oh, no, you're not," he screeched. "You've been creeping around this house looking for something."

"What?" i asked. "You're crazy."

"Oh, no, my dear, that's what they want me to think. I'm not crazy in the least. What were you looking for? Who sent you? You didn't find anything, did you? Well, you can tell them, I haven't invented anything else for them to steal."

"I don't know what you're talking about. Nobody sent me no place and i wasn't looking for anything."

"Oh, no! You were just going for a little moonlight stroll. Do you think I'm some kind of fool? I took you in off the street, out of kindness, and here you try and deceive me. They really fooled me this time. I never thought they'd send a nigger. A nigger spy."

"Your momma is a nigger," i told him, "and you're a crazy son of a bitch." I threw on my clothes as i cursed him out.

"Spy. Spy," he kept saying.

"Your mother is a spy, and you can drop dead as far as i'm concerned."

I slammed the door and walked out into the early morning. The sun was beginning to come up. I walked until i found a drugstore open and ordered tea and an English muffin. I bought a toothbrush, toothpaste, and some makeup so that i would look older. I was going to get a job if it killed me. I got my suitcase, found a bathroom to wash up in, changed clothes, and checked the suitcase again. I bought a couple of newspapers. This time i was going to be systematic about it.

I saw an ad for a waitress and counter girl. That was something i knew i could do. The place was in downtown Brooklyn. I hopped on the first train in that direction and got there about 8:30 in the morning. The cafeteria was in a factory building and was solely for the factory workers. The manager had black and white hair and was big, fat, and sloppy. He wasn't so anxious to hire me at first, so i told him a sob story about coming from down South to help my mother who was in the hospital and that i needed a job as soon as possible. Finally, after looking me up and down, he hired me and said i could start right then and there. I was grinning from ear to ear.

I was supposed to spend the morning making salads and sandwiches and other things for lunchtime. But around ten o'clock, all these men started coming for coffee break. The manager had me running around like crazy, toasting bread, buttering buns, and getting the men their orders.

"Move faster, move faster," he kept telling me. Every time he told me to move faster i tried until it seemed that it wasn't humanly possible for anyone to have moved faster. Then i noticed he was always brushing against me. His hands were always "accidentally" touching my behind. I'd move his hand away but that only seemed to make him bolder. Every time i bent over to get something out of the freezer or off the food shelves, he would try to slide his hands up my dress. After a while, i began slapping his hands away. This, too, seemed to make him bolder. Finally i told him, in a nice, quiet voice, "Would you please keep your hands off me? Would you keep them to yourself?"

"Whattaya talkin' about?" he said, acting surprised. "I ain't done nothin' to ya."

As the day wore on, he accelerated his shouting at me. "Can't you move any faster?" he would yell. "Get that lead outa your ass." He stopped putting his hands on me for a while, but in about an hour he was right back to his old tricks. He acted like it was some kind of joke or something. I didn't think it was funny worth a damn. Lunchtime was super-busy and i was moving super-fast. After lunch, we started getting ready for afternoon coffee break and after that we started getting ready for dinner. Dinner was from 4:30 to 6:30, and 7:00 was quitting time. When dinnertime came, i was tired and miserable. I needed the job desperately, but the manager was driving me wild putting his hands all over me. When i told him to stop, he would grin, throw his hands in the air, and say, "What am I doing? What am I doing?" Then he started a new trick. He'd pull the elastic of my panties through the uniform and let it pop like a rubber band.

"Stop it!" i yelled. "Just stop it!"

"Stop what? What am I doin'?"

By the time dinner was over i knew i couldn't take it anymore. Bad as i needed the job, i couldn't take that big fat pig's hands all over me. Just before i was ready to go home, i told him.

"Look, if you can't keep your hands to yourself, i'll quit. I can't take it anymore."

"Whattaya mean, you'll quit? You're fired. You got lead in your ass and you don't know how to treat your boss. Now get the hell outta here."

"Just give me my money and i will."

"I ain't gonna give you shit," he said, " 'cause you ain't did shit."

"Look, mister, you gonna pay me my money. I worked hard and i want my money."

"Come back at the end of the week."

"No, i want my money now. I need it now."

"You ain't gettin' nothin' now, I told ya. Come back at the end of the week."

"No, you're giving me my money now; i want my money!"

"Well, you ain't gettin' it."

"I'll call the cops on you," i bluffed.

"I'll call the cops on you," he said, "if you don't get your ass outta here."

"You better give me my money," i repeated, looking wild and about ready to jump out a real bag.

Some people from the factory came in and stood at the back of the cafeteria looking.

"Keep your voice down," he said, acting like he was going to be cooperative and pay me. "I'll tell you what. You come in the back with me now and I'll pay you for an extra day. I'll even let you keep your job, and, if you're good, I'll even give you a little extra change."

"I'm not going any damn where with you. Just give me my money!"

"Now, why do you want to be like that?" he asked, putting his hands on my shoulder. I was hot and fit to be tied.

"Get your hands off me," i yelled. "You don't want nobody to know what kind of a dog you are. Well, i'm gonna tell everybody. If you don't give me my money, i'm gonna make you wish you had. I'm gonna tell everybody what you are." I started to walk to where people were working in the factory part.

"All right, all right," he said. "Here's your goddamn money. Just get the hell outta here."

The people who had been standing in the back moved up

closer to see what was going on. The man went to the register and counted out my money. I was dead tired and felt like a fool, but at the same time i felt kinda good inside. I was still in the same boat, but i was thirteen dollars richer and i had enough self-respect not to let any old lecherous white man feel up and down my body.

I had enough money altogether to rent a cheap hotel room. I got my suitcase and checked into a hotel. I think it was the Hotel Albert. After i had hung up my clothes and taken a shower, i decided to get something to eat. Downstairs in the lobby, there was this big, tall Black woman, dressed to kill. She had black hair with silver streaks running through it, long false eyelashes and a lot of makeup.

"Well, look at the baby!" she said, looking straight at me. "Palease tell me how you wound up in this joint? Are you straight from Alabama, dar-ling? Where are you going, honey?"

I just looked at her.

"Do you speak, dar-ling? Can you talk? Where are you going, honey?"

"I'm going out to eat," i said, a little wary.

"Where are you going to eat, love?"

"I don't know."

"Well, come with me, honey. We can eat together. I'm having a starvation attack."

I just stood there looking at her.

"Well, come on, love. You don't want me to die of malnutrition, now, do you? Do you like Chinese food?"

"Yes," i told her, wondering why she was taking all of this interest in me and wondering how she knew i was new at the hotel. We walked around until we came to a Chinese restaurant. The whole time she talked nonstop. Suddenly i remembered how little money i had. I had intended to eat a hot dog or something.

"Look," i told her, "i don't have enough money to go in there. This place looks expensive and i'm kinda on the broke side. Maybe another time i'll come eat with you."

"Listen, love," she said, "I didn't drag you all this way to eat alone. I hate to eat alone so you're just stuck with my company. It looks like I'm gonna have to treat your broke ass to dinner."

I was extremely grateful. Miss Shirley (that's what she called herself) was one helluva talker. She sounded sophisticated and country at the same time. She was from Georgia, but she had been in New York for a long time. She had lived in the Village for a long time, too, although she said she was a gypsy. I ordered something like chop suey, the cheapest thing on the menu.

"What is you tryin' to do, honey?" she said. "Make me sick? Look, you sit there with your ears open and let me do the ordering." She ordered all this stuff and, when it came, we feasted. There was so much we could barely finish it.

"That's better, honey. Now Mother can join the living."

The waiter came and asked if we wanted anything else.

"If I can't have you," Miss Shirley said with a wink, "I'd like the check."

The waiter, a tall, thin Chinese man, blushed and hurried away. This is one bold chick, i remember thinking.

"How long is your place rented for?" Miss Shirley asked.

"Until tomorrow."

"What are you going to do after that?"

"I'll find another job," i told her. Then i told her about my job at the cafeteria. She laughed her head off.

"Well, honey," she asked me, "what in the hell are you running from or what in the hell are you running to?"

I told her the sad tale about my mother in the hospital.

"Do you actually expect me to believe that mess?"

I swore up and down that it was true.

"I ain't no fool, honey, and I been out in these streets long enough to know that you running from something, and if you don't want to tell me, that's your business. But I like you and I'll try to help you if I can." I was grateful and i didn't know what to say so i didn't say anything.

"Look, I've got this friend that works on Bleecker Street. He wants to take some time off to hang out with his friend, but he doesn't want to lose his job. You could work in his place until he comes back."

"Fine," i said. I was down for anything—well, almost. We went to the café and a skinny white dude came up to us.

"Sit down and rest yourselves. I'll be back in a minute."

We sat down at a little round table.

"You want some espresso?" the guy asked.

"Sure," Miss Shirley said. He brought two little cups of black stuff. I took one sip and thought i was gonna choke. Miss Shirley cracked up. "Well, I can see that you're not initiated. I'm gonna have to do something about your education."

I arranged to take the guy's job for four days and he showed me what i had to do. "If you forget anything, or have any questions, ask the sailor," he said, pointing to a man with tattoos up and down his arms. I was to begin work the next afternoon at four. I still didn't know how i was going to pay my rent at the hotel for the next few days because i wouldn't be paid for my work at the café until the guy came back from his vacation. I told Miss Shirley what i was thinking.

"I'll talk to Freddie," she said, "and see if he'll let my good friend have a little credit. If not, you can come up to my place and sleep on the floor. We went back to the hotel and found Freddie. He didn't want to give me any credit. Miss Shirley kept haggling.

"How much money do you have?" she asked me.

"Fifteen dollars."

"Well, give me ten and I'll lend you the rest so you can rent a room for a week."

I gave her the money and Freddie told me i had to move to another room, which was fine with me. The room was tiny, but at least it had a bathroom and i had somewhere to stay for the rest of the week. I was grateful as hell for Miss Shirley.

"Well," she told me, "you get a good night's sleep. Mother has to go to work."

"Where do you work?"

"Anywhere I have to," she said. "Anywhere I can."

I was dog-tired and the bed was like an oasis. I woke up the next afternoon. It was almost one o'clock. I took a shower, got dressed, and went to find something to eat. Then i went back to the hotel and knocked on Miss Shirley's door. She opened the door with a razor in her hand. I almost fainted. She was shaving her face. Miss Shirley was a man. When she saw my reaction, she fell out laughing.

"You got a lot to learn, sugar. Ya got a lot to learn." We both sat there laughing up a storm. Somehow, it was funny as hell.

I went to work early that afternoon. The job wasn't bad and i could eat all i wanted, which meant i didn't have to buy dinner. The tips weren't that much, but i'd be able to live on them until the guy came back.

Any Black woman, practically anywhere in amerika, can tell you about being approached, propositioned, and harassed by white men. Many consider all Black women potential prostitutes. In the Village, this phenomenon was ten times worse than elsewhere. It was almost impossible to go from one corner to the next without some white man hissing at you, following you, or jingling the money in his pockets. One morning in the park, i met a couple, about my age, from Harlem, who had run away from home and were now living in a room in the Village. I told them that i had run away, too, and we became instant comrades. We got into a discussion about how white men are always approaching Black women.

"Yeah," they giggled, "but we got something for they ass."

"Yeah?" i asked.

"Yeah. We fix them right up."

"How?" i asked. Then they told me. The Murphy game was their game. They told me how it worked and i fell out laughing. I thought it was a brilliant scheme.

"You want to try it? I know them ofays'll dig you."

I was anxious to try this new scheme because it was "big" money and i would be able to pay Miss Shirley back and get a real place of my own. The first night, after my job was over, i met Pat and Ronnie in the park. Pat and i were the bait and Ronnie was the protection. We were all to walk separately on different sides of the street so that we could see each other. I had dressed up and put on makeup to look older. About five minutes after we started walking, a white man came up to me. He said he liked the way i walked and wanted to take me someplace.

"I'm on my way to a party," i told him. "It's going to be a real hot party."

"Yeah? What kind of party is it going to be?"

"What kind of party would you like it to be?"

"A party for two," he said.

"I know a place where they've got some very nice private rooms and they're not too expensive. It's a private club. You've gotta join first."

"How much does it cost?"

"Fifteen for the room, fifteen to join the club, and fifteen for the babysitter."

"You don't look old enough to have a kid."

"The babysitter's for my little sister."

We argued about the price. He thought it was too high. I kept telling him how he was getting a deal and that, once he joined, he would be a member for a year and could go there anytime he wanted and get some action. Finally he agreed to pay. When we got to the building, i told him to give me the money so i could go upstairs and pay the people.

"By the way," i said, "would you tell me what kind of work you do? These people are very particular about who joins their club."

"I work for a bank." I could see from his face he was lying.

"I'll be right back. Don't you go nowhere."

I ran up the stairs and opened the door to the roof. Carefully, i closed it behind me. Then i went over about ten roofs until i came to the one i was supposed to come down from. I tried the door. It wouldn't budge. Somebody had locked it. I went to the next roof.

Luckily, the door opened. I ran down the stairs and came out around the corner from where the man was standing. Hurriedly, i walked to where i was supposed to meet Pat and Ronnie.

"How'd it go?" they asked.

"Easy as pie," i answered.

"Okay, let's do another one." I was scared to try another one because i was scared i would run into the man again.

"We can go up around 14th Street. We've got another building staked out around there."

"Okay," i told them, "but let's check it out first." I explained about the door that wouldn't open. We got to the new place, checked it out, then went to 14th Street. In a matter of twenty minutes Pat and i had each caught a fish. I was worried to death we would bump into each other. I rushed my man to the building, got the money, and hurried to the meeting place. I waited and waited. It seemed like an eternity until they came. Pat had seen me with my man and had the good sense to go to a different building than the one I took my man to. We were all in high spirits.

"See how easy it is?" Pat asked me.

"Yeah. It's a breeze."

We split up the money. We had each made $45. I rushed back to the hotel. Miss Shirley was there and we went up to her room for a drink. I felt like a millionaire. I had the money i had made working in the café plus the $45. I whipped out my bankroll and paid Miss Shirley back.

"Now, girl, I know you ain't got no rich uncle. How'd you get all that money?"

I told her everything. I thought i was so slick.

"Girl, is you crazy? Do you know what one of these men will do to you if they find you in the street? Girl, these people out in this street don't give a damn about you. This street will eat your ass alive. Honey, I know what I'm talking 'bout. You done run away, ain't you?"

"Yeah," i told her. "I ran away."

"I knew it all the time. Well, honey, I can't make you go home. If I tried, you'd only run away again, but you're wasting your time and your life out here. These people don't care nothin' 'bout you. All they want to do is suck your blood. You a smart girl. What you need to do is go home and finish school."

"I'm never going home."

"Well, if you insist on staying out here in these streets, you better start acting like you got some sense. Don't you never let nobody use you and make a fool outta you. What if one of those men had been a crazy man and followed you upstairs? What if the other door had been locked and you hadn't been able to get out? Where was your so-called protection? You mean to tell me that you gon risk your life for fifteen dollars? Girl, this Village ain't nothin' to play around with. They got some crazy mens around here that is killing up young girls like you and one of 'em cuts their titties off. Girl, as far as I can see, that young boy Ronnie don' wanna be nothin' but a pimp. He ain't done one thing to earn that money. You better start to use your head."

I could see Miss Shirley knew what she was talkin' about. "But what am i gonna do, Miss Shirley? You know how hard it is to find a job."

"Don't worry, honey, I'll come up with something."

The next day when i went down to the lobby, Freddie was behind the desk. "I hear you're lookin' for a job," he said.

"Uh-huh."

"You know anything about bein' a barmaid?"

"No," i told him.

"Well, ya go over to this place, Tony's, on 3rd Street and ask for a guy named Chuck. Tell him i sent you."

"Thanks. Thanks a lot." I went over to Tony's and talked to Chuck. "Do you have any openings?" i asked him.

"Sure, we always have openings for foxes like you." He laughed. "Do you know the setup?"

"No."

"Fifteen dollars a night and you get a quarter for each drink and a dollar for each bottle of champagne."

I looked at him blankly.

"Your job is to sit and look pretty and keep the customers happy and buying. You work from eight in the evening to four in the morning when the place closes. What you do after that is your business. Just don't make any deals on the premises."

"Yes," i answered warily.

"Well, then, see you tonight."

When i got back to the hotel, i told Miss Shirley about my new job. "All right, honey, but you be real careful. There are a whole lot of crazy peoples 'round here. And you keep looking for a real job so you can go to school at night. Now, come on upstairs and let me show you how to put your face on. You look like a two-bit hoe."

At ten to eight i was at Tony's. Chuck was there and introduced me to the barmaid. Her name was Joyce. "Come here for a minute, honey," she told me and went to the end of the bar. I followed her.

"You like whiskey sours?"

"I guess so. I never had one."

"Whatever you do, don't get drunk. I'm going to make your drinks without the whiskey. If a customer come in and I know he's the suspicious type, I'll make you a real one. If you want a drink with the whiskey in it, just order with your hands folded. There's not too much I can do about the champagne. I'll try to keep pouring it into the man's glass. But it's not too bad and the bottles are small."

"Okay. Thanks."

I went to the bar and sat down. In a few minutes a couple of white guys came in. They sat two seats down from me and kept looking in my direction.

"Would you like a drink?" one said.

"Okay," i answered.

"What are you drinking?"

"A whiskey sour." And so began what seemed like a never-ending parade of whiskey-less whiskey sours. It got so that even the smell of the stuff made me sick. Once in a while i would ask the barmaid to put some whiskey in one, but i have never been much of a drinker.

Most of the customers were white men who were looking for some action. I found most of them to be crude, boring, and creepy. I would sit there, making up different stories to tell them just to keep myself amused. Another object of these stories was to get them to spend as much money as possible. If i thought that the man would go for a sob story and hand over some money, i would tell him a real tearjerker. Other times i pretended to be a college girl going to NYU. This made them less likely to be bold. When i played a college girl, i usually said i was a math major because people never know the first thing about math. One night, though, after i told this guy my math major story, he asked me some questions about integrals and imaginary numbers. I didn't have the faintest idea what the guy was talking about. It turned out he taught math at NYU.

"I know you're lying," he told me.

"Of course, i am. Who in the hell is going to be interested in the life of a waitress?"

The guy broke out laughing. "That deserves a drink," he said. "Bring the lady another drink." After that, the guy (i called him Mr. Math) came by every so often to hang out. He would buy drinks and we would sit there cracking jokes.

"How's your thesis going?" he would ask.

"Fine," i'd answer. "I'm doing a chronological study about the social significance of two and two equaling four."

I had a few other regulars. Most of them came in to tell me their troubles. They either had wife trouble or job trouble. Some were drunks who just wanted somebody to drink with, and others just liked the challenge of trying to seduce a young girl.

A lot of the other girls were prostitutes. The few who weren't were either just out to make some extra money or they were alcoholics. Most of the women were very nice and protective of me. The prostitutes liked me because i was always sending them business and was always discreet about it. Soon i made friends with the guys in the jazz quartet that worked there regularly. I've always loved jazz and i would clap and shout and let them know i enjoyed the music. The piano player and i became especially tight. I called him my big brother and he was very protective of me. When the place closed, he and maybe one or two of the group would walk me home. If it was raining, he would send me home in a cab. Closing time was the roughest time of all. Some of the men thought that buying drinks entitled them to more than conversation. But Chuck was a good bouncer and could spot a problem before it became serious. If a guy was getting out of hand, Chuck would approach him, tell him that i was the sister of one of the guys in the band and that if he didn't treat me with respect, he would let him have it.

At times some real freaks and weirdos hung out there. There was one guy who had bought the panties of almost every woman who worked at Tony's, paying them each $15. I asked him what he did with them. He laughed and told me he hung them on the walls of his apartment. When i told one of the other girls, she laughed.

"Girl, you believe that? That guy takes them home and holds them over his nose. He's a sniff freak."

But any woman at Tony's had to be careful. Some of the men who came around were real dangerous. On nights when things were slow and there were no customers in the place, the women would tell horror stories about all the crazy men they had run into.

I was big for my age and well built and, with all the makeup i wore, i could usually pass for eighteen. I told everybody i was nineteen. The white people never questioned my age, but the Black people would, sooner or later, realize i was younger than i let on. Some of them even guessed i had run away and would take me to the side and encourage me to go home. After a while, all the women who worked at the place teased me about not having a boyfriend.

"This girl don't like men and she don't like women. Here's a girl that let's her fingers do the walking!"

When they teased me i wanted to crawl into a crack somewhere and hide. The more embarrassed i became, the more they laughed. A new bass player came to work for the band and i developed an instant crush on him. I was convinced i was in love. In a short time, everybody knew about my crush. But the bass player paid me no mind at all. I did everything i could think of to attract his attention, but he just ignored me. Near closing time, his white girlfriend would come and they would leave together. I hated her. She looked so smug. One weekday night, it was pouring rain outside and the place was empty. The bass player said to me, "I'm writing a song for you. You want to hear it?" I could have fainted. I was grinning from ear to ear.

"Yes, i'd like to hear it."

> Da da da ta ta da da de de.
> Da da da ta ta da da de de de Jailbait!
> Da da da ta ta da da de de,
> Da da da ta ta da da de de de Jailbait!"

The rest of the group chimed in, "Jailbait, jailbait," and the whole place cracked up. I could have died right then and there. That was the end of my crush. When i thought about it later, though, it was funny.

A lot of the Black men that i met in the Village were hung up on white women. Some of them would come right out and tell you, "Man, i can't dig no spade chick. Gimme an ofay every day." When i asked them why, they said white women are sweeter, Black women are evil; white women are more understanding, Black women are more demanding. One of the things that really infuriated me was when they called Black women sapphire. "You know how you nigga women are, sapphire, evil." A lot of these guys would have trampled over my face just to get to a white woman.

At times, i really got sick of being around so many grown people. I'd either sneak back into my old neighborhood or hang out with Pat and Ronnie. One night they were going to a party uptown. I was dying to be with kids my own age, so i told Chuck i was taking the night off. When we got to the party, it was dull and tired, so Pat and Ronnie went off to find some reefer. They loved the stuff, but i was scared of it. I waited and waited for them to get back. I started to talk to a boy, who seemed really nice, about how dull the party was. He said he knew of a boss party that was going to be happening later. I waited for Pat and Ronnie to come back, but they never did.

"Why don't you come to the party with me?" the boy asked. "It's at my house and I'm sure you'll have a good time."

Finally i said i would go. He seemed so nice. He lived in some projects near Spanish Harlem. When we got to his house, no one was there. I started to leave, but he said his friends were all at a ball game and they would be there afterward. In a little while, the doorbell rang and, sure enough, all these people came in. After a minute i noticed they were all boys.

"Excuse me," the boy said. Then they all went into another room for a minute. When they returned they were whispering and talking under their breaths and i could tell that they were up to something.

"Where are the girls?" i asked. "Oh, they're coming." One came and sat next to me. He put his hand on my leg. I moved it away.

"Come on, baby, why you wanna act like that?"

"Come here, man," one of them said. I could sense that something was wrong. I didn't know what they were up to, but i knew they were up to something. I picked up my pocketbook and my sweater.

"I'll have to be going."

"No, baby, you ain't goin' nowhere."

"I've got to go." I started walking toward the door. One of them grabbed my arm and yanked me away from the door.

"Sit your ass down, bitch. We've got plans for you."

I knew it now. They were going to rape me. I had heard people talking about "trains," but i had never thought it would happen to me. I sat still for a minute. Then i made a wild break for the door. They tried to grab me and i fought like hell. The fight didn't last too long, though, because in a minute they had me held down on the floor. They were pulling up my skirt and taking my blouse off. I cried and screamed.

"Shut up, bitch," one of them said, slapping my face. I begged them for mercy. I told them i was a virgin.

"There's always a first time, baby," someone sneered. I begged and pleaded. I cried and cried. I couldn't believe they could be so heartless. But they were. The boy who brought me there was arguing with another boy about who would be first. I couldn't believe it. It was a nightmare. They were arguing and carrying on as if i wasn't even human, as if i was some kind of thing. I felt so scared and betrayed. I had trusted this boy. The argument between them was heated. I hoped they would fight and kill each other. I kept begging for mercy, pleading with them. They paid me no attention. One of them came over to me as if he felt sorry for me.

"Don't worry, baby, it won't hurt. You'll see. You'll like it."

"Okay," i heard the boy who had brought me there say, "you can go first, man," and the other boy started toward me. I jumped up and tried to run, but i was cornered. One tried to grab me and, in the process, he knocked over an ashtray.

"Be careful, man," said the boy whose house it was. "My mother will kill me if the house gets messed up."

That was my cue. I picked up a vase and threw it at the wall. I picked up a lamp and something else, crying and screaming at the same time.

"You might get me, but i'm gonna mess up your mother's house before you do."

The boy who was supposed to go first made a leap for me and missed. I kicked over the table and knocked over a plant that was on the stand.

"Get back! Get back!" i screamed.

The boy whose house it was grabbed the boy who was supposed to go first.

"Come on, man, my mother will kill me."

"Get back! Get back!" i screamed. "I'm gonna throw this lamp straight into that mirror." There was a big mirror hanging behind the couch. "Get them out of here. Get them out of here or i'll fuck this house up." I was shaking and crying, but i was serious as hell. I was gonna mess that boy's house up so bad no one would recognize it. "Get them out of here," i said, kicking the table over.

"Come on," the boy said. "Y'all got to get out of here. My mother's gonna have a fit."

"You crazy bitch," one of them said to me. "Come on, let's jump on her, man, she can't do that much damage."

"It's the man's house," one of the others said. "Come on, let's go."

"Get 'em out of here," i screeched at the top of my lungs.

"That's okay," one of them said. "We'll wait for you outside, baby."

Slowly, in what seemed forever, they left. Only the boy who had brought me remained. I could see that he was trying to figure out some way to jump me.

"Don't come near me. You better stay back." I didn't know

what i was gonna do next. They were all waiting for me outside. I couldn't call the police because the police were looking for me.

"Get back," i told the boy who looked like he was trying to ease up close to me. "All right, get away from the door." I still had the lamp and something else in my hands. "Get back there," i told him, indicating the back of the apartment, "or i'll smash your house up." When he moved back i looked through the peephole. There was nobody in the hallway. "They must be waiting downstairs," i thought. "All right," i yelled, "get over by the door." He moved to the door. "Now get out in the hallway and knock on one of your neighbor's doors and bring a grownup back here."

"What?"

"You heard me, sucker. Now move."

"It wasn't my idea. I didn't want to do it. I had to."

"I don't want to hear that shit. Just get your ass out in that hall or i'll mess up your house so bad your mother won't even think it's her house."

"Please," the boy said.

"Please, my ass," i screamed. "If you don't get out there and knock on one of those doors, you can forget about your mother's house."

He went outside into the hallway. I slammed the door after him and watched through the peephole as he knocked on a door. A lady answered, and i opened the door and started begging her to help me.

"Please, miss, help me. They're trying to get me," i screamed, crying all over again. I still had the lamp in my hand. "Please walk me downstairs to the subway or to a cab."

"What happened, honey?" she asked.

"They tried to do it to me," i cried.

The woman looked at me and then at the boy. "You wait there for a minute, honey," she said. Then she and her husband came out. "Don't worry, nothin's going to happen to you now." They brought me downstairs and put me into a cab.

I thought a lot about those boys after that night. I hated them, but what i couldn't understand is why they hated me so much. Everybody was always saying what a dog-eat-dog world it was. There were all kinds of people in the world and most of them seemed unhappy. Everybody seemed to be in their own bag and few seemed to care about anybody else. I had read this play by Sartre. The play ended with the conclusion that hell is other people, and, for a while, i agreed.

Back then, when i was growing up, boys gang-banging or gang-raping a girl was a pretty common thing. They called it pulling a train. It didn't happen to any particular kind of girl. It happened to girls who were at the wrong place at the wrong time. The boys talked about it like it was a joke or a game, like they were "only" out to have some "fun." If a girl was caught on the wrong side of a park or in the wrong territory or on the wrong street, she was a target. It was a common thing back then for boys to down-grade girls and cuss at them in the street. It was common for them to go to bed with girls and talk about them like dogs the next day. It was common for boys to deny they were the fathers of their babies. And it was common for boys to beat girls up and knock them around. And then the girls would get hard too.

"If the nigga ain't got no money, I don't want to be bothered."

"If the nigga ain't got no car, then later for him."

The more i watched how boys and girls behaved, the more i read and the more i thought about it, the more convinced i became that this behavior could be traced directly back to the plantation, when slaves were encouraged to take the misery of their lives out on each other instead of on the master. The slavemasters taught us we were ugly, less than human, unintelligent, and many of us believed it. Black people became breeding animals: studs and mares. A Black woman was fair game for anyone at any time: the master or a visiting guest or any redneck who desired her. The slavemaster would order her to have six with this stud, seven with that stud, for the purpose of increasing his stock. She was considered less than a woman. She was a cross between a whore and a workhorse. Black men internalized the white man's opinion of Black women. And, if you ask me, a lot of us still act like we're back on the plantation with massa pulling the strings.

After my close call uptown, i became more skeptical of everybody. I was much more careful about the situations that i let myself fall into. I would talk to the men at Tony's but, more and more, i became "strickly business." The more i saw of street life, the uglier it was.

One day, as i was walking down 8th Street, i saw one of my aunt's friends. Her name was Abbie or Addie or something like that and she was as big as a truck. I turned my head hoping she wouldn't recognize me.

"Joey, Joey!" i heard her cry out. I kept walking. She kept calling. I kept walking. Then i felt her grab my arm.

"I know you," she said. "You're Joey. Your aunt and your mother are worried to death about you."

"I don't know what you're talking about," i said. "My name is Joyce and i don't know you or anyone else that you're talking about."

"Come off it, Joey," she said. "You're not fooling me. Come with me while I call your aunt." She had my arm in an iron grip. I thought of making a run for it, but she was too big to play with. She took me to some bar and told me to sit at the counter while she made the call. As soon as she started dialing i made a beeline for the door. She was right on top of me, grabbing me with that iron grip. "You're not going anywhere until your aunt gets down here." In half an hour, Evelyn was on the scene throwing questions at me left and right.

"Where have you been? What have you been doing? Where have you been staying? What have you been doing for money? How have you been eating?" she asked—and a million questions more. When Evelyn questioned me, she sounded like a lawyer cross-examining a witness. In about an hour i had broken down and told her everything. She demanded that i take her to the hotel where i was staying. After i had packed my things, she told the guy behind the desk, "Do you know that you've had a thirteen-year-old girl staying here? I could have you prosecuted for contributing to the delinquency of a minor." The guy looked at me like he just couldn't believe it. I could have crawled under the floor. Then she called up Tony's and told him the same thing. I was dying of embarrassment, but in a way i was glad it was over. I was getting tired of the streets. I was tired of being grown and i wanted to be a kid again.

Chapter 7

Kamau and i were acquitted in the bank robbery trial in the Southern District of New York on January 28, 1973, and on the following day i was returned to new jersey. When i arrived at the morristown jail, there was a clump of reporters and photographers standing around. Morristown looked just like smalltown, usa. The jail was an ugly building attached to the kourthouse. There were a few other women in the jail and i was kept away from them. The only time i saw them was when i was being taken to or from my cell. They all appeared to be white, although i found out later that one was Black. The guards were all women, as old as the hills, and they had been working at the jail for an eternity.

There was a television and a radio in the cell, and it had been so long since i had been able to watch the news on television or listen to a static-free radio station that i went crazy. And i had turned into a crochet fiend. My poor mother was the unfortunate recipient of my early "creations." Brave, devoted person that she was, she thought they were pure genius.

We learned there were few, if any, Black jurors on the panel for the new trial. The news was depressing. The panel was selected from the voting rolls, and, since candidates running for office seldom represent the interests of Black and poor people, Blacks and the poor don't vote. But failing to vote means they don't sit on juries. Any chance that we would receive something even remotely resembling a fair trial was slim. We decided to try to have the trial removed to federal court. The chance of the feds taking over was slim, but it was worth the try. If the trial was held in the federal kourt in Newark, at least we'd be assured of a few more Black jurors on the jury panel.

There were countless joint legal meetings, countless strategy sessions, and countless kourt appearances. My first look at the Morris County jury panel flung me into a terrible depression. There were only two or three Black jurors on each panel and they looked like extras in a soap opera. As a matter of fact, the whole jury panel looked like escapees from a soap opera. They dressed differently and had a whole different air about them than New York people. Morristown was supposed to be one of the ten richest counties in the country, and, looking at these people, i believed it. I could just see trying to explain to them what poor Black people in big cities go through. How could they understand someone becoming a Black revolutionary? They had so little to revolt against. They had bought the amerikan dream lock, stock, and barrel and seemed unaware that, for the majority of Black and Third World people, the amerikan dream is the amerikan nightmare.

Evelyn and i had resolved our differences and she was back on the case. She, Ray Brown, and Charles McKinney, Sundiata's lawyer, worked hard on the motion to remove the trial to federal kourt. But after a hearing, the federal judge remanded the case back to the state kourt. He hadn't even listened to our arguments. So we were right back where we had started: picking a jury in Morris County.

Jury selection droned on tediously. Sundiata and i kept ourselves from falling asleep or from having nervous breakdowns by laughing and talking. Just seeing Sundiata every day was such a comfort to me. We made up all kinds of little games and jokes, especially guessing the answers jurors would give to the trial judge's questions. We got to be pretty good at it. We could look at a person and pretty much know what he was going to say. Some glared at us hatefully while they waited to be called, as if they couldn't wait to give their opinion that we were guilty. They were so sure of exactly what happened. They recited detail after detail from newspapers and TV.

"Where were you hiding that night on the turnpike?" i wanted to scream at them. "I didn't see you!"

Others gave us crooked smiles in the hope that we would think they sympathized with us and would leave them on the jury. But there was not one bigot in the kourtroom. None of them said they had any prejudice against Black people.

"Do you have any Black friends?" the judge asked.

"Of course." But when asked if they had ever invited a Black person to their homes or been to the home of a Black person, the answer was, invariably, no. On one panel, the judge asked everybody if they had ever called a Black person a nigger. They all said no, except for one woman, who said, "Well, when I was a child, we used to say 'Eeny, meeny, miny, mo, catch a nigger by the toe.'" After that, a whole bunch of them said the same thing. Sometimes their answers were so phony they were a joke. Except the joke was on us.

One day, a man being questioned told the judge what he had read about the case in newspapers and what he had heard on radio and TV. He tried to make it seem that he had just incidentally come across the news stories and that he had not really followed the case or paid much attention to it. Further, he denied having been affected by any of it.

"Have you ever read a book called *Target Blue*?"

Only a day or two before, the defense team had asked that that question be included in the voir dire. Robert Daley, who at one time was the public relations and publicity director for the New York City Police Department, had written the book *Target Blue*. An excerpt from the book was "coincidentally" printed in *New York* magazine on almost the exact day our trial was to begin. One or two chapters were about the Black Liberation Army. The book was a collection of sensationalism, groundless accusations, and outright lies. The few facts that were in those two chapters were distorted beyond recognition. I was referred to by name. Daley implied that i had been responsible for the deaths of numerous policemen. He called me the "soul" of the Black Liberation Army, the "mother hen" that "kept them fighting and kept them moving." According to the book, i had also robbed numerous banks and blown up a police car with a hand grenade during a police chase.

"Have you ever read *Target Blue*?" the judge asked.

"Er, er, yes."

Immediately the defense team submitted requests to the judge that additional questions be asked.

"When did you read this book?"

"As a matter of fact, I'm reading it now." Not only had he been reading the book, but he had it upstairs in the jury room. Although the defense team asked for an investigation, the judge refused. It was obvious the man had brought the book to court to show to the other jurors and that they had discussed it. After a lot of arguments made by our lawyers, the judge agreed to dismiss that juror and others in the panel with whom he had been close.

One day i was informed that the nazi party was demonstrating outside the court, marching up and down, complete with swastikas, brown uniforms, and helmets. They carried "White power," "Save our police," and "Death penalty" placards. Other signs were printed with racist statements. Rumor spread that a cross had been burned in front of the home of one of our supporters. At the end of the day the nazis almost got into a fight with some of the few Black residents in Morristown.

A lot of people don't know it, but they've got more nazis and Ku Klux Klan in jersey than a little bit. Some of my friends call it "up South." Lou Myers, who was later one of my lawyers on this case, is from Mississippi. One day, in all earnestness, he told me he would rather try a case in Mississippi any day than try one in jersey.

I couldn't understand it. I was growing weaker and weaker. My energy seemed to have gone down the drain. All i wanted to do was sleep. I chided myself for trying to escape from reality instead of facing it. I had seen women in jail sleep their whole time away. I was afraid that was happening to me. I was so easily upset and reacted to everything in an exaggerated manner. My nerves were terrible. Every little thing affected me. All i did, all day, when there was no kourt, was sleep, eat, watch television, and listen to the radio. I was eating like food was going out of style. This also convinced me my nerves were going bad. I have seen people in prison gain twenty, thirty, forty, fifty pounds eating out of nerves and boredom. It gets to the point when all you have to look forward to is the meals. And that in itself is pitiful, because anyone who has ever been in prison knows how terrible the food is. Yet i was gulping that stuff down just like it was Mom's home cooking.

It wasn't until i sat down one day to do my exercises that i really suspected what could be wrong. I could barely get through ten sit-ups. Everything added up. I didn't dare hope, but, at the same time, down deep inside, i knew. As sure as i knew my own name, i knew that i was pregnant. But what was i to do next? I knew i had to see the doctor, but what in the world was i going to say? I had been in prison for eight months and it would really be weird to say, "Hey, i think i'm pregnant." I wanted to know for sure whether i was or not, but if i wasn't i didn't want the doctor to know my business. Because if i was, it would be only a matter of time before the whole world would know.

First thing the next morning, i saw the prison doctor. I told him all my symptoms, dropping hint after hint. He told me there was nothing to worry about, that i was just constipated.

As time wore on, it became harder and harder to wake up in the morning. When the guards came to wake me for kourt, i would simply roll over and continue sleeping. They did everything to get me out of bed. They called. They threatened. They banged on the bars and anything else they could think of.

"Just don't come in this cell," i would tell them, feeling evil as the day is long. "You come in here and you put your hands on me and i'ma take your head right offa your shoulders." They must have known i meant it because they kept their distance until i was awake. I didn't care what they thought or said as long as they didn't put their hands on me. I wanted them to leave me alone. All i wanted to do was sleep.

I walked into kourt whenever i got up, no matter what time it was. The judge would go on and on about my lateness and admonish my lawyers for not having me in kourt on time, but it was hopeless. I didn't care what the judge said, what the guards said, or what anybody said. All i wanted to do was sleep.

I told Sundiata and one or two of the lawyers that i thought i was pregnant. They looked at me blankly, puzzled, as if i had an overactive imagination. Each day i felt more and more weird. I felt fragile and sick. I went back to the prison doctor, dropping more and more hints. I repeated my symptoms. Queasy stomach, stomach getting bigger, sick in the mornings, sleep all the time, etc. But he still didn't get the message and kept telling me this stuff about an intestinal disorder. I didn't know what to do next.

One day i woke up and could hardly move. I was sick as a dog and dizzy to boot. I got up for a minute, then sank back down on the cot, holding onto it for dear life. They called the prison doctor. I repeated the symptoms again, and this time he ordered some tests. He asked for a urine specimen. I was sure he had sent for a pregnancy test. I waited a few days and heard nothing. Then the nurse came and asked me for more urine. I was certain this meant the pregnancy test was positive and they were retesting just to be sure. I gave her the urine sample and waited.

When the doctor called me to his office, i knew he was going to tell me i was pregnant. Instead, he was smug and acted really on the stupid side. He kept making snide little remarks and i could tell he was trying to make fun of me. I asked him what was wrong with me and he repeated the same old stuff about a bowel disorder. Then he asked me some questions about my sex life.

"Ask your momma about her sex life," i said and went out of his office, slamming the door. Later that day, Ray Brown and Evelyn came to see me. Ray was in a jovial mood, laughing his head off.

"Well, you've really done it this time. I don't know what we're going to do with you. His honor is going to give you a strong reprimand for getting pregnant during his trial."

"You mean i'm really pregnant?"

"It was in the doctor's report to the judge. Didn't you know?"

"No," i told him. "I was just in that slimy bastard's office this morning and he told me that i had something wrong with my intestines.

"He's pulling your leg," Ray said. "They did two or three pregnancy tests on you and they all came back positive. You're pregnant, all right. I can't believe it."

Evelyn was in a state of shock. "It's something," she said. Then she looked into space for a long time. "It's something."

"Judge Bachman's having a fit," Ray said. "I hear the FBI is going to conduct an investigation to determine how you got pregnant."

"Well, they better not try to come 'round me asking no questions," i told them. "I'll tell them that this baby was sent by the Black creator to liberate Black people. I'll tell 'em that this baby is the new Black messiah, conceived in a holy way, come to lead our people to freedom and justice and to create a new Black nation."

Sundiata and McKinney had joined us. Sundiata was elated. He couldn't get over it. He sat there grinning and slapping his knee. "I think it's beautiful," he kept saying. "I think it's absolutely beautiful." Everyone was in a jubilant mood. I was glad. I hadn't known how they would react.

"It's amazing," Evelyn said. "Out of all this misery a new life is conceived."

I was caught up in the mood, but i couldn't wait to get off alone in my cell to think about this. What had seemed like a remote dream was coming true. A baby. My mind was jumping and dancing.

I spent the next few days in a virtual daze. A joyous daze. A person was inside of me. Someone who was going to grow up to walk and talk, to love and laugh. To me it was the miracle of all miracles. And deeply spiritual. The odds against this baby being conceived were so great it boggled my mind. And yet it was happening. It seemed so right, so beautiful, in surroundings that were so ugly. I was filled with emotion. Already, i was deeply in love with this child. Already, i talked to it and worried about it and wondered how it was feeling and what it was thinking. I would lie in my cell wondering about his or her life, wondering what kind of life it would have. What kind of people it would love, what kind of values it would have, and what it would think of all the madness that would surround it. Sometimes i felt so helplessly protective, wondering when my baby would be called nigger for the first time, wondering when the full horror and degradation of being Black in amerika would descend on my baby. How many wolves hid behind the bushes to eat my child?

But there were so many happy things that i thought about, too. I wondered when would be the first time my child would sit down and seriously appreciate the glory of a sunset and marvel at the wonders of nature. Or when he or she would smack lips and lick fingers over a sweet potato pie, or kiss strawberries and drink lemonade. It has always intrigued me how the world can be so beautiful and so ugly at the same time. I wanted, with all my being, for my baby to experience the many types and sides of love and friendship and to know and understand selflessness and generosity, struggle and sacrifice, honesty, courage, and so many of the sentiments that have given me strength and have made my life worth living. In these days, i was in such a state of sensitivity and thought that i barely noticed what was going on around me.

The next time my mother came to see me, my sister was with her. I was so happy to see them both. When i say "see," it is something of an overstatement, because in morristown jail there are little windows that you and your visitors peek through, and there are little holes through which you are supposed to talk, but to make yourself heard you are obliged to shout.

"Honey, you look pale," my mother shouted.

"Mommy, i'm pregnant."

"What is it, honey?"

"I'm pregnant, Mommy."

My mother smiled blandly. I repeated myself and she began to laugh. "How many months are you?"

"No, seriously, Mommy, i'm pregnant."

"Well, so am I," my mother said, this time laughing heartily. "I think it was my hysterectomy that caused it."

"No, Mommy," i pleaded. "You don't understand. I'm pregnant. I'm not joking."

"Who's joking, honey? Pregnancy is a serious matter," she said, trying to keep a straight face, "especially when the baby is born under immaculate conception and god is the father." She and my sister were having a giggling fit. "What are you going to name the baby?" my sister added. "Jesus?"

They just carried on. The more i insisted i was pregnant, the more they laughed and cracked jokes. But, finally, my mother stopped laughing.

"Are you really pregnant?"

I told her that it happened in the kourt and that Kamau was the father.

"How do you feel?"

"Actually, kind of funny," i told her. "I can barely move and i'm just so tired."

In the visiting room on the prisoners' side, there were no chairs, so you had to stand up and talk. I was so tired, i just couldn't stand any longer. I sat down on the floor, leaning on the wall behind me so that they could see me. I couldn't see them, but we shouted to each other until the visit was over. I went up to my cell after the visit ended and immediately fell out. My mother went to the warden to complain about their refusal to provide chairs.

The next day Evelyn came to see me. "Your mother called me last night all the way from Morristown, as soon as she left you. She was worried to death that, with all you've been through, you'd finally been driven crazy. I told her not to worry, that you are, in fact, pregnant. I think she's in a state of shock. So's your sister. It's all over the papers. I brought them for you."

I couldn't believe it. Sure enough, there were the articles. The one in the New York *Daily News*, i remember, was especially sordid. All of the papers speculated about who the father was and how i had managed to become pregnant in jail. One of them hinted that a prison guard was the father.

"I'm sick, Auntie, i feel awful."

"Well, that's what happens when you're pregnant. You get morning sickness and all sorts of other strange ailments. It's only normal."

"Maybe you're right, but i'm having these pains down here," i told her, pointing to where the pains were. "And i can barely stand up."

She told me to go see the doctor and i told her how the doctor had acted.

"Well, go see him anyway, and have him examine you thoroughly. Meanwhile, I'll try to have you seen by a private gynecologist as soon as possible. I'll probably have to go to court."

She promised that she would do all that she could to get an outside doctor, and i went upstairs to see the jail doctor.

"Why did you lie to me and tell me all that junk about a bowel disorder?" was the first thing i asked him.

"Well, you lied. I just figured I'd get back at you. Anyway, you found out, like I knew you would."

I told him about my pains and he examined me.

"What's wrong?" i asked, anxiously.

"There's a chance you're threatening to abort."

"What?" i practically screamed.

"There's a chance that you're going to abort."

"I don't want no abortion," i cried out.

"It's probably the best course you could take now, and I'd recommend it. But that's not what I was talking about. I said that there was a chance you could spontaneously abort, have a miscarriage."

"Oh no!" i moaned. "What are you going to do?"

"Relax. It's probably nothing serious. It's nothing much to worry about."

"What do you mean, nothing much to worry about. I want this baby."

"Well, I can't force you to do anything, but my advice is to have an abortion. It will be better for you and for everyone else."

"I don't want nobody's abortion. But what are you going to do about this miscarriage thing? Isn't there something you can give me to keep me from having a miscarriage? Isn't there something that i can take to make sure i don't lose this baby?"

"No. There's nothing I can do now. We have to wait and see what happens."

"What do you mean, wait and see what happens? If i have a miscarriage, then it will be too late. Can't you call a gynecologist?"

"No. There's nothing I can do right now."

"You mean there's nothing you *will* do right now, don't you?"

"Take it any way you want to."

"Won't you at least call a gynecologist in to see me? You're not a specialist in this area."

"I don't need you to tell me what my specialties are," he said angrily. "It would be best for everybody concerned if you have an abortion, no matter which way you have it."

"Just who is everybody concerned?"

"Don't you worry about it. My advice to you is that you should go to your cell and lie down. Just lie down and rest your mind. Just lie down and stay off your feet. And if you go to the bathroom and see a lump in the toilet, don't flush it. It's your baby."

I raced out of his office and, when i got to my cell, i lay on the cot crying. I was worried to death. As far as i could see, they were out to kill my baby. I couldn't lose this baby now, not now. It was meant to be; this baby was our hope. Our hope for the future. I tried to calm myself. I didn't want the baby to feel my anguish. Finally, i fell asleep.

The next morning, i waited anxiously for Evelyn and Ray Brown. Ray came first. I told him what had happened.

"Please," i begged, "get a doctor we can trust to see me today."

"I'll try to get one as soon as I can," Ray assured me. "I'll have to make some phone calls and then I've got to talk to the judge. He's having a fit, you know. He wants to resume the trial today. Don't worry, everything is going to be all right."

Ray and Evelyn came back in about an hour. "Don't worry," they told me, "the trial has been postponed until there is a report from our doctor. The judge has permitted you to be examined by your own gynecologist, and he's coming this afternoon, so cheer up." They did their best to take my mind off everything and to make me feel better. That day i felt worse than ever before.

"Is the doctor Black?"

"No, he's a Ku Klux Klan doctor," Ray Brown joked. I felt like my insides were going to drop out on the floor at any minute. Ray went outside to meet the doctor and came back followed by a tall, brown-skinned man. The man sure as hell didn't look like no doctor. He looked like Mr. Superfly himself. He had on a long fur coat, a jumpsuit, and platform shoes. But when i looked into his face, i was reassured. He was kind and very self-assured. He was gentle when he examined me and i was truly grateful. He asked a whole lot of questions in a careful, painstaking manner. I was really impressed.

"Would you tell me your name again?" i asked him, ashamed that i had forgotten it.

"Sure. That's an easy order. Ernest Wyman Garrett." He practiced in Newark and there was an air of Newark about him. I liked him instantly. He was one of those rare breed of Black professionals who haven't lost contact with the masses of Black people. He didn't have one trace of the affected bourgie speech and mannerisms that are so popular among the Black middle class.

I waited nervously for the verdict. "There's no doubt about it. You're pregnant. But I found blood in the vaginal canal, which can be a sign that something is wrong. There's a possibility that you are threatening to abort. This doesn't mean that you are going to have a miscarriage. The chances are good that you won't. The odds and medical statistics are in your favor.

He explained the different possibilities and the treatment he was prescribing. I asked a million questions and, when he left, felt a whole lot better, just knowing there was someone i could trust taking care of me and the baby.

The days that followed are blurry in my mind. Most of the time i slept. The warden and the sheriff and the powers that were didn't like the idea of my having my own doctor, though. In their minds, the butcher, jailhouse-quackhouse doctor was good enough for me. And the fact that Dr. Garrett was Black infuriated them. They refused to let him examine me unless a white doctor, hired by the state, was present, and for the report to the judge, the white doctor had to examine me. Fortunately, he agreed with my doctor's findings. There was a lot of activity going on around me that I didn't understand. I was too out of it to try. I could see, though, that Evelyn and Ray were worried. I wanted to help them, to get to the bottom of what was happening, but i just didn't have the energy.

About two days after his first visit, Dr. Garrett came to visit me. When he finished examining me, he said, "Assata, I don't want to worry you, but I think you should be hospitalized. It's nothing serious, strictly a precautionary measure. You're in no condition to proceed with a trial. You need a few weeks of complete bedrest. There is a possibility the judge will try to push you into that trial right away, without regard for your medical condition. Assata, there is no way we are going to let that happen. I am prepared to fight all the way for your right as a human being to receive decent medical care and for your baby to be born healthy. I'm doing the same for you as I would for any other patient. You should be hospitalized. There isn't a responsible doctor in the world who wouldn't agree with that opinion. And I'm prepared to testify in any court that to deny you proper medical care would be tantamount to committing murder. I will be going, in a very short time, to give a medical report about your condition to the judge. I will do my best to convince him of the seriousness of this matter. I think he'll listen to reason. I'm sure the judge will go along with the findings of two board-certified gynecologists. But if worse comes to worst, and the judge denies our motion, I will see to it personally that this jail and the courtroom are surrounded by the right-to-life people by tomorrow morning."

I was too shot out to say much more than thank you. I was scared to death for my baby, but i knew that everything that could be done was being done and that was a load off my mind. I got dressed and waited for them to come and take me to kourt. I wanted to hear what was going on. When they didn't come for me, i became worried. What was going on? Why weren't they bringing me to kourt? Why were they taking so long? What were they going to do? Were they going to try to make me go to trial like this? What were they planning to do?

Evelyn and Ray came in strutting and beaming. I knew everything was going to be all right. "What happened? Why didn't they bring me to kourt?"

"You're too sick to go to court." Evelyn laughed. "Haven't you heard that they don't let pregnant women into court? They figure it's a disease and are afraid everybody will catch it. We felt it was much better for you not to be moved. It went fine. They'll be taking you to a hospital as soon as they can make the arrangements. Dr. Garrett did a great job. After that speech, there was no way the judge was gonna force you to go to trial in your condition. The trial has been severed and Sundiata will go on with the trial alone."

"What?" i exclaimed. "But we had agreed that we would be tried together. Why can't they wait until i'm better?"

"Now, Assata, you know they're not gonna wait for you to have your baby to try Sundiata. They claim that being here in Morristown is costing them a fortune."

"It will be cheaper to try us together," i said. "Well, can't i at least see Sundiata and say good-bye to him?"

"We'll try," they said, "but we doubt if there will be time or if the sheriff will consent to it."

"I'm going to miss Sundiata."

"Yes. We know."

Later they put me on a stretcher and wheeled me into an ambulance. "Don't worry," i told the baby, "you're gonna be all right."

LOVE

Love is contraband in Hell,
cause love is an acid
that eats away bars.

But you, me, and tomorrow
hold hands and make vows
that struggle will multiply.

The hacksaw has two blades.

The shotgun has two barrels.

We are pregnant with freedom.

We are a conspiracy.

Chapter 8

After the Village, i lived with Evelyn on 80th Street between Amsterdam and Columbus in Manhattan. She had a garden apartment in a brownstone. Nothing grew in the garden but weeds, and it was where our neighbors threw their garbage. The apartment was one big room that we used for sleeping, eating, and living; it had a kitchen and a bathroom with an old-fashioned toilet up on a platform and an overhead tank so that you had to pull on a little chain to flush it. Evelyn always referred to it as the dump. She had it fixed up nicely, but it was just too small for two people, especially if one of them was me. I was a slob, and Evelyn went to great pains to train me in neatness. In a small place like that, when just a few things are out of place it looks like a hurricane passed through. And many times after a long day's work, poor Evelyn would be greeted with a hurricane, a tornado, and an earthquake at the same time. Gradually, i learned to keep things in something vaguely resembling order.

The neighborhood, for me, was exciting, full of character and different flavors. Central Park and Riverside Park were nearby, and i immediately fell in love with both of them. Then, also, there were plenty of museums nearby; i spent hour upon hour in the Museum of Natural History and the Metropolitan Museum of Art. They were free then, and full of fascinating things. There were all kinds of stores for me to explore and examine, even though most of the time i didn't have any money. I was delighted with it all. And it was my first clear glimpse of the hierarchy of amerikan society.

Eightieth Street, like many of the nearby streets,

was changing. Most of the changing, however, had taken place before i got there. Most of the Germans had moved out and Blacks and Puerto Ricans were moving in. Evelyn told me that when she moved there it was so safe she had slept, in the summer, with the back door open and just the screen door latched. On 80th Street there might be three, four, five, or more people huddled into a one-room apartment. Sometimes the apartments were rented furnished with nothing but an old saggy bed, a chest of drawers, and a beat-up refrigerator and stove. You could usually tell them from the outside by the paper-thin plastic curtains shimmying in the wind. Most of the people on 80th Street were poor, although here and there were a few renovated apartments that catered to a clientele that was a little richer, usually "night people."

Seventy-ninth Street was directly behind us, but there was a world of difference between the two. It was an upper-middle-class street. Doctors and lawyers and a lot of performers lived there. Every day after school, i would hear an opera singer practicing. Maybe that's why i developed a profound dislike for opera. The people on 79th Street wouldn't dream of socializing with the people on 80th Street. They recognized our existence with a mixture of amusement, fear, and dislike. Eighty-first Street between Central Park West and Columbus Avenue was even richer. The lobbies were elegant and the doormen were splendidly attired. They were, for the most part, all white and not even slightly aware of the people who lived only a block away.

Farther over, toward the river, near West End Avenue or Riverside Drive, there was a middle-class neighborhood. The buildings were usually old, grandiose, and well kept. The people who lived there were mostly white, of course, with a few Blacks and mixed couples thrown in. The Upper West Side, as the neighborhood was called, was supposed to be a "liberal" stronghold. I have never really understood exactly what a "liberal" is, though, since i have heard "liberals" express every conceivable opinion on every conceivable subject. As far as i can tell, you have the extreme right, who are fascist, racist capitalist dogs like Ronald Reagan, who come right out and let you know where they're coming from. And on the opposite end, you have the left, who are supposed to be committed to justice, equality, and human rights. And somewhere between those two points is the liberal. As far as i'm concerned, "liberal" is the most meaningless word in the dictionary. History has shown me that as long as some white middle-class people can live high on the hog, take vacations to Europe, send their children to private schools, and reap the benefits of their white skin privileges, then they are "liberals." But when times get hard and money gets tight, they pull off that liberal mask and you think you're talking to Adolf Hitler. They feel sorry for the so-called underprivileged just as long as they can maintain their own privileges.

Sometimes i walked over to the East Side, on the other side of Central Park. If Riverside Drive was like another city, then the East Side was like another world. English nannies pushed fancy baby carriages (they called them trams) through the eastern side of Central Park. The only Black people you saw were servants or, like me, those just passing through. Fifth Avenue, Park Avenue, chauffeur-driven cars, diamonds, and furs. The Upper East Side was for the sho nuff rich. When i'd walk through those streets, some looked at me as if i was an object from a museum or something. Once or twice, a doorman actually stopped me and asked where i was going. But i kept walking and looking. Sometimes, i'd have some fun and walk into one of the stores. I couldn't believe there were people who paid that kind of money for things. As soon as i'd step in, the salespeople were right on me. Sometimes i said i was just looking. Other times i would ask for outrageous things, like pickled feet. Usually, they would say, "What? What? What?" and i would burst out laughing. One time, i went into a grocery store and was asked who my mistress was.

I was always crazy about art and made it a point to visit any art gallery i discovered. Sometimes they acted snooty or disgusted. At first, i felt uneasy and out of place. But after a while, whenever they acted disgusted, i made a point of asking the price of each piece. They would turn so red and swell up so much that it was comical. I remember hating some of those people, but at the same time i wanted to be rich like them. Back then, i thought being rich was the solution to everything.

Four blocks from where we lived, there was still another world: 84th Street between Amsterdam and Columbus. Before it was torn down, it was voted the worst block in the city. When i was a kid, i never would have imagined that people could live so bad. Living in some of those apartments was like living in a coffin. I swear, there was one building that, when you walked past it in the summer, it stunk so bad it made you want to drop to your knees. Usually, i'd just sit on some stoop and watch the street. There was always something going on. Men standing around with do-rags on their heads, covering greasy process hairdos, making deals, laughing and talking and looking at the women passing by. Drunks and fights and drunken fights. The street was always alive and swarming with people. Survival and life were hanging out in the open like laundry for everyone to see. Arguments, dirty deals, misery, and malice ran out into the streets like pus from open sores. There was something horrible and foreboding about the street, yet exciting at the same time.

Lil-Bit, who went to my school, lived on 84th Street. Her nickname was Lil-Bit, but i called her Fruit-fly because she was crazy about fruit. I liked to hang out with her because she was a good walker; we could walk for hours without getting tired. One day she asked me to come with her to get something from her house. When we got there i couldn't believe it. I thought i had seen some messed-up cribs before, but hers took the cake. She lived in a tiny little pea-green closet of a room, covered with wall-to-wall roaches. I just kept staring at Lil-Bit. She walked around in that horror house like it was normal. She didn't even try to kill the roaches. She just brushed them aside if they got in her way. When i left, i itched and scratched for hours.

When i met Lil-Bit's mother and started getting to know her and some of her neighbors, i got my first lesson in hopelessness. Lil-Bit's mother used to work in factories and laundries as a presser. But she burned her hand real bad and was on some kind of disability. She lived from day to day and from check to check. She was always sick, and sometimes her cough was so bad i thought she was going to die any minute. She acted like she was too tired or too weak to do much of anything. They had a hot plate, but most of the time they didn't even cook. They just ate sandwiches, usually lunch meat on white bread. Lil-Bit's mother never went anywhere except to the clinic or to the welfare office or to the bar on Amsterdam. Sometimes she would get drunk and start crying about some man she used to go with. She didn't know anything about what was going on in the world and she didn't seem to care. Eighty-fourth Street was her world and other worlds didn't really exist. When i was with Lil-bit and her mother i felt all kinds of things. Sometimes disgust and anger because they accepted anything and lived any old kind of way. Other times i felt sorry for them, and, still other times, i relaxed and enjoyed them because they were so easy and down to earth. But whenever i hung out with them it was down on the stoop. I would never go up into that house.

Evelyn kept my excursions at a bare minimum, though. She was strict and didn't play around. Every day, after school, i had to be in the house by four o'clock, and she would call home just to see that i had arrived safely. Evelyn didn't want me in the street too much because she said the neighborhood was bad and she didn't want me to get in any trouble. And she also wanted me to stay at home and do my homework. After homework, i read. I have never been too fond of television and, besides, Evelyn had an excellent library. Those books were like food to me. Fiction and poetry were my favorites, although i liked history and psychology, too. I also liked to read about other countries and about all the different religions in the world. The only books i never touched were Evelyn's law books. They were dry and boring and Greek to me.

Evelyn was a store of knowledge and she knew about a whole range of subjects. We were always discussing or debating something. Hanging out with Evelyn, i started to think that i was cool and sophisticated and grown up and that i knew it all. You couldn't tell me nothing. I was just too cool. Evelyn and i went to museums and art galleries and the theater. On Broadway, off Broadway, she was turning me on to so many things. I started to view movies as an art form instead of just entertainment. I was learning what and how to order at restaurants. And my vocabulary and control of the English language were expanding greatly.

But life with Evelyn definitely had its ups and downs. Sometimes we got along famously and other times it was terrible. Evelyn was super-honest and she just could not tolerate my lying. I would try to tell the truth and try to be honest, but sometimes, especially if i was in a tight situation, i would lie. I had been in the habit of lying and it was easy for me to fall back into the old pattern. But it was futile to lie to Evelyn because she was a lawyer and would cross-examine me until i would inevitably trip myself up. Little by little, i got out of the habit, but it was a long and constant battle between us.

Our financial situation also had its ups and downs. One week we were "rich" and the next week we were "poor." Evelyn was determined to be a trial lawyer and to be in private practice. Most of her clients were Black and poor and most of the time they didn't have money to pay her. But Evelyn would defend them anyway. She was always up in arms about some injustice or other. I used to call her the "last angry woman." But whenever somebody did pay her, we were "rich." We would go out and celebrate. For a week or so we ate steaks and lamb chops, went to restaurants, took taxis; the next week we would be right back to riding subways and eating hamburgers. Evelyn was generous and extravagant, and she had absolutely no head for business. I usually did the shopping for us since i was more tight-fisted and practical. Once in a while, i'd be tempted to give myself a "five-finger discount," but Evelyn was so honest that it rubbed off on me. I was becoming so goody-goody i couldn't stand myself. I really underwent a great change.

Evelyn had great plans for my future. I was going to Junior High School 44, but Evelyn wasn't satisfied with the education i was receiving. J. H. S. 44 wasn't a bad school, but we were learning at a much slower pace than at my school in Queens. I don't remember too much about the school except for the music classes. Most of the class was Black or Puerto Rican and we all loved music. But we hated music class with a passion. The teacher talked to us as though we were inferior savages, incapable of appreciating the finer things in life. She lectured about symphonies and concertos and sonatas and the like in a snooty voice. A boy would mimic the gestures and expressions of the teacher and the rest of us would giggle and snicker as she played music. The teacher became more and more exasperated, saying, "Listen! Can't you listen? Don't you have ears? Can't you appreciate anything? I'm trying to get you to appreciate music and you all act as though you're deaf. I want you to stop talking! I want you to stop talking and listen! Do you hear me?" We got louder and louder and the teacher became more and more disgusted. She would scream at us and call us names like hooligans and ignoramuses. And we returned her insults.

We hated her because she thought the music she liked was so superior. She didn't recognize that we had our own music and that we loved music. For her, there was no other music except Bach and Beethoven and Mozart. To her, we were uncultured and uncouth. For her, Latin music, jazz, rhythm and blues were trashy and we were trash. She was a racist who would have denied it to the bitter end. A lot of people don't know how many ways racism can manifest itself and in how many ways people fight against it. When i think of how racist, how Eurocentric our so-called education in amerika is, it staggers my mind. And when i think back to some of those kids who were labeled "troublemakers" and "problem students," i realize that many of them were unsung heroes who fought to maintain some sense of dignity and self-worth.

Evelyn strongly "suggested" that i enter Cathedral High School in the ninth grade. I was not at all happy about the idea since i hated wearing a uniform and Catholic schools had a reputation for being so strict. But Evelyn kept on strongly suggesting and i got the message. I didn't mind the Catholic religious part of it, though, since i was going to mass regularly and i was kind of holy, holy that year. I took the test for Cathedral and passed, and it was firm that i was going to enter Cathedral the next September. I even started to feel happy about it. It was a change and i have always been a person who likes a change of scenery.

I usually spent my weekends with one of my girlfriends or

with my mother as much as possible. Toni was cool to hang out with and she knew where all the parties were. But we never had deep conversations so we never got really close. Bonnie and i met through Toni and began what was to be a best-friend relationship with an argument about Abraham Lincoln. We argued for hours until Bonnie's aunt told us to shut up and go to bed, since neither of us knew what we were talking about. Bonnie lived in the same building my mother lived in, and after that night we became close friends and talked about every subject on earth. Bonnie knew more than i did about what was happening in the world and we spent hours talking about Medgar Evers, sit-ins, freedom riders, etc. We began to write poetry about love and Black people, and sometimes we wrote morbid poetry about hate and death. As soon as we finished a poem we'd call each other and read it. After a while, we read poetry together. Dorothy Parker and Edna St. Vincent Millay were our idols. We read everything they wrote and even memorized their poems. After that, we read all different kinds of poets. We were "deep" and were forever in the library or a bookstore trying to find another poet who was "deep," too. The more we read, the more we wrote. And it came in handy in the street. If we didn't like somebody, or if we had some dispute with someone, we wrote a poem about them. We made up all kinds of "dozens" poems and laughed our heads off. We were young and old, happy and sad at the same time.

Usually, every summer, i went down South to visit my grandparents. When they had the business on the beach, i loved it. But they had lost two different buildings on the beach, both destroyed by hurricanes. After the last one was leveled, they operated a restaurant on Red Cross Street. I liked working in the restaurant sometimes, but it wasn't as much fun as working on the beach.

One of the last summers that i spent down South, the NAACP rented a building a few doors from my grandparents' restaurant, which was a great source of interest to me. I was forever walking by, standing in the doorway, or sliding discreetly into the building to see what was going on. I could hear them talk about integrating the South by sitting in, praying in, singing in, and about nonviolence. I was glad because i surely wanted segregation to end. I had grown up exposed to the degrading, dehumanizing side of segregation. I remember that when we traveled from North to South and vice versa we really felt the sting of segregation more acutely than at other times. We'd drive hours without being able to stop anywhere. Sometimes we would pull into a filthy old gas station, buy gas, and then be told that we were not permitted to use their filthy old bathroom because we were Black. I can remember clearly squatting in the bushes with mosquitoes biting my bare buttocks, and my grandmother handing me toilet paper, because we could not find a place with a "colored" bathroom. Sometimes we were hungry, but there was no place to eat. Other times we were sleepy and there was no hotel or motel that would admit us. If i sit and add up all the "colored" toilets and drinking fountains in my life and all of the back-of-the-buses or the Jim Crow railway cars or the places i couldn't go, it adds up to one great ball of anger.

And so, when i saw these NAACP people, i was ready to do whatever it was that they were going to do. But they were very confusing. One day i was hanging around in the office and two men were talking about nonviolence and self-control. Then he walked around the room asking everybody questions.

"What would you do if they pushed you?"

"Nothing. I'd just keep on doing what i came to do."

"What would you do if they kicked you?"

"I'd pray to the Lord to forgive them for their sins."

"What would you do if they spit on you?"

"I'd just go on singing."

Well, that was just too much for me. I could take someone pushing me, hitting me, kicking me, but to sit there and let some craka dog spit on me, well, just the idea of it made me want to fight. To me, if someone spit on you, it was worse than hitting you, especially if they spit in your face. I tried to tell myself that i would just sit there and take it, but every muscle in my body, every instinct i had, rebelled against it. The man continued around the room asking everybody the same questions. When he came to me, i answered the same, too, except for the spitting question.

"I don't know," i told him.

"What do you mean, you don't know?"

"I just don't know."

"Well, little sister, we can see that you're just not ready. If you want your freedom, there's no sacrifice that's too big to make."

Everybody looked at me as if i was some kind of stupid idiot. I felt bad, but i still couldn't get used to the idea of letting somebody spit on me. The man said i wasn't ready, and i had to agree with him.

When i think back to those days, i feel such admiration and respect for the spirit of struggle and sacrifice that my people exhibited. They went up against white mobs, water hoses, vicious dogs, the Ku Klux Klan, trigger-happy nightstick-wielding police, armed only with their belief in justice and their desire for freedom.

I remember how i felt in those days. I wanted to be an amerikan just like any other amerikan. I wanted a piece of amerika's apple pie. I believed we could get our freedom just by appealing to the consciences of white people. I believed that the North was really interested in integration and civil rights and equal rights. I used to go around saying "our country," "our president," "our government." When the national anthem was played or the pledge of allegiance spoken, i stood at attention and felt proud. I don't know what in the hell i was feeling proud about, but i felt the juice of patriotism running through my blood.

I believed that if the South could only be like the North, then everything would be all right. I believed that we Black people were really making progress and that the government, the president, the supreme kourt, and the congress were behind us, so we couldn't go wrong. I believed that integration was really the solution to our problems. I believed that if white people could go to school with us, live next to us, work next to us, they would see that we were really good people and would stop being prejudiced against us. I believed that amerika was really a good country, like my teachers said in school, "the greatest country on the face of the earth." I grew up believing that stuff. Really believing it. And, now, twenty-odd years later, it seems like a bad joke.

Nobody in the world, nobody in history, has ever gotten their freedom by appealing to the moral sense of the people who were oppressing them. Once you study and really get a good understanding of the way the system in the United States works, then you see, without a doubt, that the civil rights movement never had a chance of succeeding. White people, whether they are from the North or from the South, whether it was in 1960 or 1980, benefit from the oppression of Black people. Those who believe that the president or the vice-president and the congress and the supreme kourt run this country are sadly mistaken. The almighty dollar is king; those who have the most money control the country and, through campaign contributions, buy and sell presidents, congressmen, and judges, the ones who pass the laws and enforce the laws that benefit their benefactors.

The rich have always used racism to maintain power. To hate someone, to discriminate against them, and to attack them because of their racial characteristics is one of the most primitive, reactionary, ignorant ways of thinking that exists.

A war between the races would help nobody and free nobody and should be avoided at all costs. But a one-sided race war with Black people as the targets and white people shooting the guns is

Chapter 9

I was taken to Roosevelt Hospital in Metuchen, new jersey, and shackled to the bed by my foot. Dr. Garrett had established that i was one month pregnant. When he visited me he demanded that the shackles be removed at once (based on the elementary principle that proper treatment, both mental and physical, of a woman threatening miscarriage would not seem to include being chained to a bedpost). My mental stability was also threatened by the round-the-clock guards who sat outside my hospital room with shotguns trained at my head.

After ten days, i was discharged from the hospital over the objections of my doctor, brought to the middlesex county jail for men, and kept in solitary confinement from February 1974 until May 1974.

At first, they wouldn't even give me milk. Since pork was served as a staple meat almost daily, i began to slowly starve. (In county jails it goes like this: one sheet, one horse blanket, a metal cup; your cell is raided if you have luxuries, like salt.) They did everything they could to thwart the care Dr. Garrett was trying to give me. They hired their own doctor and insisted that whenever my doctor saw me, their man had to be present. This meant a severe limitation on the number of visits Dr. Garrett could arrange because their doctor happened often "not to make it" out to the prison on the days examinations had been agreed to and scheduled.

My lawyers had initiated a lawsuit against the state of new jersey in federal court charging medical maltreatment and dietary abuse. Before the date the hearing was scheduled, i was extradited to the State of New York, which made the federal court action moot.

When i arrived at Rikers Island again, i was anemic and malnourished, according to my entrance physical. New jersey had been giving me iron pills, but i was anemic up to the last blood test before giving birth.

The pregnancy, or "special," diet at Rikers, in addition to the regular food, was powdered milk, juice, and a hard-boiled egg daily. This was my diet until i gave birth, and things seemed to go normally.

Meanwhile, the lawyers obtained another court order from the New York court permitting Dr. Garrett to continue treating me. When he first came to Rikers, i was in the infirmary. They told him the court order was "no good" and that he couldn't see me. I was left in a room for three days with a woman who turned out later to have active tuberculosis. It was May and they had turned the heat off. It got cold again and women who were having seizures, methadone withdrawal, and one sister who they said had pneumonia all piled blankets on their beds. The sister got worse and worse. Finally, they brought her to Elmhurst Hospital where they discovered she did have tuberculosis. I found this out later, when she was returned to Rikers, kept in isolation, and the doctors wore masks and gloves when they visited her.

I also had monilia, a vaginal discharge, which worsened because the Montefiore Hospital doctors assigned to Rikers could not agree about how it should be treated. They refused to treat the condition at all until my culture was returned from Elmhurst Hospital. By the time they managed to get the culture back, the whole inside of my thigh was chapped raw from the discharge, and i could barely walk.

Montefiore Hospital and the Health and Hospital Corporation went to court to prevent Dr. Garrett from delivering my baby. Their position was that since i was a prisoner it was not necessary for me to have the doctor of my choice. They also said he was "disruptive" because, when he did manage to see me, he "often wrote in my chart," which they found very disturbing. The kourt upheld them. I was only a prisoner!

I went into labor the morning of September 10, 1974, at 4 A.M. on 2 Main at Rikers, where i had been kept in the psycho ward. I got out of bed, took a shower, braided my hair, and packed. My labor was mild, a pinch every half hour, which rapidly became a pinch every fifteen minutes. At 11 A.M. i was sure i was on my way, but i had no doctor to confirm it, and i refused to go to the infirmary. Around noon i asked to call Dr. Garrett and they somehow got hold of him. (He was at Elmhurst Hospital trying to persuade them to let him deliver my baby.) At about 3 P.M., he arrived at Rikers and i went up to the infirmary to meet him. He told me that i was "effaced" and definitely in labor. I would not allow the other doctors there to examine me.

I was taken to Elmhurst Hospital in a motorcade. It looked to me like a million police cars buzzing around the vehicle in which i, a woman in labor, was riding. And they all followed. Into Elmhurst Hospital and up to the delivery room. They surrounded the hospital.

There was a demonstration outside of Elmhurst Hospital in support of my right to choose the doctor who would deliver my baby, and Evelyn and Dr. Garrett held a press conference at the hospital to explain the situation. There were actually two policewomen inside the labor room and several outside. I was having contractions every five minutes. Finally, i let one of their doctors, a resident, examine me to see how the labor was progressing—which turned out to be a terrible mistake. When he finished, i was bleeding. After that, there was no way I would let any of them touch me again. I ordered them to bring me a stethoscope (to see if the baby's heart was beating normally) and a few other instruments i would need because, i said, "I am delivering the baby myself."

It was a standoff for a couple of hours. Then a nurse told me to walk around to ease the pain and encourage labor. I got up, then pretended to fall out (knowing how afraid they were of lawsuits), and the doctors rushed over to pick me off the floor. I knew they were worried. I stated again, "I am delivering the baby myself." I checked the baby's heart with the stethoscope. It was beating normally.

That, or the press conference, or the demonstration outside of the building seemed to do it. They told me that if i signed a release statement absolving them of all responsibility, they would let Dr. Garrett deliver my baby. I signed, making certain that they had no control over Dr. Garrett or over anything having to do with my labor. And that was that.

He took over. He examined me, listened to the baby's heart, and, at some point, broke my water. He explained carefully everything that would happen and answered all my questions. He gave me a local anesthetic in the cervix. I didn't want Demerol or a saddle block, but the paracervical block seemed O.K. At this point i was very tired.

After that i was still in labor but felt little pain. I went to sleep for a while. I woke up about 3:30 A.M. and i could feel the baby lowering and thought i could feel the baby's head. I called the nurse. She said, without looking, that i wasn't "ready" yet. When i insisted, she looked and went running for Dr. Garrett. They wheeled me into delivery, he gave me a local anesthetic, and did the episiotomy. I pushed three times and she was here. At 4:00 A.M., Kakuya Amala Olugbala Shakur was born. I said, "Check that baby out" (just to ensure her subsequent safety). The birth itself was peaceful and beautiful—out of sight. It's very important for a woman to go through the birth experience with people she trusts.

Later that day, September 11, they still hadn't brought me the baby. Dr. Garrett had gone home to sleep and, when he returned, at 6 P.M. that day, i still hadn't seen the baby. He reminded them that i was supposed to breastfeed her. They told him he hadn't "written a prescription" for breastfeeding. Finally, they brought me the baby and i breastfed her every four hours—another incredibly beautiful experience. The nurses from the nursery were very friendly and kind and kept me informed about the baby's condition. But the staff in D-11, the psycho ward where i was kept in a tiny, guarded room, were something else again.

They allowed me only one shower a day. No toothbrush or toothpaste, only mouthwash. They don't furnish it, a friend can't bring it, and the prison won't allow it. I had to beg them for a bra while i was nursing. The prison refused to let me bring one. Many strange doctors tried to examine me to hasten my discharge and get rid of me. I came close to physically brawling with a couple of them because i refused their examinations. Finally, they discharged me anyway, without the consent of my doctor. The Commissioner of Corrections, Benjamin Malcolm, had signed a paper taking all responsibility for my discharge.

They put me in an ambulance, chained me to a stretcher, and brought me back to the Women's House of Detention at Rikers Island. They took me straight to the infirmary and said, "You will have to stay here and be examined." I was really depressed, having been separated so abruptly from my baby. I said, "I don't want to be here. I won't be examined here. Send me to PSA [punitive segregation area: solitary confinement], anywhere. I don't care. I just have to be somewhere by myself. Just leave me alone."

That's not quite what they did. When i refused examination, i walked out of the infirmary and they called the goon squad (several large female officers). They all jumped on me and started beating me. They had me on the floor—eventually my arms and legs were chained. They dragged me by the chains to PSA and stopped only when a nurse asked them to please stop. So they put me on a mattress and dragged the mattress. They took me to the observation room and left me, hands and feet cuffed. I had no sanitary napkins, no means to wash myself. The cuffs cut into my skin (the scars are still visible), and my wrists were bleeding. Later i found out that i had received an infraction for slapping an officer in the face while they were beating me.

I still refused their medical examination. They finally brought me napkins. I was left on a mattress, on the floor, no bed and no shower. I was there for two weeks. I continued to refuse all their medical attention, insisting that Dr. Garrett examine me. I refused to eat, so eventually my breasts, which were full of milk, stopped hurting. They offered doctors of all kinds and drugs (mainly tranquilizers). They sent the psychiatrist, who had the nerve to ask me if i was depressed. The Disciplinary Board met in front of my cell and gave me an additional sentence of fourteen days in PSA. All other inmates were cleared out of PSA. During this time i was still refusing most food. I was so weak i fainted a couple of times. At that time it was also Ramadan, when it is forbidden to eat until sundown for the whole two weeks. I just ate once a day, when the food was edible, and for the first few days I ate nothing at all.

After two weeks, they said, "If you agree to be vaginally searched, you can go to your floor." I did and went to my floor. The next day the captain came down to my cell and informed me that they had decided to lock me up again for refusing a complete physical from the medical staff assigned to Rikers from Montefiore Hospital. What had happened was that when i was returned to my floor they told me that Dr. Garrett had been permitted to examine me and that he was at Rikers Island, that my lawyer had gone to court and the court had ruled that i could be examined by Dr. Garrett. So i waited. A white doctor came in and said in order for me to see my doctor, i must see him and be examined by him first. I refused. Then they brought in a Black doctor, who greeted me with, "Hey, soul sister." He was really sneaky. I refused him, too. So Dr. Garrett was forced to leave and I was put back in PSA. They threatened me with administrative segregation, so i sat on the floor and refused to move when my sentence in PSA was up. They gave me an infraction and a verbal reprimand and said the vaginal search would be sufficient. Then the next day they locked me up again.

This time, i was locked in my cell for a month. I continued to refuse most food. They let me out to shower whenever they felt like it. I began a hunger strike at one point, and after a few days in the tiny cell i was sick. I wondered how long i would have to hold out.

Evelyn had filed a writ of *habeas corpus* before the brooklyn federal kourt against Commissioner Malcolm and Essie Murph, superintendent of the Women's House of Detention on Rikers, to force them to release me from punitive segregation. I was to appear in kourt for the hearing, but I didn't know the date. Then a deputy told me, "Your court date's been postponed. And your lawyer sends her advice: see a doctor." It was a lie. But I believed it. I was examined by the prison doctors under what I thought was Evelyn's advice.

So i was no longer locked. Just in jail. And separated from my child.

LEFTOVERS—WHAT IS LEFT

After the bars and the gates
and the degradation,
What is left?

After the lock ins and the lock outs
and the lock ups,
What is left?

I mean, after the chains that get entangled
in the grey of one's matter,
After the bars that get stuck
in the hearts of men and women,
What is left?

After the tears and disappointments,
After the lonely isolation,
After the cut wrist and the heavy noose,
What is left?

I mean, like, after the commissary kisses
and the get-your-shit-off blues,
After the hustler has been hustled,
What is left?

After the murderburgers and the goon squads
and the tear gas,
After the bulls and the bull pens
and the bull shit,
What is left?

Like, after you know that god
can't be trusted,
After you know that the shrink
is a pusher,

that the word is a whip
and the badge is a bullet,
What is left?

After you know that the dead
are still walking,
After you realize that silence
is talking,
that outside and inside
are just an illusion,
What is left?

I mean, like, where is the sun?
Where are her arms and
where are her kisses?
There are lip-prints on my pillow—
i am searching.
What is left?

I mean, like, nothing is standstill
and nothing is abstract.
The wing of a butterfly
can't take flight.
The foot on my neck is part
of a body.
The song that i sing is part
of an echo.
What is left?

I mean, like, love is specific.
Is my mind a machine gun?
Is my heart a hacksaw?
Can i make freedom real? Yeah!
What is left?

I am at the top and bottom
of a lower-archy.
I am an earth lover
from way back.
I am in love with
losers and laughter.
I am in love with
freedom and children.

Love is my sword
and truth is my compass.
What is left?

Chapter 10

The next several years of high school passed uneventfully. Because i was spending weekends with my mother, we became closer. During my seventeenth year, however, i decided to quit school, get a job, and live on my own.

My entrance into the working world was a rude awakening. I didn't even know what most of the want ads meant. Auditor, copywriter, accounts receivable, key punch operator were all foreign words to me.

Every day i hit the pavement with my best "office-looking" clothes on and a pair of high-heel torture shoes. Every day i came home more frustrated than the day before. I didn't know how to do anything, had no experience, and was Black to boot. Finally, i paid some employment agency one or two weeks' salary for the privilege of getting me one of those dingy, boring, $95-dollar-a-week jobs. I was one of those slaves where you pay a fifth of your salary for taxes, some more for social security, another $5 a month for union dues, and the rest was not even enough to die on.

It seemed that the whole world was made up of things i couldn't afford. After i paid the rent on my furnished room, spent carfare, and bought food, i had just enough money to buy an air sandwich. The only saving grace was that i didn't have too much time to hang out. I was going to night school, so i would leave my boring job and go to boring night school to diagram sentences, memorize garbage, and prepare for a high school diploma that meant nothing in the job market. My life was being spent pushing around meaningless papers that had nothing to do with living. I wasn't doing anything positive. I wasn't making anything, creating anything, or contributing to anything. After a while, i wanted to tell them to take their papers and their job and shove it.

But at first i wasn't like that. After weeks of looking for a job, i was grateful just to have one. I didn't think about low pay, indecent working conditions, no medical benefits, only one week vacation. I was just happy to be working. I identified with the job and talked about "our" company and told people what "we" manufactured. I wasn't making two cents over lunch money and talked like i owned the place. I remember once i was working at some joint where they made trailers. I had a job pushing papers. I told one of my aunt's friends that she should buy one of those trailers if she ever wanted one. She looked at me like i was crazy. "Why?" she asked. "Are they going to give me a discount?" I felt so stupid. It hit me. They wouldn't even give me a discount and i was working there.

The longer i worked at those places, the shorter my patience got. Half the time i didn't even want to hear that rinky-dink stuff they talked about at the office. I got sick of listening to gossip about the bosses and this and that and who was messing with who. After a while, i stayed pretty much to myself, and when i wasn't busy i would stick a book between some pages and read. That was back in the mid-sixties and papers were filled with stories about riots.

At the time, i really didn't know what to think about the riots. The only thing i can remember thinking was that i wanted to see the rioters win. In the office there was a group of secretaries who worked for the president or the vice-presidents. They looked down on those of us who worked in the general office and treated us like we were nothing. One day, i was in the bathroom and one secretary came in. She was spraying hair spray on a puffed-up French roll that was so hard it looked like it had been baked on. She began talking about this and that. I was surprised because she never talked to me. Then she started about the riots, "what a shame it was" that "those people" were so stupid and dumb for rioting because they were just tearing up their own neighborhoods and burning down their own houses. I didn't say anything. She prodded: "I said, isn't it a shame? Isn't it?" I didn't know what to say. It was true that Black people were burning down Black neighborhoods, but i didn't know how to deal with the question. She kept insisting. Finally, i said, "Yes," and walked out.

I was disgusted with myself. I hadn't wanted to agree with her, but i didn't know what else to say. I spent half the night thinking until i felt i had the answer. A few days later, the subject came up again. This time the whole bunch of front-office secretaries, who were friendly with the office manager, came into the general office. Before they had a chance to get any words out after "riot," i was on their case. "What do you mean, they're burning down their houses? They don't own those houses. They don't own those stores. I'm glad they burned down those stores because those stores were robbing them in the first place!" They stood with their mouths open.

After that, the office manager went out of her way to hassle me. Miscellaneous whites began to ask my opinion about the riots, and i made sure they weren't disappointed. I knew it wouldn't be long before they fired me. The only reason i didn't quit was that i had nowhere to go and nothing else lined up. When i was finally fired, i was relieved.

Because my girlfriend Bonnie and i read a lot of fiction and poetry, we thought we were intellectuals. Neither of us had finished high school, but we used to go to this place on Broadway called the West End, dressed in what we believed to be our scholastic finery. It was one of those real college-type places, with pastrami sandwiches and pitchers of dark beer. We sat around trying to look "deep" until someone sat down and talked to us. After a while, we made friends with some African students who were studying at Columbia.

I loved to listen to the Africans. They were intense, serious, and had so much dignity. I was introduced to African customs, and they spent hours explaining the various aspects of their cultures. Bonnie asked about their marriage ceremonies because she was dying to get married. I asked about the food because i loved it: curried chicken, groundnut stew (chicken in peanut sauce), and corn bread that you cook over the stove. You would break off a little piece, roll it into a ball, dip your thumb in the middle and make a spoon that you would fill with gravy and eat. It really made me think about how bad they've done us. We know everything about spaghetti and egg rolls and crepes suzette, but we don't know the first thing about our own food. When i was a little kid, if you had asked me what Africans ate, i would have answered, "People!"

One day, Vietnam came up. It was around 1964 and the movement against the war had not yet blown up in full force. Someone asked me what i thought. I didn't have the faintest idea. Back then, the only thing i read in the papers was the headlines, crime stories, comics, or the horoscope. I said, "It's all right, i guess." All of a sudden there was complete silence. "Would you mind explaining, sister, what you mean by 'it's all right, i guess'?" The brother's voice was mocking. I said something like "You know, the war we're fighting over there, you know, for democracy." It was clear, from the expressions around me, that i had said the wrong thing. The brother i had come with looked like he wanted to crawl under the floor. "Who's fighting for democracy?" somebody asked. "We are. The United States." And then, as an afterthought, i added, "You know, they're over there fighting communism. Fighting for democracy." The brother held his head in his hands as if he had a headache. I knew i had said something wrong, but i couldn't figure out what. Thinking i had failed to state my case strongly enough, i continued repeating everything i had heard on television. Babbling. Which only made matters worse.

When i finished, the brother asked me if i knew anything about the history of Vietnam. I didn't. He told me. He explained French colonialization, exploitation, brutalization, the starvation and illiteracy; the long fight waged and won in the North and the u.s. involvement in propping up a phony government after the French got their butts kicked.

The brother was talking about names, places, and events just like he was from Vietnam or something. I sat there with my mouth hanging open. He knew all this stuff and he wasn't even studying history. I couldn't believe that this African, who didn't even live in the u.s. or in Asia, could know more than me who had friends and neighbors who were fighting over there.

Then he defined the u.s. government's role, that it was fighting for money, to defend the interests of u.s. corporations and to establish military bases. I didn't know whether to believe him or not. I had never heard of such a thing. "What about democracy?" i asked him. "Don't you believe in democracy?" Yes, he said, but the government the u.s. was supporting was not a democracy but a bloodthirsty dictatorship. He started running all kinds of names and dates on me and there was no way i could respond. There he was, talking about the u.s. government just like somebody would talk about a criminal. I just couldn't relate to it. But my mind was blown.

Despite that, i continued saying the first thing that came into my head: that the u.s. was fighting communists because they wanted to take over everything. When someone asked me what communism was, i opened my mouth to answer, then realized i didn't have the faintest idea. My image of a communist came from a cartoon. It was a spy with a black trench coat and a black hat pulled down over his face, slinking around corners. In school, we were taught that communists worked in salt mines, that they weren't free, that everybody wore the same clothes, and that no one owned anything. The Africans rolled with laughter.

I felt like a bona fide clown. One of them explained that

communism was a political-economic system, but i wasn't listening. I was just digging on myself. I had been hooping and hollering about something that i didn't even understand. I knew i didn't know what the hell communism was, and yet i'd been dead set against it. Just like when you're a little kid and they get you to believe in the bogeyman. You don't know what the hell the bogeyman is, but you hate him and you're scared of him.

I never forgot that day. We're taught at such an early age to be against the communists, yet most of us don't have the faintest idea what communism is. Only a fool lets somebody else tell him who his enemy is. I started remembering all the stupid stuff people told me when i was little. "Don't trust West Indians because they'll stab you in the back." "Don't trust Africans because they think they are better than we are." "Don't hang out with Puerto Ricans because they all stick together and will gang up on you."

I had learned, through experience, that they were all lies told by stupid people, but i never thought i could be so easily tricked into being against something i didn't understand. It's got to be one of the most basic principles of living: always decide who your enemies are for yourself, and never let your enemies choose your enemies for you.

After that, i began to read about what was happening in Vietnam. What the Africans had said was true. There were also articles about the u.s. army in Vietnam, their involvement in torture and forcing Vietnamese women to sell their bodies just to survive.

I was so confused. It just didn't make any sense to me. "Our government couldn't do anything that bad," i told Bonnie. There had to be some other information. I couldn't even understand what "we" were doing there in the first place. Some kind of treaty, they said, but it didn't make any sense. I got so disgusted at one point that i said i wasn't going to read the news anymore.

"Ignorance is bliss," Bonnie said.

"The hell it is," i answered. I damn sure didn't want to be as ignorant as i had been. When you don't know what's going on in the world you're at a definite disadvantage. I decided i'd keep trying to follow what was happening, but i still couldn't believe the u.s. was doing all the foul things i was reading in the newspapers.

"What do you mean, you don't believe it?" Bonnie asked. "Just take a look at what they're doing to you."

The difference between the Africans and the other friends i hung out with that summer was startling. I remember one day at the beach. Everybody is hee-hee happy. It's party time. A multicolored umbrella stands defiantly against the breeze. Blankets and silly-looking beach towels color the beach, along with soda cans and bottles of Bacardi and Johnnie Walker Black. Healthy-looking Black men, wearing turned-down sailor hats and college sweatshirts with cutoff sleeves, lug ice chests and other stuff back and forth. An improvised outdoor sound system has been hooked up and Martha and the Vandellas are wailing in the background.

I am insisting on reading James Baldwin even though the wind keeps flapping the pages. Anguished voices scream and moan from the pages. Compressed ghettos threaten to explode. Poverty and fire and brimstone boil over into a deadly stew, but the "beautiful" people refuse to let me read in peace. My girlfriend has insisted on "fixing me up" with "Mr. Wonderful," who turns out to be an egomaniac decked out in monogrammed swimming trunks, a matching terrycloth robe, and a monogrammed towel to boot. Mr. Wonderful consents to grace me with his presence. His looks and manner tell me that i should be grateful because he is definitely what's happening. His ride is a red MG convertible, his crib is in Esplanade Gardens, and his gig is an assistant manager for some bank downtown. He is kool from his reel-to-reel tapedeck to his color TV, right down to his shaggy "bachelor rug," which he leeringly tells me about.

He drinks Remy Martin cognac and Harvey's Bristol Cream, uses a cologne i can't pronounce, and i wait, expectantly, for him to tell me his brand of toothpaste. He goes on and on about his trinkets and status symbols. "Look at this monogrammed motherfucker," i think to myself. He is smug and insinuating. A Black version of "Bachelor Knows Best," or some such thing. I want to go back to James Baldwin, but i am surrounded by a group of people that talk too loud, looking and thinking somewhat like Mr. Wonderful. They are talking about Karmann Ghias, Porsches, Corvettes, and other cars that are deemed "in."

The conversation drifts on to co-ops and high-rise apartment complexes. A young man, who has mentioned more than once that he is an accountant, tells us the benefits of buying "property" on the Island. An insurance salesman says that he sells insurance out on the Island and pulls some business cards out of a little silver-colored case which he "just happens to have handy" in his beach bag. A redheaded schoolteacher who has eyes for the accountant says that she has always wanted a house on the Island with a big kitchen. After talk about the Island has exhausted itself, the conversation turns to places to go. French and Mexican restaurants are definitely "in," with a restaurant that sells fifty different kinds of crepes winning hands down. One of the men, who is a poverty pimp, says that he has moved his offices to the Red Rooster bar and restaurant. Somebody laughingly asks if he isn't afraid to go into Harlem "with all them niggas." Everybody has some favorite restaurant on top of some building downtown. They don't talk about the food, just the scenery. Mr. Wonderful says he has a Playboy key and often eats at the Playboy Club.

I smile uneasily, feeling out of place. All this talk is giving me a headache. Some fraternity brothers invite me to dance. One tells me that i look like a Delta girl. "How does a Delta girl look?" i ask. "Just like you in a swimsuit." Mr. Wonderful glares at them. I am picking up snatches of conversation from all around me. Talks of grants, poverty programs, and democratic politics. Talk of the NFL, and the football season. Talk of Bergdorf Goodman, Bloomingdale's, and Saks Fifth Avenue. About speedboats and cruisers which nobody owns but everybody wants to.

Whiskey flows like water, and the speedboats turn into yachts. Everybody is just crazy about the islands: Jamaica, Bermuda, Nassau. Everybody is so chic. I'm so tired of hearing about it that I want to send them somewhere by way of foot—mine! It's a disgrace. Social workers talking about their clients like dogs, teachers who don't like to teach. A probation officer complaining about how dangerous his job is. A bunch of money-worshipers putting on a front for each other. Somebody asks me if i have my thing together. "Which thing?" i want to know. I take a walk up to the house to get away from it all. Some women are in the bathroom smoking reefer and blowing their hair dry. I go fishing in my bag for some aspirin. "Where'd you buy your suit?" one asks me. I don't want to say Klein's, but i say it anyway. "They have some nice things, sometimes," she says without conviction, dismissing me as a bargain basement case. They go back to talking about people and hair going back. They are putting on makeup to look like Black Barbie dolls on the beach.

I go back outside feeling like i'm from another planet. I feel lonely and serious. Something has been happening to me, a change that has been a long time coming. I want to be real. Am i the only bad-doing, hand-to-mouth, barely-making-it Black woman there? The struggle i've been going through and the struggle i've been seeing is too hard to lie about and i don't even want to try. I want to help free the ghetto, not run away from it, leaving my people behind. I don't want to style and profile in front of nobody. I want somebody i can relate to and talk about serious shit with.

This party is a lost cause. I get my beach towel and my book and ease on down the beach a little piece. Looking out at the ocean, i wonder how many of our people lie buried there, slaves of another era. I'm not quite sure what freedom is, but i know damn well what it ain't. How have we gotten so silly, i wonder. I get back off into James Baldwin. I don't give a damn if Sag Harbor sags into oblivion. Me and James Baldwin are communicating. His fiction is more real than this reality.

My patience was zero. I didn't want to wait for something to happen. I was into living and living for now. I was hungry, starving for life, but at the same time i was growing more and more cynical every day. I wanted to go everywhere, do everything, and be everything, all at the same time. I wanted to experience everything, know how everything felt. I had many zigzag conflicting ideas rolling around in my head at the same time. One day i was happy just to be alive and young and moving. The next day i felt like the world was coming to an end. Everything in my life was jagged, sharp, unfinished edges. Nothing happened calmly. Nothing was like i had thought it would be when i was little.

My friends were dying from OD and going into the army. My girlfriends had babies and were looking and sounding old. Nice old men sitting in the park weren't nice old men at all but were busy masturbating under their newspapers. I got so i didn't believe in anything. It seemed that everybody was in some kind of bag, the dope bag, the whiskey brown paper bag, the jesus bag, the love bag, the sex bag, the make-it bag, and none of those bags were doing anybody any good. I was looking for my own bag, but the pickings were slim. I kept on looking nevertheless, running and moving and hanging out until i was running myself ragged. One day i'd be downtown hanging out with my hippy, blippy (Black hippy) friends. The next night i'd be uptown hanging out with the hustlers. But nothing seemed like it was for real, you know? The same dudes who would be talking slick and sniffing coke out of $50 bills one day would be scrounging and begging for a loan the next. Even the most successful hustlers seemed to be nothing but flunkies and potential fall guys for the mafia. My friends from downtown weren't much better. At best, most of them were professional escape artists, into escaping the problems of the Black community or those of the white community. Some of them tried to escape through drugs, tripping over worlds that didn't exist on some kind of inner-space odyssey. But in their case, the drugs were usually not entirely self-destructive, although i know at least one who zoomed dead out of this world and didn't come back.

Through my hippy/blippy friends, i got turned on to a lot of things, though. I got into poets like Allen Ginsberg, Sylvia Plath, Ferlinghetti, all kinds of novelists, music, food, etc. I didn't relate to everything i checked out, but my horizons got a whole lot broader.

My growing impatience with petty bourgeois upward-bound "Negroes" came to a head when i went to work with a Black employment agency. Evelyn had gotten me a job there as a typist. The agency was located in Rockafella Center in the same building with Johnson Publications, the publishers of *Ebony* and *Jet* magazines. I was happy as hell to get the job since i was tired of working for white people. The people in the office were nice and the atmosphere was completely lacking in tension. The boss was decent enough, and i had a pretty good relationship with him and his secretary, under whom i worked. At first i was excited, glad to be around so many Black people who seemed to be doing so good. Everybody was into making it, moving up the ladder. Black men and women with long lists of degrees, and briefcases, were in and out of the place. They were sharp, dressed to a tee, and talking about junior executive training programs, poverty programs, etc. Some of them talked about those companies as if they were going to be the president of the board of directors in five years.

Once in a while i went to lunch with a young man who worked at Johnson Publications. But we always got into arguments. Especially about *Ebony* magazine. Half the time, in the fashion section they would have these elaborate evening gowns that cost thousands of dollars. When i asked him what Black people could afford to buy them and whether they were gonna wear them to the corner bar, he got insulted. He was one of those Black people who think that you are free if you can go in a store and buy expensive things. I told him that the only Black woman who could afford those dresses was Johnson's wife, and he got even more insulted. He told me that everything was changing, everything was so much better. I said that if things were so much better, how come every time a Black person got a good job or was a manager or something, it was news and was printed in *Ebony*. Our relationship ended abruptly when he accused me of always trying to bring Black people down and make it seem like we don't have nothing. I ended the matter by cursing him out and that was that.

These Black people went around acting as if there was no such thing as prejudice and that all you had to do was study and you could be president of the world. At the agency, we were working hard for an equal opportunity conference. The idea was to have Black college graduates from all over the country participate in interviews with representatives from the major corporations in amerika. Almost all of the big corporations were involved, and the graduates paid a substantial fee, plus transportation and hotel fees, to participate in the conference. It worked like this: students made out résumés and the corporate personnel officers decided which applicants they wanted to see. It was a big, plush affair in a major New York hotel, with the penthouse suite and quite a few lower floors rented out to the conference. I just knew that hundreds of these young, "qualified" Black people were going to get jobs. I was proud to have helped bring the conference about. It lasted a few days, and by the time it was over, i was ready to go somewhere and have a good cry.

Some of those Black graduates had spent hundreds of dollars to come to the conference and didn't have one interview. The only graduates the corporations even wanted to see were math, science, engineering, and business majors. Some corporations only wanted to interview graduates in very specialized categories, like petroleum engineering or geological engineering. Since most had majored in subjects like English, history, sociology, etc., they were out of the running from the jump.

I was shocked and upset. After the conference, i went out with one of the Black "executives" i had met in the agency. "I don't understand it," i kept telling him. "Why would those companies pay all that money to participate in the conference if they aren't really interested in hiring anybody? It doesn't make any sense."

"It makes a lot of sense, if you think about it."

"Huh? I don't understand."

"Listen," he went on, "the government says that in order for those companies to keep their contracts, they have to at least make an effort to look for 'qualified Black personnel.' The law doesn't say they have to hire anybody. The law says they've only got to look."

I was furious. They had used poor dumb me just like they use a drug dealer to conspire against his own people. I was part of the plot and i didn't even know it. There were some Blacks who got jobs, but mainly the thing was a sham, to make things look good on paper. My friend and i got stupidly drunk, singing oldies by the Sherrills on Lexington Avenue, he telling me about what bastards the bosses were and about the trials and treacheries of the democratic party machine and telling me how i was gonna get another job as a go-go dancer in the ladies' room.

About a week later, i made up a résumé, described myself as a college graduate, and was hired as a marketing assistant. I didn't believe in anything, and i wasn't gonna follow anyone's rules but my own. I got fired from that job a couple of weeks later, got another college job, and got fired from that too. I didn't care. I was going to deal with them just like they dealt with us. One time i got a job as a bookkeeper. I didn't know the first thing about it, but after i got the job i bought a couple of "bookkeeping made easy" books and when i didn't understand something I told them that we used a different system at the last place i worked.

The job involved a lot of cash and i had to be bonded. When you get bonded, they do a background check on you. The job wasn't too bad, and the boss was cool. It was an excellent way to learn bookkeeping and the insurance business. I knew they would fire me as soon as the report came in, but i didn't care. One day, my boss threw a detective's report on my desk. It had my name on it. I swallowed hard, knowing it was my last day. The more i read it, the more surprised i became. The report verified everything i had said: "Subject attended such and such high school," subject . . . graduated from such and such college," "subject worked at such and such places." They even reported that i lived on a quiet tree-lined street and that they had talked to my neighbors and learned that i was a nice person. I cracked up all the way home. Everything is a lie in amerika, and the thing that keeps it going is that so many people believe the lie.

But my patience was getting shorter and my temper was terrible. I was quick to tell people what i thought of them, and even i was surprised by my bluntness. Bonnie kept telling me, "Slow down, you're speeding, somebody's gonna give you a ticket." She was almost as restless and crazy as i was. We would check out things happening and make a joke of them. The world seemed to be so big and fixed and we couldn't think of anything to change it. Bonnie encouraged me to stop lying about going to college and go for real. "If you're smart enough to fool them, then you're smart enough to play their game." I knew that what she said made sense, but i had hated my last days in high school and had no desire to study anything else.

The only other person who stayed on my case and prodded me to go back to school was my friend from Kenya. We had grown to be serious friends. And we dug each other much more as friends than as lovers. He was studying economics out on Long Island, and we didn't get a chance to see each other much. Sometimes on the weekend we would hang out together. He was one of the few people i knew who was serious about almost everything he did in life and whose conversation was not just about his small world but about the whole world. One weekend we had arranged to hang out. I think we were supposed to go and hear somebody play at Count Basie's club. My apartment looked like some kind of hurricane had hit it, and i was trying to ease out the door without letting him in. Somehow he managed to get a glimpse inside. "No, we aren't going anywhere," he said. "How can you live like this? If your house looks like this i can just imagine what your head looks like."

I was embarrassed, but i had to admit he was right. I had everything thrown every which way, clothes flung all over the place. It was a wreck. He suggested that instead of going out he would help me clean up and get organized. "You'll be all right if you just get yourself organized. You can do almost anything you want as long as you organize yourself to do it." I decided he was right. It was time to get my life in some kind of order. It was time to take control. Life was like a bus: you could either be a passenger and go along for the ride, or you could be the driver. I didn't have the foggiest idea where i wanted to go, but i knew that i wanted to drive. I decided the first thing i would do was go back to school. I returned home to live with my mother in her new apartment in Flushing, Queens.

CULTURE

i must confess that waltzes
do not move me.
i have no sympathy
for symphonies.

i guess i hummed the Blues
too early,
and spent too many midnights
out wailing to the rain.

Chapter 11

On July 19, 1973, while i was still at the middlesex county workhouse, i was brought to the u.s. district kourt for the eastern district of New York in Brooklyn, which has jurisdiction over all federal crimes committed in the counties of Brooklyn and Queens. I was taken there by federal writ to be arraigned on an indictment in which Andrew Jackson and i were accused of having robbed a bank in the county of Queens on August 23, 1971. While there were a lot of indictments against me all over New York State i didn't even know about that summer, this is one i surely could not have missed, because the bank surveillance photo taken of the woman holding up the bank with a gun was put on wanted posters that were pasted up in every subway station, posted in every bank and post office, and blown up in full-page newspaper advertisements. They hit the streets on August 24, 1971, and remained even after my arrest on May 2, 1973.

Under the photo was the name Joanne Deborah Chesimard. Above the photo were the words "WANTED FOR BANK ROBBERY: $10,000 reward."

After the feds took a mug shot of me and fingerprinted me, i was arraigned, pled not guilty, and was returned to the workhouse on the same day. I heard nothing further about this indictment until January 1, 1975, when the feds brought me back to the eastern district kourt. Only this time it was to have me photographed.

The prosecutor has made a motion to have me photographed in the same angle, wearing the same kind of glasses, wig, and dress as the woman who had been photographed by the bank cameras during the robbery. The judge, a notorious, racist pig, is sure to grant the motion. I have decided to refuse. As far as i am concerned, the reasons are obvious. You put anybody in a monkey suit and they're gonna end up looking like a monkey. Besides, someone had told me about some trick the FBI uses. They take a photo of you in the same angle as the bank photo and superimpose a transparency of the bank photo over it. If you are unfortunate enough to have two eyes, a nose, and lips, in more or less the same place, you end up looking like the bank robber, no matter what you really look like. When i was arraigned i had permitted them to take all the photographs of me they wanted, and that, as far as i was concerned, was enough.

We enter the kourtroom. The judge is on the bench. The kourtroom has been rearranged. FBI agents, with cameras, are standing on top of tables. A group of federal marshals are buzzing around nervously like flies that smell rot. They are waiting for action. Evelyn gets up and says her piece. The judge ignores what she is saying and orders me to be photographed. I refuse, stating my objections as strongly as i can. In a hot second, the marshals and the FBI agents are crawling all over me. They seem to be trying to jerk my head off my shoulders. The judge has ordered that i am to be photographed, today, now, and that all the force necessary to take the pictures in the way the FBI wants to take them is to be used.

The FBI, the marshals, and i end up on the kourtroom floor, with me on the bottom. I hear Evelyn in the background. "Let the record reflect that the marshals are twisting my client's arms behind her back." "Let the record reflect that the marshals are choking my client." "Let the record reflect that there are five marshals manhandling my client." Evelyn goes on and on while the marshals twist me, jerk me, strangle me, kick me, and literally try to beat me into submission. The assault goes on and on with Evelyn putting it, blow by blow, into the record. Finally, it is over. The marshals lead me back into the holding pen. I lie on the bench like a rag doll with the stuffing hanging out, feeling like i have just been stampeded by a herd of buffalo.

Evelyn comes back for a lawyer's visit. She looks just as tired as i feel.

"That was unbelievable," she exclaims. "How's your arm? Are you okay?"

More or less, i tell her. My body is aching and my bad arm's numb. I sit back marveling at how cool Evelyn has been. It dawns on me how hard it must have been for her to watch what was happening and then, calmly, put it into the record. I am amazed at her control. She insists that a nurse be called to check me out.

"Did you hear that shit?" she asks me.

"Yeah, i heard it."

"I can't wait for the record to be transcribed. If they don't erase it, i think we've got that dumb asshole right on the record. If they don't erase it, then we can get the stupid moron off the case." Evelyn is looking triumphant and defiant, like she has just put her foot up somebody's butt.

"What the hell are you talking about?" i want to know.

"Didn't you hear him? He said, right on the record, that he thought you were guilty. He admitted he was prejudiced right on the record. Didn't you hear him?"

"I'm afraid i was otherwise occupied. What does it mean?"

"It means we'll be able to get rid of his stupid ass. Anybody else is bound to be better. This judge is out to hang you, and he'll go to any limits to try and convict you. If we're forced to go to trial in front of him, i'm afraid the only shot we'll have is in an appeals court."

"I sure hope they don't erase the record."

Evelyn and i sit there speculating on the chances of the record being changed. Evelyn thinks the judge is too dumb to even realize what he said. I am afraid that the judge will review the transcript and then have it changed. Evelyn thinks the judge is too racist and too arrogant to be worried about the record. It turns out that she is right. She files a motion, based on the transcript, to have the judge relieved from the case. After what seems like forever, the judge is removed and a new judge is assigned.

But before i went to trial on this case, the powers-that-be decided that i must first be tried on a state kidnapping case in brooklyn supreme kourt. I had been accused of kidnapping a drug dealer for ransom on December 28, 1972. Evelyn was my lawyer and there were two codefendants. One was Rema Olugbala (Melvin Kearney), a member of the Black Liberation Army and well known to me. The other codefendant was a young brother by the name of Ronald Myers. The pretrial motions were permeated by an aura of paranoia. Mine. No one i knew had ever heard of Ronald Myers, and no one understood why he had been targeted for this particular frame-up. In fact, i wondered if he was some kind of plant. It all seemed so strange.

Finally, we had a joint conference, which was arranged by a court order. I asked Rema about Ronald Myers. Rema told me that as far as he was concerned, Ron was just a brother who happened to have the misfortune of being framed along with us: an unsuspecting victim. But everything in this case was so strange that i couldn't figure it out. A joint legal conference was arranged between Ronald Myers, his lawyer, a young Black lawyer by the name of James Carroll, Evelyn, and me. Immediately upon seeing this brother most of my suspicions disappeared.

He was nineteen but looked like he was about sixteen. He had a quiet, soft, honest manner that i didn't think any police agent could feign. He seemed to be just as perplexed and out of it as we were. As i listened to him talk, i felt a kind of motherly protectiveness toward him. We were revolutionaries, supposedly prepared for such things. For years we had been preaching about and denouncing pig conspiracies to kill and imprison Black political activists. But looking at this soft-eyed young Black man, the thing seemed that much more horrible. Those were very cynical days, and we had developed very cynical attitudes to deal with it all. We had become masters at telling bitter, angry jokes about justice and equality and "democratic freedom." But seeing this brother awakened such a sense of righteous indignation in us so-called veterans that we were all bitten by a sudden burst of energy. I pored over the discovery material and the police records tirelessly. Rema was tense, mysterious, and determined in his manner. We knew that the state was out to get us and we were more determined than ever not to let them.

The guards came and tore my cell apart. It was clear they were looking for something, standing on chairs, kneeling on all fours; they reminded me of bloodhound bitches. They seemed desperate. I tried to speculate on what they were looking for. One of the Black guards, who was halfway decent, was looking funny at me. Another guard, who had always been hostile, looked smug. Shortly after they left my cell, i tried to hook up with the wire to see what was going on. Finally i got the news. Rema Olugbala was dead. He had plunged to his death while trying to escape from the brooklyn house of detention. The makeshift rope that he was using to lower himself had broken. I felt too numb to do anything. Or say anything. Some of the sisters helped me piece my cage together. There was nothing to say. Another Black man had died trying to be free. Everything was boiling up inside me. I had to do something, and most of my options seemed absurd.

It wasn't what i would like to have done. It didn't say half of what i wanted to say. But i guess it was the best thing i could have done at the moment. I wrote a poem.

For Rema Olugbala—Youngblood
They think they killed you.

But i saw you yesterday,
standing with your hands in your pockets
waiting for the real deal to go down.
I saw you smiling your "fuck it" smile, blood in your eyes,
your heart pumping freedom
Youngblood!

They think they killed you.
But i saw you yesterday
in the playground.
Black skin, sweaty, shiny,
hurling your ball bomb into the hoop
right on target.
Won't be no game next time
cause you ain't hardly playing.

They think they killed you.
But i saw you yesterday
with your back against the wall,
muscles bulging against the chains,
eyes absorbing truth.
Lips speaking it.
Heart learning how to love.
Head learning who to hate.
Blood ready to flow
towards freedom.
Youngblood!

Youngbloods ain't got no blood to waste
in no syringes, on no barroom floors,
in no strange lands
delaying other youngbloods' freedom.
We don't need no tired blood.
No anemic blood. No blood clots
in our new body.

They think they killed you.
But i saw you yesterday.
All them youngbloods
musta gave you a transfusion.
All that strong blood.
All that rich blood.
All that angry blood
flowing through your veins
toward tomorrow.

The next time we went to kourt, i winced when i saw the empty chairs. Slouching listlessly, i thought about Rema, completely unaware of what was being said. There was talk about this hearing and that hearing and this motion and another and none of them made the slightest sense to me. But Evelyn was on the case, letting nothing slide by, citing all of her objections "for the record." I was bored to death, completely out of it, until the jury selection process began.

There were two prosecutors: one exceedingly ugly lynch mob–looking fat guy and another thin, bearded wolfman-looking dude, rather on the young side. I don't even remember their names. The judge's name was William Thompson, and he was a Black man, which surprised me. I guess they assigned the case to him because they were so sure we would be convicted and they figured a Black judge would, at least, give the illusion of justice. Thompson was somewhat of a character, who rarely sat up on the bench but constantly walked around the kourtroom. While he clearly could not, by any stretch of the imagination, be accused of ruling in our favor, and his political career would certainly not have been helped by our being acquitted, nevertheless the kourtroom did not have that out-and-out lynch-mob atmosphere we usually encountered.

The jury selection process really stood out in my mind. If anyone can write a book about how a Black lawyer can pick a jury and eliminate hostile, racist, prejudiced jurors from the panel, then Evelyn is surely the one to write the book. I was fascinated as i watched her. She was all honey and pie as she started to voir dire the jurors. At first, almost all of the white jurors began by saying they had no prejudices. By the time Evelyn finished asking them questions, we learned they had no Black friends or neighbors, would object to their children marrying a Black person, or had referred to Black people as niggers or some other derogatory name. After a while, many of the whites asked to be excused before Evelyn even asked them any questions. Most of them preferred to be excused rather than have their feelings toward Black people, Black militants, and Black Panthers questioned and explored. When you think about the fact that the average Black defendant on trial gets to ask prospective jurors only a few perfunctory questions, you can see why so many Black people end up in jail. Even with Evelyn putting everything she had into picking the jury, it was a long uphill struggle. But at the end, we managed to get four or five Black people on the jury, a remarkable accomplishment anywhere in amerika, except for D.C. The prosecutor even had the nerve to ask for extra peremptory challenges so he could bump some of the jurors off the panel.

The hardest thing in the world for me was to keep my mouth

shut in the kourtroom, to sit quietly and suffer silently. Evelyn, well aware of that fact, happily consented to my acting as co-counsel. Although she remained skeptical about my ability to cross-examine major witnesses, she agreed that it would be an excellent idea for me to make the opening statement. Finally, after days of writing under the dim nightlight in the cell, i delivered it. I was nervous as hell, since i have never liked speaking in public, but i tried my best to express to the jury some of what i was feeling:

Judge Thompson, Brothers and Sisters, men and women of the jury.

I have decided to act as co-counsel, and to make this opening statement, not because i have any illusions about my legal abilities, but, rather, because there are things that i must say to you. I have spent many days and nights behind bars thinking about this trial, this outrage. And in my own mind, only someone who has been so intimately a victim of this madness as i have can do justice to what i have to say. And if you think that i am nervous, your senses do not deceive you. It is only because i know that this moment can never be lived again and that so much depends on it. I have to read this opening statement to you because i am afraid that if i don't, i will forget half of what i have to say. Please try to bear with me.

This will not be a conventional opening statement. First of all, because i am not a lawyer, and what has happened to me, and what has happened to Ronald Myers, does not exist in a vacuum. There are a long series of events and attitudes that led up to us being here.

When we were sitting in this courtroom, during the jury selection process, i listened to Judge Thompson tell you about the amerikan system of justice. He talked about the presumption of innocence; he talked about equality and justice. His words were like a beautiful dream in a beautiful world. But i have been awaiting trial for two and one half years. And justice, in my eyesight, has not been the amerikan dream. It has been the amerikan nightmare. There was a time when i wanted to believe that there was justice in this country. But reality crashed through and shattered all my daydreams. While awaiting trial i have earned a Ph.D. in justice or, rather, the lack of it.

I sat next to a pregnant woman who was doing ninety days for taking a box of Pampers and watched on TV the pardoning of a president who had stolen millions of dollars and who had been responsible for the deaths of thousands of human beings. For what? For peace with honor? Nixon was pardoned without ever standing trial or being found guilty of a crime or spending one day in jail. Who else could commit some of the most horrendous, destructive crimes in history and get paid 200,000 tax dollars a year? Ford stated that he pardoned Nixon because Nixon's family had suffered enough. Well, what about thousands of families whose sons gave their lives in Vietnam? And what about the millions of people who have been sentenced at birth to poverty, to live like animals and work like dogs. What about the families who have sons and daughters in prison, who cannot afford bail or even lawyers for their children? Where is justice for them?

What kind of justice is this?

Where the poor go to prison and the rich go free.

Where witnesses are rented, bought, or bribed.

Where evidence is made or manufactured.

Where people are tried not because of any criminal actions but because of their political beliefs.

Where was the justice for men at Attica?

Where was the justice for Medgar Evers, Fred Hampton, Clifford Glover?

Where was the justice for the Rosenbergs?

And where is the justice for the Native Americans who we so presumptuously call Indians?

I am not on trial here because i am a criminal or because i have committed a crime. I have never been convicted of a crime in my life. Ronald Myers is not on trial because he has committed a crime. He was nineteen years old when he turned himself in, after seeing his picture in the newspapers. He thought that the police would immediately see their mistake. I met Ronald Myers for the first time about eight months ago in the lawyers' conference room. It was a strange meeting, something i hope i'll never have to go through again. I was shocked to see how young he was. And no matter what the outcome of this trial, i will always feel a bitterness about what has happened to Ronald Myers and what has happened to me.

I do not think that it's just an accident that we are on trial here. This case is just another example of what has been going on in this country. Throughout amerika's history, people have been imprisoned because of their political beliefs and charged with criminal acts in order to justify that imprisonment.

Those who dared to speak out against the injustices in this country, both Black and white, have paid dearly for their courage, sometimes with their lives. Marcus Garvey, Stokely Carmichael, Angela Davis, the Rosenbergs, and Lolita Lebrón were all charged with crimes because of their political beliefs. Martin Luther King went to jail countless times for leading nonviolent demonstrations. Why, you are probably asking yourself, would this government want to put me or Ronald Myers in jail? In my mind, the answer to that is very simple: for the same reason that this government has put everyone else in jail who spoke up for freedom, who said give me liberty or give me death.

During the voir dire process, we asked you about the word "militant." There was a reason for that. In the late sixties and the early seventies, this country was in an upheaval. There was a strong people's movement against the war, against racism, in the colleges, on the streets, and in the Black and Puerto Rican communities. This government, local police agencies, the FBI, and the CIA launched an all-out war against people they considered militants. We are only finding out now, because of investigations into the FBI and the CIA, how extensive and how criminal their methods were and still are. In the same way that witches were burned in Salem, this government went on a witch-hunt for people they considered "militant."

Countless numbers of people were either killed or imprisoned. The Berrigans, the Chicago 7, the Panther 21, Bobby Seale, and thousands of antiwar demonstrators were all victims of this witch-hunt justice. Maybe some of you are saying to yourselves, no government would do that. Well, all you have to do is check out for yourselves the history of this country and to look around and see what is going on today. All you have to do is ask yourselves, who controls the government? And who are the victims of that control?

Since you have been in this courtroom you have heard the name Black Liberation Army mentioned over and over. Those of you in the jury have been questioned as to what you have read or seen on television and what your opinions were about the BLA. Most of you have stated that you thought the Black Liberation Army was a militant organization. You have said that what you have read or heard has come from the establishmentarian media. The major TV and radio networks, the Times, *the* Post,*and the* Daily News. *I have read the same articles that you have read. I have seen the same news programs that you have seen. When it comes to the media, i have learned to believe none of what i hear and half of what i see. But i can tell you, if i were just Jane Doe citizen and if i did not know better, i would've read those articles and come to the same conclusion: that JoAnne Chesimard, Ronald Myers, and all other people called militants were a bunch of white-hating, cop-hating, gun-toting, crazed, fanatical maniacs—fighting for some abstract, misguided cause.*

But one percent of the people in this country control seventy percent of the wealth. And it is that one percent, the heads of large corporations, who control the policies of the news media and determine what you and i hear on radio, read in the newspapers, see on television. It is more important for us to think about where the media gets its information. From the police department or from the prosecutor. No major newspaper or television station has ever asked my lawyers or myself one question concerning anything. People are tried and convicted in the newspapers and on television before they ever see a courtroom. A person who is accused of stealing a car becomes an international car theft ring. A man is accused of participating in a drunken brawl and the headlines read "Crazed Maniac Goes Berserk."

During the seventies, the media created a front-page headline, guaranteed to sell newspapers: the Black Liberation Army. According to them, the BLA was everywhere. Almost every other thing that happened was attributed to the Black Liberation Army. Headlines that are sensational sell newspapers. The media shape public opinion and the results are often tragic.

Before you were sworn as jurors, you were asked about your knowledge of what the Black Liberation Army is or what it stands for. However, most of you did say you believed that the Black Liberation Army was a "militant" organization. I would like to talk about that for a moment. The Black Liberation Army is not an organization: it goes beyond that. It is a concept, a people's movement, an idea. Many different people have said and done many different things in the name of the Black Liberation Army.

The idea of a Black Liberation Army emerged from conditions in Black communities: conditions of poverty, indecent housing, massive unemployment, poor medical care, and inferior education. The idea came about because Black people are not free or equal in this country. Because ninety percent of the men and women in this country's prisons are Black and Third World. Because ten-year-old children are shot down in our streets. Because dope has saturated our communities, preying on the disillusionment and frustration of our children. The concept of the BLA arose because of the political, social, and economic oppression of Black people in this country. And where there is oppression, there will be resistance. The BLA is part of that resistance movement. The Black Liberation Army stands for freedom and justice for all people.

While big corporations make huge, tax-free profits, taxes for the everyday working person skyrocket. While politicians take free trips around the world, those same politicians cut back food stamps for the poor. While politicians increase their salaries, millions of people are being laid off. This city is on the brink of bankruptcy, and yet hundreds of thousands of dollars are being spent on this trial. I do not understand a government so willing to spend millions of dollars on arms, to explore outer space, even the planet Jupiter, and at the same time close down day care centers and fire stations.

I have read the Declaration of Independence, and i have great admiration for this statement:

"We hold these truths to be self-evident, that all men are created equal, that they are endowed by their Creator with certain unalienable Rights, that among these are Life, Liberty, and the pursuit of Happiness. That to secure these rights, Governments are instituted among Men, deriving their just powers from the consent of the governed. That whenever any Form of Government becomes

destructive of these ends, it is the Right of the People to alter or abolish it, and to institute new Government, laying its foundation on such principles and organizing its powers in such form, as to them shall seem most likely to effect their Safety and Happiness."

These words are especially meaningful in the year of this country's bicentennial. I would like to help make this a better world for my daughter and for all the children of this world; for all the men and women of this world.

But you understand that the BLA is not on trial here. I am on trial here. Ronald Myers is on trial here. And the charge is kidnapping and armed robbery, where the so-called victim is a drug pusher, a seller of heroin, a man called James Freeman.

We live in New York, and it is impossible not to see the horror, the degradation, and the pain associated with heroin addiction. Most of you have seen the staggering numbers of young lives sucked into oblivion, into walking deaths by the use of drugs. Many of you have seen helpless mothers watch their children turn into nodding skeletons, whom they can no longer trust. And seen the dreams, the potential of a whole generation of youngsters drain away, down into the bottomless pit of a needle. And these victims also have their victims: the countless number of people who have been mugged, burglarized, and robbed by drug-made vampires, who care about nothing else but their poison.

We will show you that James Freeman is a liar. We will show you that the other prosecution witnesses are all friends, relatives, lovers, or employees of James Freeman and that they are liars. You will see for yourself that they have conspired and that they have been coached.

Men and women of the jury, human lives are serious matters. I have already told you that i have no faith in this system of justice, and, believe me, i don't. I have seen too much. If there was such a thing as justice, i wouldn't be here talking to you now. You have been chosen to be the representatives of justice. You and you alone. You have said that you could try this case on the basis of evidence. What i am saying now is not evidence. What the prosecutor says is not evidence. You may or may not agree with my political beliefs. They are not on trial here. I have only brought them up to help you understand the political and emotional context in which this case comes before you.

Although this court considers us peers, many of you have had different backgrounds and different learning and life experiences. It is important that you understand some of those differences. I only ask that you listen carefully. I only ask that you listen, not only to what these witnesses say, but to how they say it.

Our lives are no more precious or no less precious than yours. We ask only that you be as open and as fair as you would want us to be, were we sitting in the jury box determining your guilt or innocence. Our lives and the lives that surround us depend on your fairness. Thank you.

As the prosecution began its case, one witness after the other took the stand. I don't remember how many there were, but they were a never-ending parade. The trial was a circus. The carefully planned, carefully rehearsed case of the FBI and local New York police began to fall apart from the moment the witnesses were cross-examined. The prosecution was so desperate to get a conviction in this case that they resorted to stupid, theatrical devices that backfired. One witness, also a drug dealer, hobbled up to the witness stand with the "aid" of a cane, looking like he was two steps from the grave. When asked about the source of his "injuries," he stated that he had received them several years ago at the time of the "kidnapping." Both he and the prosecutor must have forgotten that just a few days ago he had bebopped into the kourtroom to pick me out in an identification hearing, looking perfectly healthy. Under cross-examination, he was forced to admit that he had entered the kourtroom just a few days before without any visible limp and without the "aid" of his cane. He was the only witness who claimed he could positively identify me, because i "had spent weekends at his house." But he didn't know the color of my eyes.

The so-called major witness, James Freeman, the supposed "victim," told a real tearjerker about his kidnapping and the forced ingestion of drugs during it. The prosecution had lightly glossed over the fact that Freeman was a convicted drug dealer. We knew he was connected with the FBI in some way, but it was not until he was cross-examined by James Carroll, Ronald Myers' lawyer, that the real picture of collusion between him and the FBI came out. Freeman testified that he was a paid informant for the FBI. When asked if he had been paid by the FBI to frame me, he said he "couldn't talk about it."

At the end of the people's case, our motions for a verdict of dismissal of the indictment were denied, and we put on our defense. Evelyn and Martha Pitts, a good friend of mine, were working around the clock. Since we could not afford to pay investigators, they did all the leg work. Martha, a registered nurse, investigated Freeman's claim of being drugged. Evelyn was running around like crazy after kourt was over looking for witnesses to testify. Most of it seemed futile to me, since i could not conceive of how one finds defense witnesses in a frame-up. By the time we called our first witness, Evelyn was looking smug and rubbing her hands together.

"We've got their ass this time," she grinned. "They didn't use enough dirt to cover their tracks."

And they didn't. Records subpoenaed from the state Liquor Authority proved that the bar was owned by someone else, not by the witness who had testified to be the owner. The real owner testified that he had closed the bar before the alleged kidnapping, that he had visited it every day during the period of time it has hosted the "kidnapping," and had locked the door as he left and had given no one permission to use it. The bar had been closed for one year before the alleged crime. The irrefutable and obvious conclusion was that, in fact, there was no bar, no "scene" of the alleged crime, and, therefore, no crime. Subpoenaed medical records and expert medical testimony showed that Freeman's stomach contained only a couple of aspirin, hardly supporting his testimony that he had been drugged with some drugs he could not identify, which he had been forced to swallow and which had left him knocked out for several hours.

Sure enough, on December 8, 1975, after four months of trial, the jury acquitted Ronald Myers and me.

Chapter 12

When i entered Manhattan Community College i fully intended to major in business administration and then graduate into a job in marketing or advertising. Instead, i took only one business course. History, psychology, and sociology interested me more than learning how to sell somebody something.

I had truly lucked up. I had gone back to school at a time when struggle and activity were growing, when Black consciousness and nationalism were on the upswing. I had also lucked up on the school.

Manhattan Community College had a very high percentage of Black and Third World students, more than fifty percent. The level of activity was high, both on campus and off. The Golden Drums, the Black organization on campus, whose president was a principled, disciplined brother named Henry Jackson, was pushing for more Black studies courses, Black teachers, programs more responsive to the needs of Black students, and cultural awareness. They gave all kinds of programs on African dancing, drawing, and more. By word of mouth or by the bulletin board, we were turned on to concerts, plays, poetry readings, etc. The Last Poets, a group of young Black poets, knocked me out. I had always thought of poetry in a European sense, but The Last Poets spoke in African rhythms, chanted to the beat of African drums, and talked about revolution. When we'd leave their place on 125th Street—i think it was called the Blue Guerrilla—we'd be so excited and fired up we didn't even notice the long subway ride home.

If i was running myself ragged before i went back to school, now i was flying. I was learning and changing every day. Even my image of myself was changing, as well as my concept of beauty. One day a friend asked me why i didn't wear my hair in an Afro, natural. The thought had honestly never occurred to me. In those days, there weren't too many Afros on the set. But the more i thought about it, the better it sounded. I had always hated frying my hair—burnt ears, a smokey straightening, and the stink of your own hair burning. How many nights had i spent trying to sleep on curlers, bound with scarves that cut into my head like a tourniquet. Afraid to go to the beach, afraid to walk in the rain, afraid to make passionate love on hot summer nights if i had to get up and go to work in the morning. Afraid my hair would "go back." Back to where? Back to the devil or Africa. The permanent was even worse: trying to sit calmly while lye was eating its way into my brain. Clumps of hair falling out. The hair on your head feeling like someone else's.

And then i became aware of a whole new generation of Black women hiding under wigs. Ashamed of their hair—if they had any left. It was sad and disgusting. At the time, my hair was conked, but the hairdresser said it was "relaxed." To make it natural, i literally had to cut the conk off. I cut it myself and then stood under the shower for hours melting the conk out. At last, my hair was free. On the subway the next day, people stared at me, but my friends at school were supportive and encouraging. People are right when they say it's not what you have on your head but what you have in it. You can be a revolutionary-thinking person and have your hair fried up. And you can have an Afro and be a traitor to Black people. But for me, how you dress and how you look have always reflected what you have to say about yourself. When you wear your hair a certain way or when you wear a certain type of clothes, you are making a statement about yourself. When you go through all your life processing and abusing your hair so it will look like the hair of another race of people, then you are making a statement and the statement is clear. I don't care if it's the curly conk, latex locks, or whatever, you're making a statement.

It was a matter of simple statement for me. This is who i am and this is how i like to look. This is what i think is beautiful. You can spend a lifetime discovering African-style hairdresses, there are so many of them, and so many creative, natural styles yet to be invented. For me, it was important not just because of how good it made me feel but because of the world in which i lived. In a country that is trying to completely negate the image of Black people, that constantly tells us we are nothing, our culture is nothing, i felt and still feel that we have got to constantly make positive statements about ourselves. Our desire to be free has got to manifest itself in everything we are and do. We have accepted too much of a negative lifestyle and a negative culture and have to consciously act to rid ourselves of that negative influence. Maybe in another time, when everybody is equal and free, it won't matter how anybody wears their hair or dresses or looks. Then there won't be any oppressors to mimic or avoid mimicking. But right now i think it's important for us to look and feel like strong, proud Black men and women who are looking toward Africa for guidance.

I wasn't in school but a hot minute when a brother in my math class told me about the Golden Drums. After a couple of meetings i was hooked. They addressed me as sister, were glad to see me at meetings, worried about how I was making out in school, and were really concerned about me as a person.

The subject of one of the many lectures scheduled by the Drums was about a slave who had plotted and planned and fought for his freedom. Right here in amerika. Until then my only knowledge of the history of Africans in amerika was about George Washington Carver making experiments with peanuts and about the Underground Railroad. Harriet Tubman had always been my heroine, and she had symbolized everything that was Black resistance for me. But it had never occurred to me that hundreds of Black people had got together to fight for their freedom. The day i found out about Nat Turner I was affected so strongly it was physical. I was so souped up on adrenalin i could barely contain myself. I tore through every book my mother had. Nowhere could i find the name Nat Turner.

I had grown up believing the slaves hadn't fought back. I remember feeling ashamed when they talked about slavery in school. The teachers made it seem that Black people had nothing to do with the official "emancipation" from slavery. White people had freed us.

You couldn't catch me without a book in my hand after that. I read everything from J. A. Rogers to Julius Lester. From Sonia Sanchez to Haki Madhubuti (Don L. Lee). I saw plays by Black playwrights like Amiri Baraka and Ed Bullins. It was amazing. A whole new world opened up to me. I was also meeting a lot of sisters and brothers whose level of consciousness was much higher than mine—Black people who had gained knowledge not only by reading but by participating in the struggle, who talked about Denmark Vesey, Gabriel Prosser, Cinque, as well as Nat Turner, because they had gone out of their way to learn about our history and our struggle.

Many of us have misconceptions about Black history in amerika. What we are taught in the public school system is usually inaccurate, distorted, and packed full of outright lies. Among the most common lies are that Lincoln freed the slaves, that the Civil War was fought to free the slaves, and that the history of Black people in amerika has consisted of slow but steady progress, that things have gotten better, bit by bit. Belief in these myths can cause us to make serious mistakes in analyzing our current situation and in planning future action.

Abraham Lincoln was in no way whatsoever a friend of Black people. He had little concern for our plight. In his famous reply to editor Horace Greeley in August, 1862, he openly stated:

> My paramount objective in this struggle is to save the Union, and is not either to save or destroy slavery. If I could save the Union without freeing any slave, I would do it and if i could save it by freeing some and leaving others alone, I would also do that.

Lincoln was elected president in 1860. Immediately afterward, South Carolina had a convention and unanimously voted to withdraw from the Union. Before he had even been inaugurated, Florida, Georgia, Alabama, Mississippi, Louisiana, and Texas followed suit. In his inaugural speech on March 4, 1861, Lincoln said that slavery was legal under the constitution and that he had no right and no intention to abolish slavery. He further promised to enforce the Fugitive Slave Act, which permitted Southern slave owners to "reclaim" their escaped slaves in Northern states. What the law actually did was give any white man with a "certificate of ownership" the right to kidnap any "free" Black man, woman, or child in the North and force them into slavery. Because of this position, Lincoln received a great deal of criticism from Black abolitionists. Ford Douglas, a runaway slave who accompanied Frederick Douglass on his anti-slavery tours in the West, blasted Lincoln's position, saying,

> In regard to the repeal of the Fugitive Slave Law, Abraham Lincoln occupies the same position that the old Whig Party occupied in 1852. . . . Here, then, is Abraham Lincoln in favor of carrying out that infamous Fugitive Slave Law, that not only strikes down the liberty of every black man in the United States, but virtually the liberty of every white man as well, for, under that law, there is not a man in this presence who might not be arrested today upon the simple testimony of one man, and, after an ex-parte trial, hurried off to slavery and to chains.

On April 12, 1861, Southern troops fired on Fort Sumter, South Carolina, thus starting the Civil War. The response of the Northerners was electrifying. Millions who had been indifferent or lukewarm to the secession of the South jumped on the bandwagon to defend the Union. But the enthusiasm was short-lived. They already viewed Black workers in the North as competitors for their jobs, and the white Northerners, for fear of losing even more jobs to the Blacks, refused to enlist in sufficient numbers for the North to win the war. When the draft law was enacted, tens of thousands of white workers in New York City took to the streets and brutally beat and murdered every Black person they could find. It has been estimated that between four hundred and a thousand Blacks were killed as a result of the so-called New York draft law riots. Draft riots and the murder of Blacks also took place in other Northern cities.

Lincoln had originally opposed Blacks fighting in the Civil War, stating:

> I admit that slavery is at the root of the rebellion, and at least its sine qua non. . . . I will also concede that emancipation would help us in Europe. . . . I grant, further, that it would help somewhat at the North, though not so much, I fear, as you and those you represent imagine. . . . And then, unquestionably, it would weaken the Rebels by drawing off their laborers, which is of great importance; but I am not so sure we could do much with the Blacks. If we were to arm them, I fear that in a few weeks the arms would be in the hand of the Rebels. (History of the Negro Race in America, Vol. II, p. 265.)

Northern whites were more than happy at the prospect of Black people fighting in the war. A popular verse published in the newspapers of the day reflected the sentiment of many Northerners:

> Some say it is a burnin' shame
> To make the naygurs fight
> An' that the trade o' bein' kilt
> Belongs but to the white;
>
> But as for me upon me sowl,
> So liberal are we here,
> I'll let Sambo be murthered in place o' meself
> On every day in the year.

It was not until 1863 that Lincoln in fact issued the Emancipation Proclamation. But the document had very little immediate effect. It freed slaves only in the Confederate states; the slaves in states loyal to the Union remained slaves. Lincoln clearly did not believe Black people could live in the u.s. as equal citizens. In the Lincoln-Douglas debates, he stated:

> If all earthly power were given to me, I should not know what to do as to the existing institution. My first impulse would be to free all the slaves and send them to Liberia—to their own native land. But a moment's reflection would convince me that, whatever of high hope . . . there may be in this, in the long run its sudden execution is impossible. . . . What then? Free them all and keep them among us as underlings? It is quite certain that this betters their condition? I think I would not hold one in slavery at any rate, yet the point is not clear enough for me to denounce people upon. What next? Free them and make them politically and socially our equals? My own feelings will not admit of this, and, if mine would, we well know that those of the great mass of whites will not.

Lincoln was a firm believer in the massive exportation of Black people anywhere. In 1865, at the end of the war, he asked General Butler to explore the possibility of using the navy to remove Black people to Haiti or to other areas in the Caribbean and South America.

It's also important to understand that the Civil War was not fought to free the slaves. It was a war between two economic systems, a war for power and control of the u.s. by two separate factions of the ruling class: rich, white Southern slave owners and rich, white Northern industrialists. The battle was between a plantation slave economy and an industrial manufacturing economy.

An industrial revolution was taking place in the years before the Civil War. Inventions such as the cotton gin, the telegraph, steamships, and steam trains completely changed methods of manufacturing, transportation, mining, communications, agriculture, and trade. The amount of goods produced was no longer determined by the number of people working in the process but by the capacity of the machines. Amerika was no longer a country that produced raw materials for the manufacturing nations in Europe. By 1860, the census reports that 1,385,000 people were employed in manufacturing and that one-sixth of the whole population was directly supported by manufacturing. The number was much higher when clerks, transportation workers, and merchants were added.

As manufacturing centers began to grow, European immigrants were imported as a source of cheap labor. More than five million entered the u.s. between 1820 and 1860. Although the South had many cotton mills functioning, the factories were small and their numbers grew slowly. In 1850, the value of manufactured goods produced in the Northern "free" states was four times the output of the Southern "slave" states. And with the rise of industry came the rise of economic crisis and the threat of industrial collapse.

Even though there had been economic crises in the past, people had generally lived on farms and the economic depressions didn't create such a great hardship for the masses. But with many people living in cities, economic crises meant unemployment and no way to pay for food, clothing, and shelter. The first big crash came in 1825, followed by further depressions in 1829, 1837, 1847, and a severe depression in 1856. The recession in 1857 almost completely destroyed the early labor movement. The poverty in Northern and Southern cities was staggering. Rags, filth, squalor, hunger, and misery were words used to describe the ghettos of the 1800s.

To solve the problems in industrial cities, many called for reforms such as the abolition of debtors' prison, an end to the laws that kept white men who did not own property from voting, free education, the right to strike, an end to child labor, establishment of a ten-hour workday, and granting of land in the West to poor people in the cities. Big business proposed the expansion of capitalism and industry to other parts of the country. And this was where Northern capitalists clashed with Southern slave owners.

Northern capitalists wanted new states to enter the Union as "free" states. Slave owners wanted new states to enter as "slave" states. To maintain a balance of power, the North and the South had entered into several compromises. The main one was the Missouri Compromise. Northern capitalists were afraid slave owners would open factories and produce goods more cheaply because they didn't have to pay for labor. White workers were afraid of losing their jobs because of slavery. Southern plantation owners, of course, wanted the system of slavery to expand across the country.

All the differences between the North and the South were economic, not moral. For capitalists to control the economy and the political system, the slave system had to be defeated.

In 1856, the newborn republican party ran Abraham Lincoln, a former whig, as their first presidential candidate. He lost. In 1860, he ran again with a strong, three-point platform:

1. To shut slavery out of the territories.
2. To establish large protective tariffs.
3. To enact a homestead law giving a medium-size farm free to anyone willing to till the land.

The platform was designed to appeal to rich Northern capitalists, poor white laborers, farmers, and abolitionists. For only a tiny portion of the population was the abolition of slavery a moral issue, and the overwhelming majority of the white people who supported the abolition of slavery or who fought in the Union's army did so because they believed it was in their interests, not for love or concern for Black people.

I was gradually becoming more active. I began to control my life. Before going back to college, i knew i didn't want to be an intellectual, spending my life in books and libraries without knowing what the hell was going on in the streets. Theory without practice is just as incomplete as practice without theory. The two have to go together. I was determined to do both.

The major way i got hip to things was by listening to people. The Black students going to Manhattan Community College belonged to every type of organization. There were Black Muslims, Garveyites, Malcolm X's Organization of Afro-American Unity (OAAU), members of various community and cultural organizations, and a few who were young turks of the NAACP. We got together and talked about everything under the sun. I did a whole lot more listening than talking, but i asked questions about anything i didn't understand. Sometimes the discussions and debates got so heated that they lasted until eleven o'clock, when night school ended and the building was being closed up.

One of the first organizations i checked out was a Garveyite group that had a big hall on 125th Street. I had just read a book on Marcus Garvey. In fact, i had only recently learned he existed. It was a shame. Here he had headed up one of the strongest movements of Black people in amerika and i hadn't heard about him until i was grown. One of the brothers who was studying there invited me to a meeting.

The meeting was upstairs. There seemed to be hundreds of chairs in the room. I arrived a little early and hardly anyone was there. I spotted the brother who had invited me, and he introduced me to the ten or fifteen people already there. We sat around in a little group talking and waiting for the others to arrive. They never came. It was obvious that everyone knew each other and had been coming to these meetings for a long time. After a while, a speaker climbed the podium. He welcomed me to the meeting, then gave an impassioned speech. One after another got up and gave speeches as if they were talking to a roomful of people. The others applauded loudly. I felt sad. They were such nice people, and so sincere, but their circle had grown so small they were reduced to giving speeches to each other.

No movement can survive unless it is constantly growing and changing with the times. If it isn't growing, it's stagnant, and without the support of the people, no movement for liberation can exist, no matter how correct its analysis of the situation is. That's why political work and organizing are so important. Unless you are addressing the issues people are concerned about and contributing positive direction, they'll never support you. The first thing the enemy tries to do is isolate revolutionaries from the masses of people, making us horrible and hideous monsters so that our people will hate us.

All we usually hear about are the so-called responsible leaders, the ones who are "responsible" to our oppressors. In the same way that we don't hear about a fraction of the Black men and women who have struggled hard and tirelessly throughout our history, we don't hear about our heroes of today.

The schools we go to are reflections of the society that created them. Nobody is going to give you the education you need to overthrow them. Nobody is going to teach you your true history, teach you your true heroes, if they know that that knowledge will help set you free. Schools in amerika are interested in brainwashing people with amerikanism, giving them a little bit of education, and training them in skills needed to fill the positions the capitalist system requires. As long as we expect amerika's schools to educate us, we will remain ignorant.

The parents in the Ocean Hill–Brownsville section of Brooklyn, like Black parents all around New York at that time, were pushing for control of the schools in their communities. They wanted a say in what their children were taught, in how their schools were run, and in who was teaching their children. They wanted the local school boards to have hiring-and-firing power over teachers in their districts, but the city's board of education and the American Federation of Teachers was against them.

A whole bunch of us from Manhattan Community College loaded on the subway and took the train out to a demonstration called by the Ocean Hill–Brownsville parents. As soon as we got off the train we ran into some students from CCNY. It seemed like the whole train had been heading for the demonstration, and it was just the kind of demonstration i like.

An energetic sea of Black faces. Proud, alive, angry, disciplined, upbeat, and, most of all, with that sisterly, brotherly kinship i loved. Several of the parents spoke to the crowd, along with the Black principal the parents had insisted on hiring. A Black teacher, head wrapped in a galee, talked about the importance of Black people controlling our schools. She made sweeping gestures with her bangled arms as she spoke. Everybody dug what she said. We were all high on the atmosphere. It seemed like a kinetic dance was boogying in the air.

When it was over, i hated to go home. There aren't too many experiences that give you that good, satisfied feeling, that make you feel so clean and refreshed, as when you are fighting for your freedom.

Most of us felt that taking control of our neighborhoods was the first step toward liberation. We sat in the subway station tripping. When a train did come, we just let it pass. First we would take control of the schools; then we would take control of the hospitals; then we would take control of the colleges, the housing, etc., etc. We would have community-controlled employment, welfare centers, and city, state, and federal agencies.

"Hold on for a minute," somebody said. "Where are ya'll gonna get the money to run all that stuff?"

"We'll take community control of the banks," someone else answered.

"You'd better take control of the army, too, because those banks aren't gonna just let you take their money lying down."

"We'll take control of the political institutions in our community. Then we'll take control of the congressional seats, the senate seats, the city council seats, the mayor's office, and every other office that we can take control of. We'll take control of the political offices so we can allocate money to the people who need it."

"Y'all just wishing and hoping," someone said. "You can control the social institutions and the political institutions, but unless you control the economic and military institutions, you can only go but so far."

Everybody just sort of got quiet, thinking.

"Well, what are we supposed to do, then? Just sit back and do nothing?"

"Fighting for community control is just the first step. It can only go so far. What you need is a revolution."

Everybody started talking about what the brother had said. We were all confused, but we were all enthused. That was the one thing i dug about those days. We were alive and we were excited and we believed that we were going to be free someday. For us, it wasn't a matter of whether or not. It was a question of how.

We always started out talking about reform and ended up talking about revolution. If you were talking about anything except a few little jive crumbs here and there, reform was just not going to get it. I was long past the day when i thought that reform could possibly work, but revolution was a big question mark. I believed, with all my heart, that it was possible. But the question was how.

I had heard a lot about the Republic of New Afrika and had promised myself to check it out. The Provisional Government of the Republic of New Afrika advocated the establishment of a separate Black nation within the u.s., to be made up of what is now South Carolina, Georgia, Alabama, Mississippi, and Louisiana. At the time, i thought the group was kind of wild and far out, but i got a good feeling being around them and the idea of a Black nation appealed to me.

The first time i attended a Republic of New Afrika event, i drank in the atmosphere and enjoyed the easy audacity of it all. The surroundings were gay and carnival-like. A group of brothers were pounding out Watusi, Zulu, and Yoruba messages on the drums. Groups of sisters and brothers danced to motherland rhythms until their skins were glazed with sweat. Speeches were woven between songs and poems. Vibrant sisters and brothers with big Afros and flowing African garments strolled proudly up and down the aisles. Bald-headed brothers, wearing combat boots and military uniforms with leopard-skin epaulets, stood around with their arms folded, looking dangerous. Little girls running and laughing, their heads wrapped with galees, tiny little boys wearing tiny little dashikis. People calling each other names like Jamal, Malik, Kisha, or Aiesha. Sandlewood and coconut incense floated through the air. Red, black, and green flags hung from the rafters alongside posters of Malcolm and Marcus Garvey. Serious-looking young men, wearing jeans and green army field jackets, passed out leaflets. Exotic-looking sisters and brothers, decked out in red, black, and green, sat behind felt-covered tables and sold incense, bead earrings, and an assortment of other items.

"Peace, sister," a voice said. "Do you wanna be a citizen?"

"What?" i asked, without the slightest notion of what she was talking about.

"A citizen," she repeated. "Do you want to be a citizen of the Republic of New Afrika?"

"How do i become a citizen?"

"Easy. Just sign your name in the citizens' book."

"That's all?"

"Yeah. You want a name?"

"A name?"

"Yeah, sista, a name. If you want an African name, just ask that brother over there to give you one."

The brother she pointed out was wearing a long bubba with matching pants and a matching fez-type hat. He was wearing various necklaces made of beads, bones, shells, and pieces of wood. His left ear was pierced and his face was strained in concentration, the veins in his forehead throbbing.

Without giving it a second thought, i went over to have my name changed. The brother looked at me, asked me a couple of questions which i don't remember, and then began shaking a container furiously. He hurled out the contents, which turned out to be shells, onto a soft cloth. After a long, concentrated stare at the shells and after glancing back and forth at me, the brother decided that my name was Ybumi Oladele. He spelled the name out to me as i wrote it down, then i hurried over to the sister's table and became a citizen of the Republic of New Afrika. Ybumi Oladele. I liked the way it sounded. Soft and musical, kinda happy-sounding. I filed my new name away in my pocketbook and continued sucking in the atmosphere, tripping out on the idea of a Black nation in Babylon, a nation of Black people smack dab in the middle of the belly of the beast. Imagining Black youth flourishing and being nourished in Black schools, taught by teachers who loved them and who taught them to love themselves. Controlling their lives, their institutions, working together to build a humane society, ending the long legacy of suffering Black people have endured at the hands of amerika. My mind spaced out on the idea and in a minute i was imagining red, black, and green buses, apartment buildings with African motifs, Black television shows, and movies that reflected the real quality of Black life rather than the real quality of white racism. I imagined everything from cities called Malcolmville and New Lumumba to a reception for revolutionary leaders around the world at the Black House. Sure enough, i liked the idea of a Black nation, but i didn't give it any serious consideration as a possible solution. Back then, the idea just seemed too farfetched. I guess, at the time, having an African name seemed a little farfetched, too. I told my friends about the name, talked about it for a few days, and then promptly forgot about it.

It wasn't until years later—after college and more revolutionary activism and marriage—that i began to seriously think about changing my name. The name JoAnne began to irk my nerves. I had changed a lot and moved to a different beat, felt like a different person. It sounded so strange when people called me JoAnne. It really had nothing to do with me. I didn't feel like no JoAnne, or no Negro, or no amerikan. I felt like an African woman. From the time i picked my hair out in the morning to the time i slipped off to sleep with Mingus in the background, i felt like an African woman and rejoiced in it. My big, abstract black and white inkblot-looking painting was replaced by paintings of Black people and revolutionary posters. My life became an African life, my surroundings took on an African flavor, my spirit took on an African glow. From the paintings on my walls to the big, fat pillows on my floor, from the incense burning in the air to the music dancing through the rooms, my whole life was moving to African rhythms. My mind, heart, and soul had gone back to Africa, but my name was still stranded in Europe somewhere. JoAnne was bad enough, but at least my mother had given it to me. As for Chesimard, well, i could only come to one conclusion. Somebody named Chesimard had been the slavemaster of my ex-husband's ancestors. Chesimard, like most other last names Black people use today, was derived from massa. Black folks went from being Mr. Johnson's Mary and Mr. Jackson's Paul to being Mary Johnson and Paul Jackson. Sometimes, before dozing off to sleep, i would lie in bed and think about it, wondering how many slaves Chesimard had owned in Martinique and how often he beat them. I would stare up at the ceiling wondering how many Black women Chesimard had raped, how many Black babies he had fathered, and how many Black people he had been responsible for killing.

So the name finally had to go. I thought about Ybumi Oladele, but there was one problem. I didn't know what the name meant. My new name had to mean something really special to me. At the time, there were little pamphlets being put out listing names and their meanings, but i had a hard time finding one i liked. A lot of the names had to do with flowers or songs or birds or other things like that. Others meant born on Thursday, faithful, loyal, or even things like tears, or little fool, or one who giggles. The women's names were nothing like the men's names, which meant things like strong, warrior, man of iron, brave, etc. I wanted a name that had something to do with struggle, something to do with the liberation of our people. I decided on Assata Olugbala Shakur. Assata means "She who struggles," Olugbala means "Love for the people," and i took the name Shakur out of respect for Zayd and Zayd's family. Shakur means "the thankful."

At first, the Golden Drums society concentrated its efforts on Black culture and history. But after a while we started to examine our role as students. We didn't want to be tape recorders, recording whatever information, facts, lies they gave us and then playing them all back during examinations. We began to talk about an education that was relevant to us as Black people, that we could take back to our communities. We didn't want to learn Latin or classical Greek. We wanted to learn things that we could use to help free our people.

One of our first struggles centered on student government. Most of us were from working-class or poor families and we wanted a student government that was responsive to what we needed. We didn't need a student government that was brownnosing the administration in return for favors and good grades. We wanted a student government that supported a Black studies program, more Black faculty members, and other Black causes. As a result, the Golden Drum Society and the Students for Democratic Society (SDS) ran a joint ticket and won by a landslide.

It soon became evident that having control of the student government wasn't enough. It had no real power. We would pass resolutions and come up with proposals, which the administration would promptly deny. The only power we had was over the student government budget. Instead of inviting reactionary "scholars" or politicians to speak, we invited the Young Lords or the Black Panther Party or some other group who was saying something relevant.

One of our proposals was for students to work during the summer in remedial programs to improve the level of kids who had trouble with reading and math. Our idea was to have a few kids assigned to each student-teacher. In that way, each one would receive the individual attention he or she needed. The academic curriculum was to be supplemented with courses that would enhance the students' sense of self-worth and give them more of a sense of their history. Student-teachers would work with parents, visit the kids' homes, and create a kind of day camp by offering sports, trips, crafts, etc. Several of the Black faculty members helped us with the proposal. As soon as it was submitted it was rejected.

The administration claimed there was no money. A small investigation into finances, aided by some concerned Black and white faculty members, revealed that the president of the college was living in a house rent-free, that taxpayers were also providing him with chauffeur and maid services, and that student fees, which had not been spent in previous years, were being invested on the stock market. A rather strange financial picture was emerging. After we made some of our investigation results known to the administration, we were informed that the money for the project had been found.

As a student-teacher i taught reading and math in the morning and arts and crafts in the afternoon. The morning classes were tiny, while the afternoon classes were larger, combining various morning groups. The curriculum included Black history, dancing and drumming, physical education, arts and crafts, in addition to reading and math. There was an excursion every Friday afternoon.

My mother thought my teaching reading and writing was a joke. My spelling is terrible, and my skills in mathematics are limited to two and two equaling four. To prepare myself for the day's lesson, i had to study just as hard as the kids. My students shocked the hell out of me. Through conversation, it was obvious just how bright they were, yet they scored way below their grade levels in reading and math. There was such a big contradiction between the intelligence they exhibited in class and their test scores that i didn't know where to begin. The books we had to work with were Reader's Digest–like textbooks that i couldn't even imagine using. I didn't even want to read those things and i knew sure as hell that my students wouldn't want to use them. So every day, i took the vocabulary out of those books and wrote a little story, something i thought the students would find interesting, typed it on a stencil, and ran it off. I brought all kinds of books to school for them to read, and as long as they found the books interesting, those students would read until the cows came home. I was learning just as much as the kids. I found it oppressive playing teacher all the time, so every day i rotated the thing around. Everybody got to be teacher for a while. It was also great for discipline, since if somebody acted up in your class, you were free to act up in theirs. Nobody wanted people to act up in their class so everyone was more or less cool.

In order to teach, each one of us had to prepare our lesson and know what we were talking about. One of the boys in the class worked so hard on his lessons that he would just lay me out. I don't know where he is now or what he's doing, but if he isn't a teacher, it's a damn shame, because he would have been a great one. He would cut out pictures and even make up math games for us to play.

My class in the afternoon was usually exhausting. Clay, paint, papier-mâché over everything and everyone, especially me. The first days of that class i wanted to do nothing but go somewhere and have a good cry. On the first day of the arts and crafts class i had nothing really prepared, so i asked everyone to draw themselves. When i looked at the drawings i felt faint. All of the students were Black, yet the drawings depicted a lot of blond-haired, blue-eyed little white children. I was horrified. I went home and ransacked every magazine i could find with pictures of Black people. I came in early the next day and plastered the walls with pictures of Black people. We talked about what was beautiful. We talked about all the different kinds of beauty in the world and about all the different kinds of flowers in the world. And then we talked about the different kinds of beauty that people have and about the beauty of Black people. We talked about our lips and our noses. We made African masks out of clay and papier-mâché, made African sculptures, painted pictures of Black people, of Black neighborhoods. Over the summer i felt the classroom changing. The kids were changing and so was i. We were feeling good about ourselves and feeling good about being with each other.

I was so involved in working at the school that i had time for little else. If one of the students didn't come to school, i was at his or her house that very day wanting to know why. I would go home and spend hours rewriting some story or preparing for the next day. Half the time my mother would find me asleep with a book in my hands and all the lights on. I loved working with the kids, and i loved teaching. My mother helped me quite a lot and we grew closer than we had ever been before. I thought about becoming a teacher but decided against it.

For the first time, i became aware of what my mother had been going through all those years trying to teach in New York schools. Most of these principals are caught up in bureaucracy and they force the teachers to be caught up in it too. They care more about what the teachers have written in their plan books than what they are actually teaching in the class. My mother was working in an environment where white teachers often showed a hostile, condescending attitude toward Black children and where some teachers thought of themselves as zookeepers rather than teachers.

As much as i loved working with kids, i knew that i could never participate in the board-of-education kind of teaching. I wasn't teaching no Black children to say the pledge of allegiance or to think George Washington was great or any other such bullshit.

That fall, the level of activity on campus surpassed anything that we had dreamed of. Large numbers of students became involved in the antiwar movement. It seemed that there was no time to catch up with all of the things that were happening. I would be at the construction workers' demonstration one day and then marching with the welfare mothers the next. We got down with everything—rent strikes, sit-ins, the takeover of the Harlem state office building, whatever it was. If we agreed with it, we would try to give active support in some way. The more active i became the more i liked it. It was like medicine, making me well, making me whole. I was home. For the first time, my life felt like it had some real meaning. Everywhere I turned, Black people were struggling, Puerto Ricans were struggling. It was beautiful. I love Black people, i don't care what they are doing, but when Black people are struggling, that's when they are most beautiful to me.

As usual, i was speeding. My energy just couldn't stop dancing. I was caught up in the music of struggle, and i wanted to dance. I was never bored and never lonely, and the brothers and sisters who became my friends were so beautiful to me. I would mention their names, but the way things are today, i'd only be sending the FBI or the CIA to their doors.

There were a lot of communist groups on campus. I had no idea at the time that there were so many different kinds of communists and socialists. I had been so brainwashed i had thought that all communists were the same, that there were Marxists, Leninists, Maoists, Trotskyites, etc. Most of the so-called communists i met weren't in any party at all, but just related to the philosophy of communism. Most followed very different political lines and policies, and it was difficult for them to sit down and agree on the time of day, much less hatch up some "communist plot."

I was surprised to learn that there were all different types of capitalist countries and different types of communist countries. I had heard "communist bloc" and "behind the iron curtain" so much in the media, that i had naturally formed the impression that these countries were all the same. Although they are all socialist, East Germany, Bulgaria, Cuba, and North Korea are as different as night and day. All of them have different histories, different cultures, and different ways of applying the socialist theory, although they have the same economic and similar political systems. It has never ceased to amaze me how so many people can be tricked into hating people who have never done them any harm. You simply mention the word "communist" and a lot of these red, white, and blue fools are ready to kill.

I wasn't against communism, but i can't say i was for it either. At first, i viewed it suspiciously, as some kind of white man's concoction, until i read works by African revolutionaries and studied the African liberation movements. Revolutionaries in Africa understood that the question of African liberation was not just a question of race, that even if they managed to get rid of the white colonialists, if they didn't rid themselves of the capitalistic economic structure, the white colonialists would simply be replaced by Black neocolonialists. There was not a single liberation movement in Africa that was not fighting for socialism. In fact, there was not a single liberation movement in the whole world that was fighting for capitalism. The whole thing boiled down to a simple equation: anything that has any kind of value is made, mined, grown, produced, and processed by working people. So why shouldn't working people collectively own that wealth? Why shouldn't working people own and control their own resources? Capitalism meant that rich businessmen owned the wealth, while socialism meant that the people who made the wealth owned it.

I got into heated arguments with sisters or brothers who claimed that the oppression of Black people was only a question of race. I argued that there were Black oppressors as well as white ones. That's why you've got Blacks who support Nixon or Reagan or other conservatives. Black folks with money have always tended to support candidates who they believed would protect their financial interests. As far as i was concerned, it didn't take too much brains to figure out that Black people are oppressed because of class as well as race, because we are poor and because we are Black. It would burn me up every time somebody talked about Black people climbing the ladder of success. Anytime you're talking about a ladder, you're talking about a top and a bottom, an upper class and a lower class, a rich class and a poor class. As long as you've got a system with a top and a bottom, Black people are always going to wind up at the bottom, because we're the easiest to discriminate against. That's why i couldn't see fighting within the system. Both the democratic party and the republican party are controlled by millionaires. They are interested in holding on to their power, while i was interested in taking it away. They were interested in supporting fascist dictatorships in South and Central America, while i wanted to see them overthrown. They were interested in supporting racist, fascist regimes in Africa while i was interested in seeing them overthrown. They were interested in defeating the Viet Cong and i was interested in seeing them win their liberation. A poster of the massacre at My Lai, picturing women and children lying clumped together in a heap, their bodies riddled with bullets, hung on my wall as a daily reminder of the brutality in the world.

Manhattan Community College had not one course on Puerto Rican history. The Puerto Rican sisters and brothers who knew what was happening became our teachers. I had hung out all my life with Puerto Ricans, and i didn't even know Puerto Rico was a colony. They told us of the long and valiant struggle against the first Spanish colonizers and then, later, against the u.s. government and about their revolutionary heroes, the Puerto Rican Five—Lolita Lebrón, Rafael Miranda, Andres Cordero, Irving Flores, and Oscar Collazo, each of whom had spent more than a quarter of a century behind bars fighting for the independence of Puerto Rico. Once you understand something about the history of a people, their heroes, their hardships and their sacrifices, it's easier to struggle with them, to support their struggle. For a lot of people in this country, people who live in other places have no faces. And this is the way the u.s. government wants it to be. They figure that as long as the people have no faces and the country has no form, amerikans will not protest when they send in the marines to wipe them out.

I had begun to think of myself as a socialist, but i could not in any way see myself joining any of the socialist groups i came in contact with. I loved to listen to them, learn from them, and argue with them, but there was no way in the world i could see myself becoming a member. For one thing, i could not stand the condescending, paternalistic attitudes of some of the white people in those groups. Some of the older members thought that because they had been in the struggle for socialism for a long time, they knew all the answers to the problems of Black people and all the aspects of the Black Liberation struggle. I couldn't relate to the idea of the great white father on earth any more than i could relate to the great white father up in the sky. I was willing and ready to learn everything i could from them, but i damn sure was not ready to accept them as leaders of the Black Liberation struggle. A few thought that they had a monopoly on Marx and acted like the only experts in the world on socialism came from Europe. In many instances they downgraded the theoretical and practical contributions of Third World revolutionaries like Fidel Castro, Ho Chi Minh, Augustino Neto, and other leaders of liberation movements in the Third World.

Another thing that went against my grain was the arrogance and dogmatism i encountered in some of these groups.

A member of one group told me that if i was really concerned about the liberation of Black people i should quit school and get a job in a factory, that if i wanted to get rid of the system i would have to work at a factory and organize the workers. When i asked him why he wasn't working in a factory and organizing the workers, he told me that he was staying in school in order to organize the students. I told him i was working to organize the students too and that i felt perfectly certain that the workers could organize themselves without any college students doing it for them. Some of these groups would come up with abstract, intellectual theories, totally devoid of practical application, and swear they had the answers to the problems of the world. They attacked the Vietnamese for participating in the Paris peace talks, claiming that by negotiating the Viet Cong were selling out to the u.s. I think they got insulted when i asked them how a group of flabby white boys who couldn't fight their way out of a paper bag had the nerve to think they could tell the Vietnamese people how to run their show.

Arrogance was one of the key factors that kept the white left so factionalized. I felt that instead of fighting together against a common enemy, they wasted time quarreling with each other about who had the right line.

Although i respected the work and political positions of many groups on the left, i felt it was necessary for Black people to come together to organize our own structures and our own revolutionary political party. Friendship is based on respect. As long as much of the white left saw their role as organizing, educating, recruiting, and directing Black revolutionaries, i could not see how any real friendship could occur. I felt, and still feel, that it is necessary for Black revolutionaries to come together, analyze our history, our present condition, and to define ourselves and our struggle. Black self-determination is a basic right, and if we do not have the right to determine our destinies, then who does? I believe that to gain our liberation, we must come from the position of power and unity and that a Black revolutionary party, led by Black revolutionary leaders, is essential. I believe in uniting with white revolutionaries to fight against a common enemy, but i was convinced that it had to be on the basis of power and unity rather than from weakness and unity at any cost.

TO MY MOMMA

To my momma,
who has swallowed the amerikan dream
and choked on it.

To my momma,
whose dreams have fought each other—
and died.

Who sees,
but cannot bear to see.
A volcano eating its own lava.

To my momma, who couldn't turn
hell into paradise
and blamed herself.
Who has always seen
reflected in her mirror
an ugly duckling.

To my momma,
who makes no demands of anyone
cause she don't think she can afford to.
Who thinks her money talks
louder than her womanhood.

To my butchfem momma,
who has always
taken care of business.
Who has never drifted
hazily to sleep
thinking, "he will take care of it."
Who has schemed so much
she sometimes schemes against herself.

To my sweet, shy momma.
Who is uneasy with people
cause she don't know how
to be phony,
and is afraid to be real.

Who has longed for sculptured gardens.
Whose potted plant
dies slowly on the window sill.

We have all been infected
with a sickness
that can be traced back
to the auction block.

You must not feel guilty
for what has been done to us.
Only the strong go crazy.
The weak just go along.

And what i thought was cruelty,
I understand was fear
that hands, stronger than yours,
and whiter than yours,
would strangle my young life
into oblivion.

Momma, i am proud of you.
I look at you
and see the strength of our people.
I have seen you struggle
in the dark;
the world beating on your back,
dragging your catch
back to our den.
Pulling your pots and pans out
to cook it.
A mop in one hand.
A pencil in the other,
marking up my homework
with your love.

The injured have no blame.
Let it fall on those who injure.

Leave the past behind
where it belongs—
and come with me
toward tomorrow.

I love you mommy
cause you are beautiful,
and i am life that springs from you:
part tree, part weed, part flower.

My roots run deep.
I have been nourished well.

Chapter 13

I am at school when i hear about it. Electric shocks are zooming down my back the way they do when i am about to go temporarily insane. On the train, headed uptown, i am ready to riot. I am having daymares on the subway, imagining myself with a long knife slashing slits in white sheets. Ku Klux Klan blood is spilling. You wanna look like a ghost, you wanna look like a ghost, my mind keeps chanting, you wanna look like a ghost, well, i'll make you one. Sitting on the subway, bloody fantasies. I look out of my daymare. Nobody is moving. Everybody screams. Everybody has a frozen face. The train is slowing down. Everybody is tensely looking at the door. 125th Street. I am going to a riot. I want to kill someone.

Martin Luther King has been murdered.

The street wakes me up. There is no blood yet. Everybody is getting into position. The wind is blowing rumors. The people are waiting. The streets are rumbling. The tanks are coming. The natives are restless. The tanks will quiet the natives. The tanks are coming. I feel absurd and impotent.

Who am i going to attack? Where is a George Lincoln Rockwell? I am ready to kill him. He will get a chance to utter exactly two syllables before i cut him off. He isn't there. Only the rumors and the rumble of the tanks and the waiting. The store windows are filled with shit. You can't exchange Martin Luther King for shit in the store window. Smashing windows will do me no good. I am beyond that. I want blood. The tanks are waiting to crush the resistance, squelch the disturbance. It crosses my mind: i want to win. I don't want to rebel, i want to win. The revolution will not be televised on the six o'clock news. I have to get myself ready. Revolution. The word has me going.

I am back on the subway. Nobody is looking at anybody. I think i have my period. Sweat is rolling down my legs. I go home. My mother is glad to see me. She knows that i am half crazy. The television is wet with crocodile tears. REBELLION, REBELLIOUS CHILDREN, *TEMPER TANTRUMS,* REBELLION, REVOLUTION. *I like the word.*

The grim reapers are abuzz. Reports about the natives. They are excited. This is the stuff that news is made of. We are looking at each other. Impassioned speeches sizzle on their tongues, causing sour ashes to fall from our mouths. We are just sitting there. I am thinking about revolution. The tonic. Abstract. Revolution. I am tired of watching us lose. They kill our leaders, then they kill us for protesting. Protest. Protest. Revolution. If it exists, i want to find it. Bulletins. More bulletins. I'm tired of bulletins. I want bullets.

While i was going to CCNY, after i graduated from Manhattan Community College, i decided to get married. My husband was politically conscious, intelligent, and decent, and our affair was frantic, high-pitched, and charged with emotion. Somehow, i believed that our shared commitment to the Black Liberation struggle would result in a "marriage made in heaven." I spent most of my time at school, meetings, or demonstrations and whenever i was at home my head was usually stuck in some book. It was unthinkable to allow more than five minutes on mundane things like keeping house or washing dishes. To complicate matters, my husband's ideas about marriage stemmed mostly from his parents' life, where his mother was the homemaker and his father was the breadwinner. Spaghetti was about the only thing i could cook, and he was profoundly shocked to learn i had none of his mother's domestic skills. After a while, it became clear to me that i was about as ready to be married as i was to grow wings and fly. So after a confused and unhappy year, we decided we made much better friends than marriage partners and called it quits.

I decided to go to California. It was becoming increasingly clear to me that, although it was important for students to participate in the struggle, no revolution had ever been won by students alone. Struggling around school issues had narrowed my perspective and i was getting bogged down. I wanted to expand that struggle to the Black community. At that time California, especially the Bay area, was where everything was happening. Some of my favorite professors were going out West for the summer and they offered to hook me up with a place to stay. As usual, i was flat broke, but a good friend gave me the money to make the trip, with a little spending change thrown in.

My friends found a place for me in Berkeley, the most radical, progressive place i had ever been in. Revolutionary posters were plastered all over the walls, along with "people's murals." The fronts of banks and other official buildings were bricked up as a result of the demonstrations and street fighting that followed the People's Park struggles. Red stars and Mao's *Red Book* were sold on street corners, and food cooperatives sold health food at cheap prices. People's collectives were dedicated to surviving, struggling, and teaching. I was impressed with the kinds of informal solutions they had cooked up to deal with the problems they faced, and i enrolled in the practical skills classes they gave (printing and layout, first aid, etc.).

There were books and pamphlets in the San Francisco and Berkeley bookstores i had never seen in New York, and for the first time i read the theory of urban guerrilla warfare as outlined by Che Guevara, Carlos Mariguella, and the Tupamaros. I had been more aware of imperialism in Vietnam or Cambodia, and the extent of u.s. imperialism in South and Central America surprised me. The u.s. government had invaded more than fifteen countries there, not once or twice but in some cases more than ten times, and the guerrilla movements were waging armed struggle in most of them. Reading about guerrilla warfare in South America and Vietnam was one thing, but thinking in terms of guerrilla war inside the u.s. was another.

Back then, people used the word "revolution" just because it sounded hep. Half the time what they were really talking about was change or some kind of vague progress. Some meant a separate Black nation, and others dealt with Black revolution as part of an overall revolution waged by whites, Hispanics, Orientals, Native Americans, and Blacks. Malcolm said it meant bloodshed and land. To me, the revolutionary struggle of Black people had to be against racism, capitalism, imperialism, and sexism and for real freedom under a socialist government. But the reality of achieving it seemed a long way off.

In Berkeley and San Francisco, the revolution didn't seem too far away. A lot of white radicals, hippies, Chicanos, Blacks, and Asians were ready to get down. But i hadn't forgotten the hardhats and the rednecks and the bible belt and the so-called middle amerikans who had elected Nixon. I couldn't imagine the "new left" talking to those people, much less organizing them and changing their minds. I decided the only way i would come up with some answers was to keep on studying and struggling. I didn't know how half of what i was studying would fit in, but i figured it would all come in handy some day. I read about guerrilla warfare and clandestine struggle without having the faintest idea that one day i would go underground. It's kind of funny when i think about it, because reading all that stuff probably has saved my life a million times.

As part of my first aid skills class, i worked as an assistant to a doctor who volunteered once a week at Alcatraz. At the time, Alcatraz had been taken over by Native Americans who were protesting against a long series of broken treaties, genocidal policies, and racist exploitation. Alcatraz symbolized the strength and dignity of Indian people as well as their resolve to fight to preserve their cultural traditions. I enjoyed everything about going there except the trip. The doctor was a motorcycle fanatic who insisted on zooming across the Golden Gate Bridge on that thing, with me hanging on for dear life. Once on the other side we would jump into a rickety little boat with water in the bottom and limp across the bay to the island. By the time we got there i felt as if i had done a day's work.

The first thing that hit me was the spirit of the people. I felt the tremendous pride, tremendous determination, and tremendous calm from the time i landed on the island until the time i left. They were Native Americans from all over North America, including Canada, from different tribes and backgrounds. They were young and old. Little babies wiggled in their mother's arms, and one old man who had spent many years in Alcatraz prison said that when he arrived on the island he had taken a sledgehammer and reduced the cell he had once been locked in to rubble. The prison, one of the most infamous and sadistic ever to exist, loomed in the background.

There were many different Indian nations, each with its own rich culture, religious traditions, history, and folklore. Everybody was into learning and teaching each other their own history and culture. It was a surprise to find out how many Native Americans had been raised in cities and knew nothing about who they were. In that respect, they were very similar to Black people. Most of them were from the West Coast, and so i told them about the Indian Museum and the Museum of Natural History in New York. Suddenly, i stopped short. I wondered how i would feel going into some museum and seeing the houses and stolen artifacts of my people stuck away in some exhibition hall. As i spoke i realized that most of the "history" i had been taught about the Indians was probably lies invented by the white man.

It wasn't until later, for instance, that i learned that scalping was an old European custom. In the 1700s, the state of Massachusetts was paying the equivalent of $60 for a scalp and Pennsylvania paid $134. It wasn't until more than a hundred years later, in response to the massive genocide at the hands of whites, that the Indians themselves started scalping. None of the little museum exhibits featuring tepees and feather headdresses had ever mentioned how men, women, and children were mowed down at Wounded Knee or how the u.s. army had purposely given the Indians smallpox-infected blankets. As i listened to those sisters and brothers at Alcatraz i realized that the true history of any oppressed people is impossible to find in history books.

I will always be grateful for having had the opportunity to visit Alcatraz. I will never forget the quiet confidence of the Indians as they went about their lives calmly, even though they were under the constant threat of invasion by the FBI and the u.s. military. They didn't fit into any of my preconceived notions or the stereotyped images shown on TV and in the movies. They were really open with me and, after a while, we talked about the struggle in general. They had many of the same problems we had: education, organizing the people to struggle, and raising consciousness. They damn sure had the same enemy, and they were doing as bad as we were, if not worse. They told me to check out Akwasasne when i returned to New York. It was a territory they had liberated on the border between New York and Canada. I told them if they ever came to New York they should visit me and check out Harlem. "Sure. When are you going to liberate it?" they asked.

There were a million groups in the Bay area i wanted to check out. There was so much activity i would have had to spend twenty-eight hours a day just to keep up with it all. Someone i was studying with arranged for me to hook up with the Brown Berets, a Chicano group that had been started recently in California and Texas. It was a brief meeting since the brother with whom i had the appointment had to be on the move. He ran down to me some of the conditions they were dealing with and some of the work they were doing. I had always thought of the Chicano movement as a rural rather than an urban one. Most of the information we had received was about the Chicano farmworkers' struggle and people like Cesar Chavez fighting to organize them and abolish the unbearable living conditions and slave wages they were forced to work for. I was not aware that Chicanos in the city were fighting against unemployment, police brutality, and inferior schools, just like Black people. In the same way that the Black Panther Party was trying to organize and politicize street gangs in Chicago, the Brown Berets wanted to politicize Chicano street gangs in Los Angeles. The brother also told me that they had been doing a lot of work around Los Siete de las Razas, seven Chicano brothers who had been accused of killing a San Francisco policeman. (They were later acquitted.) I wanted to rap some more about this case because i was seeing the same pattern everywhere—sisters and brothers being locked up all over the country, accused of killing pigs or of conspiring to. The brother had to run, though. We promised that we would hook up again, but it never happened.

Next i wanted to check out the Red Guard, a group of young revolutionary brothers and sisters who were struggling in Chinatown, San Francisco. I was especially anxious to meet up with them because it was so hard to get information about them back East. The West Coast has the largest Asian population in the country and i really wanted to get a good idea about what was going on in the Asian communities. A lot of people think Asians do not experience racism, that they are professionals and business owners, unaware that many are poor and oppressed.

Finding the Red Guard was not at all easy. Half the people i ran into had never heard of them, and the other half only had a minimal knowledge of who they were and what they were all about. Someone gave me an address and since i didn't have the faintest idea where it was, i got a brother to drive me over to Chinatown to look for their headquarters. We ended getting lost and never did find the address. Instead, we ended up eating at a Chinese restaurant and getting into a big debate. He couldn't understand why a Black woman wanted to hook up with Chinese revolutionaries in the first place: "ain't nobody gonna free Black folks but Black folks"; "those Chinese don't give a damn about you and me. All they care about is their own people and what's going on in China." I told him that i thought there were a whole lot of us in the same predicament and that the only way we were going to get out of it was to come together and break the chains. The brother looked at me as if i was spouting empty rhetoric. Some of the laws of revolution are so simple they seem impossible. People think that in order for something to work, it has to be complicated, but a lot of times the opposite is true. We usually reach success by putting the simple truths that we know into practice. The basis of any struggle is people coming together to fight against a common enemy.

When i finally did get around to meeting some brothers from the Red Guard, it was quite by accident and somewhat embarrassing. I was hanging out in the park with a sister and some brothers from the Black Students Union. We were exchanging experiences, talking politics, and smoking reefer. The day was blue and beautiful and we just sat there lazing in the sun without a care in the world, listening to some rock music that was playing in the background. I had brought a whole pile of leaflets and newspapers from New York to give to them. Everybody was feeling laid-back and mellow when all of a sudden a bunch of pigs descended on a group of hippies and proceeded to beat them mercilessly, kicking them and hitting them with clubs. We were all so high, we just sat there watching, like it was a movie or something. By the time we got our voices together to cry out in protest, the pigs were carrying the hippies off.

Two Asian brothers came up to us and pointed to the newspapers.

"You'd better get rid of those before the pigs see them," one said. "More are on the way. If you've got any grass on you, you'd better get out of here fast."

We were a picture of confusion, stuffing sheets of paper under shirts and into pocketbooks. The Asian brother led our half-dazed procession out of the park.

"You need a lift?"

"Yeah, that's cool."

"To where?"

"Oh, anywhere. Anywhere from here," one of us answered. We were too high to make any decisions. We piled into a rickety-looking jeep. They told us they would drive us over to Shattuck Street and drop us off. As we were driving, everybody started to talk about the pigs beating up on the hippies. The image was burning in everyone's mind.

"That was a trip," drawled one of the BSU brothers. "Did you see those pigs? I thought they were gonna kill those dudes."

I was still high, feeling too stunned and eerie to talk.

"That's why we need a revolution," the sister was saying. "They just think they can do anything they want to."

"What started the shit?" somebody asked the Asian brothers.

"It was some hassle about some ID or something. They just wanted to hassle somebody. You're lucky they didn't see you first."

We were all silent for a minute, imagining ourselves being beaten and carted off to jail.

"It's a good thing they didn't see those leaflets," the other Asian brother said. "They would have hassled you for sure."

The sister, who was obviously angry, got off into a political rap. Everybody kind of jumped into the conversation, talking about the situation in the Black community, the Black students' struggle, and the overall piggishness of amerika. Everybody was into the rap, all of us presenting ourselves as political activists and revolutionaries.

"Are you guys in the movement?" one of the Asian brothers asked us. Everybody jumped at the opportunity to say yes, giving credentials and naming organizations.

"Right on," they said.

They told us they were Red Guard cadre and that they were having some kind of forum on the revolution in China. In my tongue-tied, confused state of marijuana intoxication, i tried to communicate to them that i had been trying to get in touch with their organization to check it out. The brother who had been doing most of the talking reached down under the seat and handed me a leaflet which had the date and time of the forum.

"Make sure you come and check us out," he said. "Put this somewhere where you won't lose it," making direct reference to my confused, disjointed state of consciousness. "You guys should really be careful with that grass, especially when you've got leaflets or newspapers on you. A lot of good comrades have been busted like that."

"Yeah," said the other one. "You've got to be alert to deal with this situation. You've got to be disciplined and ready to deal with the enemy at all times."

The Red Guard brothers dropped us off and we thanked them and said good-byes amid a hail of "Right ons" and "Power to the people." Carefully avoiding each other's eyes, we wandered aimlessly, looking for someplace where we could plop down and get our heads together. I was feeling guilty and stupid, silly and politically backward. I was embarrassed to be bumbling down the street in the middle of the day not in full control of my faculties, too high to deal with reality, much less change it. I wondered what the brothers from the Red Guard had thought of us, sitting there in a stupor, having to be virtually led out of the park. It was obvious my stuff was raggedy and that i needed to get my act together. If i wanted to call myself a revolutionary i was going to have to earn the title. I had heard somebody say that revolutionaries get high on revolution and that it was the best high in the world. "I'm gonna check out that high," i said aloud. "Huh? What did you say?" "Nothing," i answered. "I was just talking out loud." "Oh," somebody said, "I can dig it."

We stopped off at a coffee shop and had some tea. Everybody looked sheepish and lost in their own thoughts. Finally, we waved our good-byes and made our separate ways. I walked back to where i was staying, wondering what i was going to have to do to become who i needed to become. Revolution is about change, and the first place the change begins is in yourself.

The most important organization on my list to check out was the Black Panther Party headquarters in Oakland. I had a whole lot of respect for the Party and had been heavily influenced by it, as had almost everyone around my age that i knew. Every time we heard about Huey Newton and Bobby Seale standing up to the power structure, we slapped five and said, "Yeah!" As far as i was concerned, the Panthers were "baaaaaad." The Party was more than bad, it was bodacious. The sheer audacity of walking onto the California senate floor with rifles, demanding that Black people have the right to bear arms and the right to self-defense, made me sit back and take a long look at them. And the more political i became, the more i appreciated them. Panthers didn't try to sound all intellectual, talking about the national bourgeoisie, the military-industrial complex, the reactionary ruling class. They simply called a pig a pig. They didn't refer to the repressive domestic army or the state repressive apparatus. They called the racist police pigs and racist dogs.

One of the most important things the Party did was to make it really clear who the enemy was: not the white people, but the capitalistic, imperialistic oppressors. They took the Black liberation struggle out of a national context and put it in an international context. The Party supported revolutionary struggles and governments all over the world and insisted the u.s. get out of Africa, out of Asia, out of Latin America, and out of the ghetto too. I had gotten to know some of the Panthers in New York when they spoke at the lectures we invited them to at Manhattan Community College. I made it my business to drop by some of the New York Black Panther Party offices and offered to help them with this or that, whatever needed to be done. I was happy to do it. I barely opened my mouth. I just looked, listened, and worked. Some of the comrades would ask why i didn't join. "I probably will, someday," i'd always answer.

When i heard on the radio that the New York Panthers had been busted, i was furious. The so-called conspiracy charges were so stupid that even a fool could see through them. The police actually had the audacity to charge them with plotting to blow up the flowers in the Botanical Garden. And the 21 were some of the baddest, most politically educated sisters and brothers in the Party. It was an insult. I thought about joining the Party right then, but i had some other things i wanted to do and i needed a low profile in order to do them.

As much as i dug the Party, i also had some real differences with its style of work. As i opened the front gate of the Oakland headquarters, i felt just as nervous about going inside as i did about the Doberman pinschers running around the yard. A brother opened the door and i nervously blurted out that i was from New York and had come to check out the Party. He acted like he was glad to see me and brought me into a room to meet some of the other Panthers. A group of sisters and brothers were sitting around the room, laughing and talking. They greeted me casually, passing over a chair for me to sit in. Artie Seale was there and i had to control myself to keep from gawking at her. I wondered how she felt with her husband in jail, being railroaded and bound and gagged in kourt. I recognized the names of others. It was strange to be there in a room with those people. It was like sitting down on the pages of a history book.

They asked me about New York, and i told them what was happening with the Black students at Manhattan Community College, CCNY, and the Black student movement in general, the antiwar movement, Black construction workers, and whatever other work i was involved in at the time. I told them i had done some work for the New York Panthers and ran off a list of the ones i knew. Somebody asked my why i had never joined the Party.

Half stammering, i told them i had thought about it but had decided not to. "Why?" everybody wanted to know. It was hard for me to say it because i felt so much love and respect for the sisters and brothers seated there, but i knew i'd hate myself if i didn't say what was on my mind: that i had been turned off by the way spokesmen for the Party talked to people, that their attitude had often been arrogant, flippant, and disrespectful. I told them i preferred the polite and respectful manner in which civil rights workers and Black Muslims talked to the people rather than the arrogant, fuck-you style that used to be popular in New York. I said they cursed too much and turned off a lot of Black people who would otherwise be responsive to what the Party was saying.

When i had finished, i waited nervously, fully expecting them to jump all over what i had said. To my profound surprise, nobody did. Everybody agreed that if that was, in fact, how Party members were relating to the people, they should change at once. One of the sisters pointed out that there was a leadership crisis in the New York chapter caused by the arrest and imprisonment of the Panther 21. It was well known by everybody in the movement that the New York police had kidnapped the most experienced, able, and intelligent leaders of the New York branch and demanded $100,000 ransom for each one. One of the brothers explained that the Panthers were facing the same problem all over the country because of persecution by the pigs. We spent the rest of the afternoon rapping about the Black struggle in New York and in the u.s. in general. I was deep in a discussion about strategy and tactics when Emory Douglas came in. I was as happy as a bee in a pollen factory to meet him. I dug his artwork a lot and had even taped a piece he had written on revolutionary art to my closet door. We hit it off at once and, when everybody finished rapping, he took me up to see how the Black Panther newspaper was put together.

I was truly impressed by the Panthers in Oakland. After my first visit, i dropped in at their offices regularly. I visited some of the other branches in the area, talking to the people and asking my usual ton of questions. I spent a couple of nights working at the distribution center for the Party paper, which was located in the Fulton district in San Francisco. It was a trip! The papers wouldn't get picked up from the printer until late in the evening, and people would work until the wee hours sorting them out and preparing them for distribution to the Panther offices all around the country. Panthers worked there, but the majority seemed to be sisters and brothers from the neighborhood who had just dropped in to give the Panthers a hand. A lot of young people were there and some elderly sisters and brothers. As we wrapped the papers in bundles, printed addresses, and counted out papers, we sang Panther songs and marching chants. Every now and then, a few stepped outside to sip a little bitter dog. This was supposedly a Panther invention made of red port and lemon juice. It wasn't too bad, once i got used to it, and by the time 1 A.M. came around, i loved it. Working on the paper distribution didn't even seem like work—it was more like a party. Somebody always gave me a lift home and i would fall into a happy sleep feeling refreshed and renewed.

It was splashed across the papers, blaring on the radio, and yet i still couldn't believe it. The face of the serious young man with the gun refused to leave my thoughts. I must have picked up the same newspaper and put it down a hundred times. This shit was serious! Seventeen years old with a rifle under his raincoat. Seventeen years old and taking freedom into his own hands. Seventeen years old and defying the whole pig power structure in amerika. Seventeen years old and dead. Tears i didn't even know i had poured out. I got on the phone to find somebody who could explain it all. Who was Jonathan Jackson? Who was the young man who came to free a revolutionary Black prisoner, holding a district attorney and a pig judge hostage, shouting, "We are the revolutionaries! Free the Soledad Brothers by 12:30"? Who was he?"

I had only vaguely heard of the Soledad Brothers. A brother who knew all about the case broke it down to me. Three unarmed Black prisoners were shot down in the yard by a white guard. A grand jury ruled it "justifiable homicide." After the verdict, a white guard was found dead. Three politically conscious Black prisoners were charged with the murder and thrown into solitary. They all faced the death penalty. John Clutchette, Fleeta Drumgo and George Jackson were the brothers charged with the murder. George Jackson, a brilliant revolutionary theorist and writer, was Jonathan Jackson's brother.

I couldn't get the whole thing out of my head. Why were grown men and women living while Jonathan Jackson lay dead? What kind of rage, what kind of oppression, and what kind of country shaped that young man? I felt guilt for being alive and well. Where was my gun? And where was my courage?

I was dry-eyed when i attended the funeral. There were hundreds of people. We could barely get into the church. They set up a loudspeaker outside so that people could hear the sermon. Black Panthers, solemn and determined, marched in military formation. I was so, so glad they were there. Black people need someone to stand up for us or we will always be victims. I held my arms real close to me, feeling a bit unraveled. Life for us gets so ugly. If i stay a victim it will kill me, I thought. It was time for me to get my shit together. I wanted to be one of the people who stood up. These were serious times.

Angela Davis was running for her life. They had hooked her up with Jonathan Jackson, charged her with kidnapping and murder at the kourthouse, even though she was nowhere on the set. They charged her with murder because they claimed that some of the guns used belonged to her. She was one of the most beautiful women i had ever seen. Not physically, but spiritually. I knew who she was, because i had been keeping clippings of her in my file. She was the sister who got fired from her job teaching at a California college because she told everybody she was a communist and if they didn't like it, they could go to hell.

But i wasn't surprised. They will charge Black people with anything, using any flimsy excuse. We were very glad they hadn't caught her. I hoped they never would. The air was charged, everything was happening so fast, and i wasn't blind anymore. I was seeing things straight, seeing them more clearly than ever before. I had so many things to do. If you are deaf, dumb, and blind to what's happening in the world, you're under no obligation to do anything. But if you know what's happening and you don't do anything but sit on your ass, then you're nothing but a punk.

I tried to explain how i felt to some of the people i knew. I wanted to struggle on a full-time basis. They urged me to join the Panther Party. I went over in my mind all the criticisms i had of the party. They had said, "You'll be good for the Party, and the Party will be good for you. The Party is only as strong as its people." It made a lot of sense to me. For the first time in months i felt calm and sure of what i was going to do. I told them that the first thing i was going to do when i returned to New York was join the Party.

I thought about it all the way home. Of all the things i had wanted to be when i was a little girl, a revolutionary certainly wasn't one of them. And now it was the only thing i wanted to do. Everything else was secondary. It occurred to me that even though i wanted to become a revolutionary more than anything else in the world, i still didn't have the slightest idea what i would have to do to become one.

Chapter 14

"You're the property of the feds now," one of the marshals told me like he really believed it. "We're taking you to MCC [the federal prison, manhattan correctional center] where you'll stay while you stand trial for bank robbery." It was January 5, 1976, fifteen days after i had been acquitted on the kidnapping charge in Brooklyn supreme kourt; i was still on Rikers Island. He busied himself tying me up with what seemed an endless amount of chains and shackles. Another stupid-looking marshal told me how sorry he was to see me again. He said i'd given him hell the last time. I didn't even recognize him. He said he had worked on the last, other bank robbery trial and had gotten "chewed out" because i got pregnant. "You were framed," i told him . He looked at me all dumb, scratching his head. "Yeah, yeah. That's right." I started to laugh. Even the other marhsals started to crack up. "It's not so funny," he said. "I lost my commendation that went down in my record." I laughed even harder.

The only way i can describe MCC is modern gray, with dabs of colored paint here and there. It's one of those ugly inner-city fortress buildings, antinature, antihuman, and cold to all the senses. There was no fresh air because the entire building was air-conditioned, and the only natural light came in from narrow glass slits cut into the side of the building and wired with alarms. The guards looked like space age robotons, with blue blazers, gray pants, walkie-talkies, and beepers. After i had been issued the standard uniform for women (a yellow jumpsuit and tennis shoes), i was led up to the women's section. To my absolute surprise i was placed in "general population," given a key to my cage, and told that there was no "lock-in" time. We were supposed to stand by the cell doors at various times of the day to be counted. The women's section was a relatively small area, comprising a central area for eating and recreation, a TV room, and three split-level tiers. There were a few offices, one or two rooms that served as classrooms, and that was it. The only other place the women could go, once in a while, was to recreation on the roof, which was covered with huge metal antihelicopter bars.

After spending more than a month in that confining little place, the women were climbing the walls, and i'm sure the men felt the same way. A few of the federal prisoners were big time, with money and connections; they'd been arrested for more "sophisticated" crimes than the average state prisoner. But the majority were poor, Black, or Third World, just like in the state jails. But just like in the street, money talks. A lot of the men on the honor floor, which was on the same floor as the women, had money, and rumor had it that they would send their favorite guards out to buy them Chinese or Italian food or send them to the Jewish delicatessen, depending on their mood. One drug dealer made frequent visits to the women's section in the wee small hours for conjugal visits with his wife. Since the men on the honor floor had contact with the women, many tried to buy them by sending them huge quantities of commissary items. Others tried to impress the women with tall tales about how much they had ripped off or how big they were on the street. I was sitting on the bench with this white guy, waiting for them to take me to kourt one morning, and he was steady talking one and two million dollar deals he had pulled off. He was some kind of con artist, busted for stock fraud. "You shouldn't be here," i told him. "You should be in the White House with all the other big-time con artists." "I was trying," he said, "I was trying like hell."

There were two sisters who i knew from Rikers. I was really happy to see them both. Skeets was a strong, stand-up sister who kept her mouth shut, minded her business, and didn't take any shit from anybody. She was a real warmhearted person, generous and open, and maintained a whole lot of humanity, even though she was facing a hunk of time on a bank robbery case. I was shocked when i ran into Charlie, who i had known on Rikers as Charlene. She had changed completely. She was no longer the thin, round-faced young sister i had known on the rock. It was as if she had aged overnight. She had written some dynamite poetry and had been part of our drama group. But this time she had been arrested for parole violation on a technicality and just didn't give a damn about anything anymore. She was bitter and tired and her whole attitude can be summed up in the two words that she frequently used: "Shove it." She told me that her freedom depended on whether or not she passed a high school equivalency test. Everybody encouraged her to study, but she just didn't seem to care anymore. She said she was tired of jumping through hoops and didn't give a damn what happened. I understood how she felt, but i hated to see her so bitter and so hurt and nowhere to go with it, nothing positive to apply it to. I wanted to help her, but i didn't know how, and i was only going to be there for a hot minute. The only thing that perked her up was the struggle the women got into to improve medical care at the jail.

At the time, the health situation was horrible. Women came in off the street and were given no physical exam, no tests, no nothing. They had trouble seeing gynecologists and having their most basic needs met, medical or otherwise. Since we were a tiny minority of the prison population, our needs were ignored. The women got together and wrote complaints to the warden. Charlie was one of the women who worked the hardest to get better medical conditions. It's kind of ironic when i think about it now. A little more than a year later, i heard over the prison grapevine that Charlene had died from undiagnosed cancer of the uterus.

The Queens bank robbery trial, which I was here for, was one of the wildest trials i ever went through. We had just finished with the Brooklyn kidnapping case and i was not at all looking forward to going to trial again so soon.

For almost three years, now, Evelyn had worked on my cases continuously. She had quit her job as a professor at New York University Law School on the day I was arrested on the turnpike to become my lawyer. One of the few cases she had accepted since my arrest—mostly to earn some money—was ready for trial, and she couldn't postpone it any longer. So i had to get someone else for my trial. Some of the brothers and sisters recommended Stanley Cohen to me. They said he was a good lawyer and would do a good job on this kind of case. I was hesitant because i had always had Black lawyers representing me. I felt that they would probably be more understanding and more sensitive to the situation i was dealing with. I'm not talking about any old Black lawyer, because some of them make a whole lot of money and think like Richard Nixon. I'm talking about those who are concerned with the plight of Black people.

I was especially sensitive to the issue after months of listening to some of the sisters at Rikers. They were so brainwashed they thought a white lawyer, any white lawyer, was better than a Black lawyer. They also felt the same way about white doctors, white dentists, white teachers, etc. "I ain't going to court with no Black lawyer," they'd say. "I want me a white lawyer who is friendly with the judge and ain't gonna make him mad." I tried to tell them that it didn't matter what color their lawyer was, if the lawyer went against the judge and really put up a fight for the client, the judge was gonna get mad. Few, if any, Black defendants have ever been freed because the judge liked their lawyer. If you had a dime for every time a judge and a defense lawyer sat down to lunch and discussed some Black client rotting away in jail, you'd be able to stop working and live on the interest.

I decided to talk with Cohen and see whether i thought he would be good for the case. Stanley was a middle-aged, Jewish, fiesty-looking man who somehow reminded me of W. C. Fields. He had a dramatic streak in him and could change the tone and mood of his voice from indignant to pleading in a matter of seconds. He had a long list of acquittals in his record and told funny stories about the strategies he used in this or that trial. He had once been a member of the Communist party and continued to have progressive politics. "Why do you like being a criminal lawyer?" i asked him. "How can you stand to fight in the kourt system, knowing how much racism and injustice is involved?" It was a loaded question, put out there to see how he would answer it. I expected him to say something like somebody had to do it, somebody had to make the sacrifice. "I like to win," he said. "I do it because I like to win." I liked him and decided i wanted him to defend me on the bank robbery case.

Evelyn gave Stanley the transcripts from the time i was beaten up in kourt by the u.s. marshals trying to photograph me, together with all of the other documents in her file, and worked with him on the trial strategy. Andrew Jackson had pled guilty, so i was on trial alone. Everything was rush, rush, rush. The railroad train was whistling and it could hardly wait to take me up the river. The new judge assigned to the case wanted the case over with and he wanted it over with fast. We wanted to question the prospective jurors about their opinions, what they had seen and heard in the media, etc. The judge was determined not to have a long voir dire, and so we compromised. A questionnaire was made up asking some of the questions we submitted and others that the prosecutor submitted. After we went through the answers we were to pick or eliminate jurors, asking additional questions as needed. Some of the answers were so contradictory and such a study on the level of racism in amerika that it would take a book just to report on them. In one hundred percent of the cases we were able to tell whether the prospective juror was Black, white, or "other," just by reading the answers.

The trial had a lighthearted feel to it. Everyone had kind of decided that we would enjoy the fight and fight as hard as we could, without worrying about whether we were gonna win or lose. I don't think that there was a single one of us, with the possible exception of Afeni Shakur, who really thought we were going to win. Afeni, who was working as a legal assistant, kept telling me, "We're going to win this one, Assata." But i sure as hell didn't believe it. They had taken a bank picture of a woman robbing a bank, printed my name under it as being positively identified, and then placed that picture in newspapers, subway stations, and, i think, even on the sides of buses. They had this picture posted in every bank in New York. There was not a person in New York who went to the bank, rode the subway, or walked the streets who had not seen that photograph with my name printed under it a thousand times. There was no way of even counting how many times that picture had been flashed on television, with the announcer calling out my name. The public had been so saturated with that image that i felt it was crazy to take this trial seriously. After Stanley was familiar with some of the facts, i had asked him what he thought my chances were. "I'd be lying if I told you that they looked good. In reality, they look pretty lousy. But, I believe you, and I'm going to fight for you. And, believe me, I like to fight." We agreed that i would act as co-counsel on the case. "You're a lousy lawyer," he would tell me every time we got into an argument over some strategy, "but you're better than a lotta lawyers I know who passed the bar."

The atmosphere was electric. The kourtroom was packed every day with sisters and brothers who had come to watch the circus. I couldn't stop staring. I have always said that the best thing about being on trial is getting to see and smile at the spectators. Seeing so many beautiful people in the kourtroom gave us the push we needed to get down and take care of business. I felt that way during all of my trials, but this trial had an atmosphere that made it even more special. People from all over the Black community dropped by. The Muslim sisters and brothers brought their prayer rugs and broke out into prayer in the hallway of the kourthouse. People brought their children, explaining what was happening. One little girl broke up the whole kourtroom when she asked out loud, "Is that the fascist pig, Mommy?" pointing up at the judge. It was as if

Black folks had just taken over the kourtroom, letting everybody know that they were watching what was going down.

The first thing we did was ask for a lineup. The way i had been "identified" was from a photo. The FBI had selected my photograph from the "militant casebook." This book contained the photographs of all the "militants" the FBI wanted to send to prison. After they had gotten my photograph out of the "militant casebook," they put it in with a few other photographs of women. Of course, mine, a mug shot, was the only one with numbers across the front of it. The rest were normal. The FBI then showed this group of pictures to the robbery witnesses and asked them to identify someone who "somewhat resembled" or "bore a likeness" to the woman who robbed the bank. Two of the people who were in the bank signed affidavits saying that the photograph with the numbers across it, my mug shot, looked somewhat like the woman. The rest who had been in the bank at the time of the robbery made no such identification. We told the judge we wanted a lineup because we thought the initial identification of me as the bank robber was suggestive and tainted. But before the judge had arranged for the lineup, the prosecutor called one of the so-called witnesses to testify. Since i was the only Black woman sitting in the defendant's chair, of course he identified me. We protested the procedure, but the judge admitted his testimony anyway. We finally did arrange for a lineup, and, of course, the other so-called witnesses picked out another woman.

Since the photo identification part of the case was based on nothing more than "all niggers look alike," the FBI tried to use "scientific" evidence to gain a conviction. Their plan to superimpose the bank surveillance photo over my photograph failed because they had only one photo of me that was taken at the same angle as the bank robbery picture. It was one of the photographs taken when they assaulted me in the kourtroom before the trial began when I refused to let them take my picture. The FBI had blocked out the faces and hands of the marshals and FBI agents choking and assaulting me. They had cropped the picture so that the only thing the jury could see was my face. But my facial expression in the photograph was one of such agony that it was hard for them to convince the jury of anything else.

So the FBI came up with a brilliant idea. They brought in some dude from the FBI who said he was an expert on identifying photographs by examining them under a microscope. He was a real pro, slick as grease. He had charts and diagrams and whatnot, and i was worried to death that the jury would go for that crap. He sounded real good, until it came time for cross-examination. It turned out that he was a specialist in paleontology and had spent a lot of time studying rocks. He tried to claim that his expertise at examining rocks made him able to identify people. Under cross-examination, all his carefully constructed "expertise" turned into a pile of rocks, and this new technical breakthrough in crime fighting proved to be nothing but a fraud. Because the prosecution had been allowed to introduce this new, "scientific" evidence, the judge said we had the right to find a photographic expert to rebut the testimony. Since i didn't have a dime, the kourt agreed to pay for it. The day our photograph expert testified i slumped down in the seat. He was a real straight-looking white guy who looked like he subscribed to *Reader's Digest*. But the guy had credentials in photography a mile long, and you could tell from the way he talked that he loved photography and that he was incensed over what the FBI was trying to do. He explained to the jury the chemical process of photography and that what the FBI agent said was absolutely impossible. He said that if you look at a photograph under a microsocpe all you will see is little dots. His testimony was so correct and his facts so together that the prosecutor barely bothered to cross-examine him.

The capper came when the manager of the bank came forward to testify in my behalf. He said that i was definitely not the woman who robbed the bank and that the robber was a different height and weight from mine. We could see the prosecutor quietly creep under his table. His last hope was the summation.

In his closing statement, he tried to make up for everything he had not proved with the evidence. He painted me as an evil, conniving monster. He told the jury that i was hiding the fact that i had big fat arms like the woman who was shown robbing the bank, that i was concealing my arms because i had not worn a sleeveless dress in kourt (the trial was held in the middle of January). As he was talking, i politely rolled up my sleeves right there in the kourtroom, exposing my very thin arms. When he got to the final part of his closing, he grew strangely confident. "Ladies and gentlemen of the jury, this woman is very clever, very conniving. She has tried to deceive this jury in every way. But she made one mistake, ladies and gentlemen, she made one fatal error." He then held up a picture of the woman robbing the bank and, in the other hand, he held up my mug shot picture. "She made one mistake," he kept repeating. "She forgot to change her earrings. She has the same earrings on."

The prosecutor was so dramatic. The scene was straight out of the movies. You could tell he had been watching the late show. Both the woman in the bank and i had on hoop earrings. When Stanley summed up, he just said, "Will all the women in the courtroom who have on hoop earrings, please stand up?" Half the women rose to their feet.

While the jury was out deliberating i paced back and forth in the holding pen. "They're gonna convict me anyway," i told Afeni. "They probably weren't even listening. "That jury isn't going to convict you, Assata," Afeni replied. "Didn't you see the faces of those jurors, especially the Black ones?" It was true, i had seen them look at me differently after the truth started coming out. And i knew that the Black jurors in the deliberating room would make all the difference in the world. If nothing else, they remind some of the more racist whites that Black people are human beings. It's a shame that too many Black people try to avoid jury duty, instead of trying to slow down the railroad. A lot of times it's a matter of simple economics. Black people often feel they can't afford to sit on a jury, that the money they would lose would mean a sacrifice for their family. And they are probably right. But their sitting on a jury might mean that their neighbor's son or daughter doesn't end up frying in the electric chair or rotting away behind bars.

A verdict had been reached. I could tell what it was before we even entered the kourtroom. The pigs were upset, to put it mildly. The female guard who escorted me to kourt every day seemed glad. The jury read the verdict. Acquittal. The kourtroom broke into a loud cheer. The judge just gave up calling for order. He had to wait for the shouting to die down. It was a long time coming. All the spectators were jumping around hugging each other. The marshals led me out of the courtroom and handcuffed me. They brought me back to Rikers Island where i was put into solitary confinement.

Chapter 15

A bundle of energy walked into the Black Panther Party office on Seventh Avenue. If a light had been plugged into me, i'm sure i would have lit up half of Harlem. I was fired up and raring to go. When i joined the BPP, i was determined to give it everything i had.

The officer of the day gave me a form to fill out. He couldn't find the second sheet so i went back with him to look for it. He was searching through a file cabinet which was in a state of anti-order. It was a complete mess. I offered to arrange it for him and the brother consented. In a minute i was knee-deep in paper, indexing and putting everything in alphabetical order. After everybody's "security files" were filed, i cut index markers out of a manila folder, thinking about how lax security was. I had just walked in off the street and they let me go through all the files. I explained the new system to the brother, happy at least that the experience gained from all those boring office jobs was put to some revolutionary use.

That same evening i was on the bus to Philadelphia. The Party had called for a constitutional convention to write a new constitution that would guarantee the rights of the poor and oppressed and would be antiracist and antifascist. We were attending the plenary session for the convention to be held later in D.C. This session was a definite up. Everybody's spirits were soaring. It took my breath away to see all those revolutionaries get up and tell it like it was. I was happy as a dog in boneville. My "hotel room" was a pool table in the basement of a church. I slept better than a princess on twenty mattresses.

When i got back to New York, i was assigned to

the medical cadre. Joan Bird was my immediate supervisor. She had been a nursing student and was one of the defendants in the New York Panther 21 case. She was out on $100,000 bail and busy working on the trial. She had been beaten, tortured, and hung upside down out of a police station window. She had big, soft eyes, nervous lips, and the face of someone who had been forced to grow up too soon. She reminded me of someone who had led a very sheltered life and then, all of a sudden, found herself in the cold, cruel world. She was sort of shy, and i felt sorry for her because she seemed to be under so much pressure. She took everything to heart; nothing seemed to slide off her back. She worried about everything and everyone. She was facing thirty years in prison, so i had to do most of the medical cadre work, and she worried herself sick about that.

The medical cadre was responsible for the health care of the Panthers. We made medical and dental appointments for them and taught them basic first aid so that they could help the people in emergencies. Periodically, we set up a table on the street corner and gave free TB tests or gave out information on sickle-cell anemia. It was also my job to work with the Black medical students and doctors who we were counting on to help us set up a free clinic in Harlem. The Panther Party had bought a brownstone on 127th Street, and as soon as it was renovated we planned to open a free clinic there.

Every week all the medical cadre members from the Bronx, Brooklyn, Harlem, Jamaica, and Corona branches met at the Bronx Ministry of Information. On my first trip to the Ministry, i carried a big stack of Panther newspapers. I was a lousy paper seller, and most of the time i got some of my doing-good friends to chip in and buy them. Then we'd give them away to the people.

The head of the medical cadre was Alaywa, and from the first moment she gained my respect and admiration. She was serious about everything that concerned Black people, but when it came to their health she was a fanatic. She demanded that we take our jobs seriously, and woe be to the medical cadre who showed up at the weekly meeting with nothing on their progress reports. Alaywa had a young daughter, but she nevertheless did the work of two people.

I got expelled from the Party, though, that first night after the medical cadre meeting. When i came out of the meeting, my stack of Panther papers was gone. I asked around, but no one had seen them. Finally, Robert Bey, the head of the whole East Coast branch of the Party, said that he had seen them.

"Where are they?" i asked.

"I threw them away."

"What do you mean, you threw them away?" i asked, thinking it was some kind of joke.

"I threw them away," he insisted. "Ya'll know that you're not supposed to leave the papers out here on the desk. This will teach you to put the papers up on the rack where they belong."

I explained that it was my first time coming up to the Ministry and that i had no way of knowing the procedure.

"You should have asked," he replied arrogantly. "I threw them away and that's that."

I was losing my patience. "Look, man, why don't you just give me my papers so that i can get out of here. I don't have time to stand here all night."

"I told you i threw the papers away, and that's that."

"Then you're either a liar or a fool," i shot back. He had made me mad, gone and stepped on my last nerve. Then he tried to get all bad, getting all up in my face, trying to defend his stupid arrogance. I was in no mood for fooling around. I cursed him out royally and walked out of the office.

The next day, when i walked into the Harlem office, Bashir, the officer of the day, told me i would have to leave. "What do you mean, leave?" i asked. He said that he was sorry, but Robert Bey had called and told him that i was no longer in the Party. I was burnt. I got the Bronx Ministry and told them to put Bey on the phone and proceeded to call him the unprincipled, arrogant idiot he was. In addition to being cowardly, he hadn't even told me to my face that i was expelled. I was so warm i wasn't even surprised when he apologized and told me i was reinstated. I hate arrogance whether it's white or purple or Black. Some people let power go to their heads. They think that just because they have some kind of title in front of their name you're supposed to bend over and kiss them on the ass. The only great people i have met have been modest and humble. You can't claim that you love people when you don't respect them, and you can't call for political unity unless you practice it in your relationships. And that doesn't happen out of nowhere. That's something that has got to be put into practice every day.

The first day i was assigned to the breakfast program i overslept. To get there on time i had to get up at 4:30 in the morning. I was the picture of shame and remorse as i came plodding into the office. "Fancy meeting you here," the sister who i was supposed to be helping said. "So nice of you to come." Later on that evening i criticized myself for being late. "That's all right, sister," the brother who was leading the meeting said. "you can do penance by working on the breakfast program for life."

"For life?" i repeated.

"Yep, you can show your sincerity to the hungry children of Harlem by working on the breakfast for as long as you're in the Party."

I have always hated to get up in the morning, and the sheer idea of getting up every day at 4:30 made me groan. But i thought about the children i'd let down. Getting up early should be an easy thing for a revolutionary. I thought about those who had given their lives for our struggle and decided it wasn't so hard after all. Later, one of the sisters told me, "Don't worry. They'll just assign you to the breakfast program every day until you're used to it and they can count on you to be disciplined. The same thing happened to me."

I was glad it had happened to others because i felt like such a dumbbell. Got to try harder, i told myself.

Working on the breakfast program turned out to be an absolute delight. The work was so fulfilling. The Harlem branch had breakfast programs in three different churches, and i rotated among all three. From the first day i saw those kids, my heart went out to them. They were such bright, open little people, each with his or her own personality. I spent the first two weeks or so just getting my cooking act together. One little girl came over to me and tapped me on the back.

"There's something wrong with your pancakes."

"What's wrong with them?"

"They don't taste good."

Making breakfast for a whole bunch of hungry kids in the morning is no easy task, especially when you don't know how many are coming or how much they're going to eat. There was one little boy who i was convinced had a tapeworm. He put away so much food it was unbelievable. One day i saw him stuff some food into his pockets.

"Would you like some paper to wrap that in?" i asked him, tearing off a piece of foil.

"I wasn't stealing." Tears welled up in his eyes.

"Of course you weren't. Everything is free here and you can take as much as you want. But don't you want to wrap it up so your pockets don't get all greasy?"

"It's for my mother. We don't have no food and the stove is broke."

"You can tell your mother that she can come down if she wants to, and you can take as much food home as you want to." A few of the other kids were looking at us. "That goes for everyone. If you want to take a sandwich or something with you, just let me know and i'll give you some wrapping paper for it." After that i would try to remember to ask if anybody wanted anything to go. Most of the kids were interested. "Give me an egg sandwich to go." "I want two sausages to go." We rarely met the parents. When a new kid joined the program, the parents might drop by to check it out, but in general they would only come to leave the kids or pick them up.

The breakfast program in East Harlem was the poorest. In the middle of winter some of the kids were without hats, gloves, scarves, and boots and wore just some skimpy coats or jackets. When it was possible, we tried to hook them up with something from the free clothing drive. Only once in a while, when everything went smoothly and we were through early, did we get a chance to spend some time with the children. Usually we were in a rush making sure they got out to school on time. Some of the Panthers wanted them to learn the ten-point program and platform and others wanted to teach them Panther songs. I preferred talking to them, sitting down with them and exchanging ideas. So we just sort of combined these approaches. We were all dead set against cramming things in their heads or teaching them meaningless rote phrases. The children were so naturally curious we had to take care not to let the food burn while we answered their questions.

My closest friends in the Party were Dhoruba, Cetewayo, and Jamal. They were all out on bail from the Panther 21 case. They came over to my house and we sat for hours talking politics, the Party, North Korea, and what was happening on 116th Street. I learned more in one night than i learned in City College in a month. They had a hard time dealing with me, though. I can be stubborn as six mules and will argue anyone down until i'm convinced one way or the other. Although i no longer hated white people and no longer saw all of them as the enemy, i was still not too fond of them. As far as i was concerned, it was the duty of Black people to work in the Black community and it was the job of white people to go into the white community and organize white people. The brothers were in one hundred percent agreement with that. We also agreed that it was necessary for Black, white, Hispanic, Native American, and Oriental people to come together to fight. We disagreed on who and what i should study.

Usually, after a disagreement, they suggested i read this or that, often Marx, Lenin, or Engels. I preferred Ho Chi Minh, Kim Il Sung, Che, or Fidel, but i ended up having to get into Marx and

Lenin just to understand a lot of the speeches and stuff Huey Newton was putting out. It wasn't easy reading, but i was glad i did it. It opened up my horizons a hell of a lot. I didn't relate to them as the great white fathers or like some kind of gods, like some of the white revolutionaries did. As far as i was concerned, they were two dudes who had made contributions to revolutionary struggle too great to be ignored.

The more i studied, the more critical i became of the political education (PE) program in the Party. There were three different political education classes: community classes, classes for BPP cadre, and PE classes for Panther leadership. In the community classes, Panthers explained the ten-point program and the general objectives and philosophy of the BPP as well as various articles that appeared in the Black Panther newspaper. As far as i was concerned, these were the best PE classes the party ever gave. If the teachers were good, the classes were interesting and fun.

With a few exceptions, PE classes for Party members turned out to be just the opposite. We reviewed articles in the BPP paper, read passages from Mao's *Red Book,* and discussed certain speeches and articles by various Party members. Most of the time whoever was giving the class discussed whatever we were studying and explained it, but without giving the underlying issues or putting it into any historical context. The basic problem was not whether the teacher was good or bad. The basic problem stemmed from the fact that the BPP had no systematic approach to political education. They were reading the *Red Book* but didn't know who Harriet Tubman, Marcus Garvey, and Nat Turner were. They talked about intercommunalism but still really believed that the Civil War was fought to free the slaves. A whole lot of them barely understood any kind of history, Black, African or otherwise. Huey Newton had written that politics was war without bloodshed and that war was politics with bloodshed. To a lot of Panthers, however, struggle consisted of only two aspects: picking up the gun and serving the people.

That was the main reason many Party members, in my opinion, underestimated the need to unite with other Black organizations and to struggle around various community issues. A lot of the sisters and brothers had joined because they were sick and tired of the oppression they had been suffering. Most of them had never been in the struggle before. Quite a few joined thinking the Party was going to issue them a gun and direct them to go out and shoot pigs. Most of these brothers and sisters had attended inferior schools which either taught them lies or nothing at all. Education of every kind was sorely needed. Without an adequate education program, many Panthers fell into a roboton bag. They repeated slogans and phrases without understanding their complete meaning, often resulting in dogmatic and shortsighted practices. For example, one day an African brother who was working with one of the African liberation movements came into the office and gave us a beautiful calendar put out by one of the African liberation groups. It was baaad. It had beautiful pictures of African freedom fighters and said something like "International support for African liberation." The first thing i did was hang it up. When i came to the office the next day the calendar was gone. When i asked what had happened to it, they said, "The calendar said 'international' and we're not internationalists, we're intercommunalists."

I am convinced that a systematic program for political education, ranging from the simplest to the highest level, is imperative for any successful organization or movement for Black liberation in this country. The Party had some of the most politically conscious sisters and brothers as members, but in some ways it failed to spread that consciousness to the cadre in general. I also thought it was a real shame the BPP didn't teach Panthers organizing and mobilizing techniques. Some members were natural geniuses at organizing people, but they were usually the busiest comrades with the most responsibility. Part of the problem was that the Party had grown so fast that there wasn't a lot of time to come up with step-by-step approaches to things. The other part of the problem was that almost from its inception, the BPP was under attack from the u.s. government.

At first i didn't feel the repression too deeply. I knew the Party was under attack, but it felt like it wasn't so near, like it was lingering in the background. What made me maddest was the media treatment of the BPP, which gave the impression that the Party was racist and violent. And it worked. The pigs would burst into a Panther office, shoot first, and ask questions later. The press always reported that the police had "uncovered" a large arsenal of weapons. Later, when the "arsenal" turned out to be a few legally registered rifles and shotguns, the press never printed a word. The same thing goes on today. Nobody gets upset about white people having guns, but let a Black person have a gun and something criminal is going on. The only time white amerika is in favor of Black people having guns is when we are using them to do amerika's dirty work. They've got a lot of Black people so scared they are scared even to think about owning a gun. But the way the tide of racism is rising in this country, Black people better be more scared to not have a gun than to have one. With the Ku Klux Klan and all these other racists running around, Black people have got to be suicidal if they don't own and know how to operate a gun. If you don't own a gun now, you'd better rush out and buy one because in a few years, the way this country is moving, it might be against the law for Blacks to buy guns.

One of the best things about struggling is the people you meet. Before i became involved, i never dreamed such beautiful people existed. Of course, there were some creeps, but i can say without the slightest hesitation that i have been blessed with meeting some of the kindest, most courageous, most principled, most informed and intelligent people on the face of the earth. I owe a great deal to those who have helped me, loved me, taught me, and pulled my coat when i was moving in the wrong direction. If there is such a thing as luck, i've had an abundance of it, and the ones who have brought it to me are my friends and comrades. My wild, big-hearted friends, with their pretty ways and pretty thoughts, have given me more happiness that i will ever deserve. There was never a time, no matter what horrible thing i was undergoing, when i felt completely alone. Maybe it's ironic, i don't know, but the one thing i do know is that the Black liberation movement has done more for me than i will ever be able to do for it.

Becoming Zayd's friend was something really important. After i joined the party he would drop by my house every so often. We would listen to music and talk politics. I was forever teasing him about being part of the leadership (he was Minister of Information) since he was the only leader up at the Bronx Ministry, with the exception of Afeni Shakur, i had any respect for. He would laugh at my Robert Bey jokes, but he never once said a disparaging word about any of the other comrades. I also respected him because he refused to become part of the macho cult that was an official body in the BPP. He never voted on issues or took a position just to be one of the boys. When brothers made an unprincipled attack on sisters, Zayd refused to participate. Whenever we hooked up for a meeting at somebody's house, he was the first to volunteer to cook dinner or, if dinner was already cooked, the first to roll up his sleeves and wash the dishes. I knew this had to be especially hard for him because he was small and his masculinity was always being challenged in some way by the more backward, muscle-headed men in the party.

Zayd always treated me and all the other sisters with respect. I enjoyed his friendship because he was one of those rare men completely capable of being friends with a woman without having designs on her. We communicated on such an intense, honest level that afterward i wondered if it had been real. And he was cultured. When you say "cultured," most people think you're talking about the opera and Amy Vanderbilt's etiquette book, but that's not what i'm talking about. He was well versed and well educated about every aspect of Black life. He could not only recite Langston Hughes by heart and give a biographical rundown of Coltrane, Bessie Smith, or James Cleveland, but he could also sit down and have an intelligent conversation about dreambooks or Argo starch eaters.

After a while Zayd asked me to work with him on Party projects. It was mostly dealing with white support groups who were involved in raising bail for the Panther 21 members still in jail. I hated it. At the time, i felt that anything below 110th Street was another country. All my activities were centered in Harlem and i almost never left it. Doing defense committee work was definitely not up my alley. I think that one of the reasons Zayd insisted on bringing me to some of these events is that he knew how much i hated them. I was the perfect angry Panther. I hated standing around while all these white people asked me to explain myself, my existence. I became a master of the one-line answer.

"What made you become a Panther?"

"Oppression."

"What do you think about Huey Newton?"

"He's a right-on Black revolutionary leader."

"What do you think white people should be doing?"

"Organizing other white people in their communities, supporting Black and Third World liberation struggles, and helping to free the Panther 21."

Once a guy asked if i was really going to off the pigs.

"Not tonight."

I couldn't get over how personal some of those people tried to get even though i'd never seen them before. One came over to me and asked if Zayd was my Panther husband. When i looked at her as if she was crazy for asking me a question like that, she said, giggling all over herself, "I mean, I mean, is he your cat?" Another woman came over and stuck her hands all in my hair. "Oh, I just had to touch your hair. It's so . . . kinky."

Zayd would be steady trying to convince the defense groups to raise more money. He explained how important it was to have the Panther 21 out on the street, organizing and educating people about what was going on in amerika. Zayd was polite and understanding and patient. After he gave his little speech, he would turn to me and ask, "What do you think about that, sister?" Rapping in my best Panther cadence, i would say something like "Black people have been oppressed for four hundred years. We are still being oppressed. The Panther 21 don't need any moral support. They need concrete support. They don't want to hear that you sympathize with them, they want to hear that you are willing and ready to help liberate them." When we were finished, a second donation would be given.

Zayd was usually cool and poised at these functions, except once. We were at a meeting with the Computer People for Peace, a group that was helping to raise the money to bail out Sundiata Acoli. Zayd said Sundiata should be the next Panther to be bailed out because his leadership qualities were sorely needed in the Party. One guy kept interrupting him, implying that Zayd was pushing for Sundiata's release because they were friends, that he was being subjective and dealing from an emotional rather than a scientific, objective analysis. Zayd's face underwent a complete change. I could see that he was trying to control himself to keep from going off on this dude. "What do you mean, I'm being subjective? Don't you ever open your mouth to me to tell me I'm subjective as long as you live. My brother Lumumba, my own flesh and blood, has also been locked up for more than a year, and I haven't asked you for a dime to bail him out." Lumumba Shakur was one of the Panther 21. A complete hush came over the room. The computer people said they would do everything they could to raise money for Sundiata's bail, and that's what they did. The only thing was that, once the $100,000 cash bail was raised, pig judge Murtagh refused to release him or any of the others. We were furious and helpless.

After a while, everything seemed strange to me. I was catching all these weird vibrations and sensations. I couldn't quite put my finger on it, but i could sense a whole lot of stuff going on. I felt like i was standing on top of a river with currents swirling down underneath the surface. All these strange things were starting to happen. I would go to the laundromat and find a Black policeman there who said he wanted to join the Party. Every once in a while i'd turn around and see strange men following me. Even though i had no money to pay my telephone bill and had long stopped paying it, the telephone kept working and, after a while, i stopped receiving any bills.

Politically, i was not at all happy with the direction of the Party. Huey went on a nationwide tour advocating his new theory of intercommunality. The essence of the theory was that imperialism had reached such a degree that sovereign borders were no longer recognized and that oppressed nations no longer existed, only oppressed communities, within and outside the u.s. The problem was that somebody had forgotten to tell these oppressed communities that they were no longer nations. Even worse, almost no one understood Huey's long speeches explaining intercommunalism. Huey Newton was not what you would call a good speaker. In fact, he had a kind of high-pitched monotonous voice and his rambling for three hours about the negation of the negation was sheer disaster. People walked out in droves. Instead of criticizing what was happening, most of the Party members defended it. When i said that Huey needed speaking lessons they jumped down my throat. When Huey changed his title from defense minister to the ridiculous-sounding "Supreme Commander" and then to the even more ridiculous "Supreme Servant," damn near nobody said a word. That was one of the big problems in the Party. Criticism and self-criticism were not encouraged, and the little that was given often was not taken seriously. Constructive criticism and self-criticism are extremely important for any revolutionary organization. Without them, people tend to drown in their mistakes, not learn from them.

Because i was still a college student, i was often called on by the BPP to do student work. I didn't mind working with students to coordinate this or that, but i was deathly afraid of speaking in public. But they insisted i had to learn in order to be effective on campus. I had an old rickety tape recorder that was on its last legs. I decided to use it to practice public speaking. On and on i went, bla, bla, bla, into the microphone. The telephone rang. I put the mike down, turned off the recorder, and rushed to the phone. "Hello, JoAnne? Stop making tapes," the voice said. The phone clicked. I stood there with the receiver in my hand. I had to get out of there. I ran to get my coat. I needed some privacy to think.

Every day at the office, things were getting stranger and stranger. Rumors that the pigs were going to attack the office were rampant. Convinced of the invasion, the leadership decided to "secure" the office. The big storefront window was removed and replaced by a wooden partition. Windows without glass were cut into the wood, covered by little wooden doors. "What are all those little holes for?" i asked. "To shoot out of," they told me. Piles of sandbags were brought into the office. I didn't believe that shit! Everybody was talking about defending the office. "Why do we have to defend the office?" i asked. They told me something about executive mandate number three. It said Panthers were supposed to defend the office against pig attacks. I was all in favor of self-defense, but i couldn't see giving my life up just to defend the office. "It's the principle of the thing," they told me.

I didn't understand what principle they were talking about. One of the basic laws of people's struggle was to retreat when the enemy is strong and to attack when the enemy is weak. As far as i was concerned, defending the office was suicidal. The pigs had manpower, initiative, surprise, and gunpowder. We would just be sitting ducks. I felt that the Party was dealing from an emotional rather than a rational basis. Just because you believe in self-defense doesn't mean you let yourself be sucked into defending yourself on the enemy's terms. One of the Party's major weaknesses, i thought, was the failure to clearly differentiate between aboveground political struggle and underground, clandestine military struggle.

An aboveground political organization can't wage guerrilla war anymore than an underground army can do aboveground political work. Although the two must work together, they must have completely separate structures, and any links between the two must remain secret. Educating the people about the necessity for self-defense and for armed struggle was one thing. But maintaining a policy of defending Party offices against insurmountable odds was another. Of course, if the police just came in and started shooting, defending yourself made sense. But the point is to try and prevent that from happening. One day, in the not too distant future, any Black organization that is not based on bootlicking and tomming will be forced underground. And as fast as this country is moving to the fascist far right, Black revolutionary organizations should start preparing for the inevitability. Fascist governments do not permit revolutionary or progressive opposition groups to exist, no matter how peaceful or nonviolent they are. It doesn't matter whether the fascist government simply outlaws the groups like in Nazi Germany or mounts a counterintelligence campaign to destroy opposition groups, like in the u.s.

It was growing more and more impossible to get work done. Everything seemed to be in a continuous state of chaos. The Party decided at one point to open a Saturday Liberation School for children, and i was assigned to the project. I was really ecstatic about it because i love working with children and i was really tired of adults at the time. Being my usual reserved self, i threw every bit of energy i had into the project. I collected books, materials, paints, photographs, children's Black history stories, children's records, etc. Two other comrades were assigned to the project. Everybody pitched in and after a few weeks we had a whole pile of children attending. Just as we got the program on its feet, i was called aside and taken into confidence. The Party had information that the pigs were going to raid the office in about two weeks. "If the pigs were going to attack the office, why would they bother to tell us?" I asked. "We have our sources, sister," i was told. "Just like the pigs have their sources, we have ours." I was skeptical, but i figured they knew more about it than i did. In preparation for the coming attack i was asked to prepare a child care place, a safe house for Panther children. It sounded kind of wild, but i agreed to do it. In the back of my mind i half thought they were testing me to see how i would respond in a crisis.

I put the child care thing together. Two weeks came and went, but there was no invasion.

In addition, a lot of things were going on that i was not too happy about. Plans, priorities, and procedures changed daily, and most of the time the changes were ill-conceived. Everything had an arbitrary air to it, and i certainly did not have the feeling that we were waging a step-by-step analytical struggle. There was little internal conflict in either the Harlem branch or the New York Chapter. For the most part Panthers were a friendly, open group of people who really went out of their way to be kind and helpful and, in spite of all the pressure and hardships they had to deal with, managed to be principled and to fight as hard as they knew how for our people. We had a bit of a leadership problem with Robert Bey and Jolly, who were both from the West Coast. Bey's problem was that he was none too bright and that he had an aggressive, even belligerent, way of talking and dealing with people. Jolly's problem was that he was Robert Bey's shadow. Bey later became Huey Newton's bodyguard, a job for which he was much more suited.

Cotton had come to Harlem from California. Everybody loved him. He was everybody's main man. He had known Bunchy Carter, Lil Bobby Hutton, the chief (David Hilliard), and, of course, the rage (Eldridge Cleaver). Cotton had been sent to New York and put in charge of fixing up the brownstone the Party had bought on 127th Street. According to the grapevine, Huey wanted to move BPP headquarters to New York and Cotton was to prepare the security for the house. He used to mosey over to the Harlem office with a bottle of cheap pluck in his back pocket and tell war stories. He would sip his wine and talk about what had gone down on the coast.

The first time i went over to inspect the 127th Street house, Cotton gave me a guided tour. He explained the whole futuristic security plan. He was going to hook up the security system so that if so much as a foot was put on the front steps of the building an alarm would alert the security officer inside. If it was the pigs, huge floodlights would be turned on, blinding them. Thick metal doors would glide into place and a lot of other fantastic things would happen that i don't remember. I kept my mouth shut because i knew absolutely nothing about security, but i silently wondered why he didn't put in stuff that was more conventional, like a closed-circuit TV. I had a special interest in the building since the ground floor and the basement were designated to be the free health clinic. At the time, the basement was a disaster, with no plumbing, no heat, no electricity, and a mountain load of bricks, powder, and debris. Cotton assured me that the basement would be fixed up within six months.

Next he showed me Huey's room. It was the only room in the house somewhat fixed up. He had put up wooden paneling. There was a small table and a single bed which, he carefully explained to me, was made up in military style, ready at all times for the minister. I looked at him like he was crazy. Of all the things i could imagine Huey doing, sleeping in that freezing house on that Spartan bed was not one of them. Cotton talked about Huey with this eerie reverence that made me sick. And it sounded sure enough weird, how Cotton talked about the minister's bed.

I visited the house on 127th Street many times over the next few months. Hard as i tried, i could not find one shred of progress. I came to the conclusion that Cotton was a big mouth and a drunk. But everybody kept telling me how hard he was working, so i figured he was working on something secret they had obviously decided not to tell me about.

During one of my trips to the house, Cotton's assistant told me he didn't feel well. I made an appointment with the doctor and called to tell him the time. A few days later, when i came into the office, everyone looked at me like i had committed some crime against the people.

"What's wrong?" i asked.

"Cotton says that the brother who works for him is sick and that you refused to do anything for him."

"What?" I was completely surprised. "That's not true."

"Cotton says that's what happened."

Fired up mad, i tried to get Cotton on the phone, but it was out of order. It took me several days to get the thing straight, but finally the assistant confirmed that i had made the doctor's appointment for him but that he had neglected to keep it and had gone home instead. I tried to figure out why Cotton had made such a fuss. The only conclusion i could come to is that he was annoyed with me because i kept pushing him to get the clinic in order. Several years later, after the Freedom of Information Act was passed, it was revealed that Cotton had been working undercover for the police.

Things seemed to be going from bad to worse. Although there wasn't much dissension in the New York branch, there was beaucoup dissension and disunity on the national level. Every other weekend somebody was going out to the West Coast to deal with "contradictions." Everybody was uptight and miserable. And then everything started to happen at once. First there was an article stating that Huey was living in a $650-a-month apartment in Oakland. The Harlem branch was shocked because, in those days, that was a whole lot of rent and it contrasted sharply with the living conditions of the Panthers in New York. Panthers who owned little more than the clothes on their backs were out in the street in the freezing cold weather selling papers, with big pieces of cardboard in their shoes and with flimsy jackets that did nothing to hold back the hawk. The party issued a statement that Huey was living in the apartment for "security purposes," but a lot of Panthers were not at all convinced. I wanted to believe the security story, but it didn't fit my sense of logic. Then came the long series of expulsions, which proved to be the last straw.

Many long-standing, loyal Panthers were being expelled by Huey. One of the first to go in Huey's private purge was Geronimo Elmer Pratt. Geronimo was widely respected, somewhat of a Panther folk hero. When i heard about it, the first thing i did was go to someone who would know and try to find out the real deal. Although paranoid and upset, the person broke down the story to me, just enough to let me know the expulsion was probably unjust. I couldn't imagine Geronimo being an enemy of the people, anymore than i could imagine myself being one. Then came the expulsions of the Panther 21, supposedly for writing an open letter to the Weathermen that was somewhat critical of BPP policies. I had read the letter and could find nothing in it to merit such extreme action, especially since it might prove prejudicial to their ongoing trial. I was becoming more and more critical of what was going on in the Party, but i loved it nevertheless and wanted to see it functioning on the right track.

For the first time i questioned whether i could continue within the Party. Almost every project i was working on was frustrated and barely able to get off the ground. The Saturday liberation school, the free health clinic, and a lot of the student work were all on hold. I felt frustrated and a bit demoralized. This Party was a lot different from the Blank Panther Party i had fallen in love with. Gone were the black berets and leather jackets (because of police harassment, Panthers had been ordered not to wear the uniform, except for special occasions). Gone were the Panther marches, the Panther songs. Gone were the "Free Huey," "Free Bobby" songs sung to the tune of "Wade in the Water." Gone were the big Panther buttons and big Panther flags flapping in the wind. Everything felt different. The easy, friendly openness had been replaced by fear and paranoia. The beautiful revolutionary creativity i had loved so much was gone. And replaced by dogmatic stagnation.

It was around this time that Zayd and i had our big falling out. I had made a list of the criticisms of the Party, along with a list of things i thought were positive and a lot of suggestions i thought might correct some of the problems the Party was facing. I called Zayd and told him i needed to talk to him. When he arrived, i bared my heart and soul to him. I must have talked for a good two or three hours, raising all of the political and tactical concerns i had. Zayd listened to everything i said without taking any position one way or the other. Then he told me he had to leave and would talk to me another time. I was furious. I felt he was acting in his role as "leadership" and using our friendship to gain information about how i thought, to gauge the level of dissension within the ranks. Throughout my days in the Party i've always been outspoken and blunt. Zayd and i had always been frank with each other, and i interpreted his silence as a declaration that he supported and defended policies i considered unprincipled and politically incorrect. After that, we didn't see or speak to each other for a long time. I had no way of knowing the thin tightrope he was walking or the pressure he was under.

Zayd was acting as peacemaker between Huey and the Panther 21, furiously trying to get Huey to rescind his expulsion order. Zayd felt that to take any position in reference to problems within the Party might jeopardize his role and result in dire consequences for the Panther 21. Cetewayo and Dhoruba, who had not been expelled because they were out on bail and had not signed the letter, were also attempting to get the Panther 21 reinstated. They were under a lot of pressure from both sides. Huey wanted them to support the expulsion and the expelled Panthers wanted them to criticize Huey's actions. Like Zayd, Cet and Dhoruba honestly believed they could straighten out the madness. And were it not for the FBI, they probably could have. Nobody back then had ever heard of the counterintelligence program (COINTELPRO) set up by the FBI. Nobody could possibly have known that the FBI had sent a phony letter to Eldridge Cleaver in Algiers, "signed" by the Panther 21, criticizing Huey Newton's leadership. No one could have known that the FBI had sent a letter to Huey's brother saying the New York Panthers were plotting to kill him. No one could have known that the FBI's COINTELPRO was attempting to destroy the Black Panther Party in particular and the Black Liberation Movement in general, using divide-and-conquer tactics. The FBI's COINTEL program consisted of turning members of organizations against each other, pitting one Black organization against another. Huey ended up suspending Cet and Dhoruba from the Party, branded them as "enemies of the people," and caused them to go into hiding, in fear for their very lives. No one had the slightest idea that this whole scenario was carefully manipulated and orchestrated by the FBI.

When they brought the Black Panther newspaper to the office, the one that branded Dhoruba, Cet, and Cet's wife, Connie Matthews Tabor, as enemies of the people, i refused to sell it and attacked it as an outright lie. I had been so outspoken about my criticisms that i knew it was just a matter of time before i, too, would be expelled. Sick and disgusted, i decided it was time for me to leave the Party.

Most of the Panthers understood why i left, and i stayed on good terms with them. They would call me and ask if they could drop by or sleep over at my crib. Almost daily i got a blow-by-blow description of what was going on in the Party. The tension had increased even more, the differences between the New York cadre and the West Coast leadership growing even wider. I tried to stress to the comrades what i saw to be the importance of everybody sitting down and resolving their differences. No such thing occurred. In fact, a group came to my house jumping for joy. They had split from the West Coast leadership. It really saddened me that they had not been able to sit down together and mend their differences.

After i left the Party, my life became more and more impossible. Everywhere i went it seemed like i would turn around to find two detectives following behind me. I would look out my window and there, in the middle of Harlem, in front of my house, would be two white men sitting and reading the newspaper. I was scared to death to talk in my own house. When i wanted to say something that was not public information i turned the record player up real loud so that the buggers would have a hard time hearing. It was so weird. I still hadn't received a telephone bill and months had gone by since i'd paid the last one, yet the telephone was always working.

Strange people visited my neighbors, asking questions. I hated to move from my apartment because the rent was so cheap. I was paying something like $65 a month and, if you could get used to the fifth-floor walkup, it wasn't at all bad. It was one of those rent-controlled buildings right across the street from City College, where i was enrolled. I had no choice but to leave. It was impossible to live amid all those bugging devices. I decided to donate the apartment to the Panthers and look for somewhere else to live, and to spend time with some friends, passing a few days here and a few days there, until i found another place.

One day, as i was zipping up the avenue, on my way home, a friend called me over.

"What's up?" i asked.

"Don't go home."

"What do you mean, don't go home?"

"Your place is crawling with pigs. They're waiting for you."

I walked around for a while, trying to get my head together. What could they do to me if i went home? I hadn't done anything. I thought about the Panther 21. They hadn't done anything either. Anyway, they can do anything they want. I thought about my crib. Maybe they had been taping my voice and hooking up pieces of conversation to make it seem like there was a conspiracy to do something. Maybe they would charge me with harboring a fugitive or with conspiracy to harbor a fugitive. Everybody said they were tailing me so tough because they thought i would lead them to Cet, Dhoruba, or some other comrade that had been forced into hiding. Maybe they would try to interrogate me, beat and torture me until i signed some phony confession or something. I decided one thing right then and there. I definitely wasn't going home, and i definitely wasn't answering anybody's questions about anything. I thought of going to Evelyn's but i figured that as soon as i showed, the pigs would be there waiting for me. I decided the best thing i could do was lay low until i found out what was going on and could come to some decision.

Chapter 16

My initial image of the underground was pure fantasy. When Zayd talked about the underground i actually pictured people in some basement, passing through some hidden bookcase door and disappearing into thin air. I had pictured all kinds of elaborate "I Spy" kinds of hookups, outrageous disguises, false panels, stuff right out of "Mission: Impossible." I was shocked when i ran into a brother i knew in a supermarket. I knew the pigs were looking for him. He had shaved all the hair off his face, but he looked almost the same. I had to catch myself to keep from calling out to him. I just kept walking, feeling that, somehow, seeing me would make him nervous. Even though i had always thought that someday i'd probably be involved in clandestine struggle, i had never given any serious thoughts to going underground. I had, more or less, thought of a clandestine struggle in terms of leading a double life. I thought the ideal way to struggle was to have a regular job or whatever as a front and then go out at night or whenever and do what needed to be done, careful to leave no trails. I still think that is the best way, but you have to anticipate being discovered and be prepared for whatever might happen.

At the end of the sixties or the beginning of the seventies, it seemed like people were going underground left and right. Every other week i was hearing about somebody disappearing. Police repression had come down so hard on the Black movement that it seemed as if the entire Black community was on the FBI's Most Wanted list. The repression had come down so fast that many people had no chance whatsoever to get organized. I was kind of in limbo, slipping back and forth between above and below. As far as i could tell, i was only wanted for questioning. I hadn't done anything and i didn't feel that the situation was too grave. I had to be discreet and change some of my habits, but i felt relatively free to move around aboveground and underground without too much problem. I had no intentions of answering anybody's questions, and so i figured i'd just lay low until the heat was over.

There were so many things that needed to be done. Basically, i was working with the railroad (support network) stations, trying to find the basic necessities for people and trying to help them get to where they wanted to go. It was a job that required real caution and a lot of concentration on detail. Over a short period of time, i found that my powers of observation had increased many times over. I had to keep my eyes on everything that was going on, looking ahead and, at the same time, glancing over my shoulder. The work was interesting and well suited to my restless, active temperament. But i found it kind of hard to change my way of relating to people. I had always been open and trusting and i was finding it really hard to change. It took my almost getting killed for me to develop a more suspicious nature.

I was running into quite a few people, some of whom i knew and others whom i didn't: different collectives, members of different organizations, from different parts of the country. I was surprised at how disorganized many people were, and i was all for seeing them organize themselves in a much more disciplined manner. I was straining to understand some of the things i saw, but people were moving so fast it was hard to keep track of what they were dong. The whole situation was new to me and i guess all of us were trying to make heads or tails out of it, trying to get a good grip on what was happening and where we fit into it.

I had heard it on the radio, had seen some of the reports on TV. My reaction was WOW! The tables were turning. As many Black people as the New York Police Department murdered every year, someone was finally paying them back. The media were filled with countless adjectives: senseless, brutal, vicious, deadly, bloody, etc. On May 19, Malcolm X's birthday, two police had been machine-gunned on Riverside Drive. I felt sorry for their families, sorry for their children, but i was relieved to see that somebody else besides Black folks and Puerto Ricans and Chicanos was being shot at. I was sick and tired of us being the only victims, and i didn't care who knew it. As far as i was concerned, the police in the Black communities were nothing but a foreign, occupying army, beating, torturing, and murdering people at whim and without restraint. I despise violence, but i despise it even more when it's one-sided and used to oppress and repress poor people. But i was still in a state of shock, the shit was so real. I mean, it was happening. Somebody was doing what the rest of us merely had fantasies about.

I had an early morning meeting. My friend went to the corner to pick up the papers and something to munch on. He came back, all excited.

"Look at this, sister. I think you should look at this."

"I don't want to look at anything right now. I want something to eat. What did you buy to eat?"

""This is serious, sister. Will you come over and look at this?"

"Man, i don't wanna read no paper, i'm starving," i said. Nevertheless, i went over and picked up the papers. "Oh shit. Oh shit!" was the only thing that would come out of my mouth. Hungrily, i read every word of the article. I stared down at my picture on the front page of the *Daily News*. The paper said i was wanted for questioning in relation to the machine-gunning. "Shit!" I walked aimlessly around in circles. I couldn't believe it, but i was looking at it.

"You've got to get out of here, sister," my friend said.

"Where am i supposed to go?"

"I don't know, but we've got to get you out of here. Maybe you can go and hook up with the people."

I knew that i had to hook up with some people in the underground, but this was no time to go around hunting for people. Strangely enough, i felt calm and i wanted to stay that way. I asked my friend to go and get me a wig and some other things to enable me to move around a little bit. While he went to get the things i needed, i went though my address book and made mental notes of the people who the pigs could easily trace me to. I had to stifle the desire to call my mother and tell her that, at least for the moment, i was relatively safe and that i loved her.

Once i got out into the street, i could feel the tension in my body. I walked down the street searching for signs on people's faces. I walked a few blocks before i realized that not a soul in the world was paying me any mind. I heard some feet running behind me and swung around, only to find it was a bunch of children. I had planned to go to my girlfriend's house and decided i'd still head that way. She lived alone, in a quiet neighborhood, and i knew that it would be damn near impossible for anyone to trace me to her. Her life consisted almost completely of working and going to school at night.

I was a little nervous when i got to her door. Maybe i was doing the wrong thing, getting her hooked into all of this. Maybe she would be angry at me for coming at all. I decided that i wouldn't stay. I would just stop by to explain to her why i was late and to tell her good-bye. She answered the door with a towel wrapped around her head.

"What the hell took you so long?"

How did i begin? A funny thing happened to me on the way to your house? "There's something i've got to tell you," i began. "I just stopped by to say good-bye. The police are looking for me. My picture is plastered all over the *Daily News*. I don't believe this is happening, but it is."

"I know. I know," she told me. "What I want to know is, what took you so long to get here?"

I stared at her, completely surprised. I didn't understand. If she knew what happened, why was she expecting me? "I just dropped by for a minute to let you know what happened and to let you know that i'm okay."

"Are you okay?"

I told her that i was.

"Where are you going?"

I told her that i was going to try to hook up with some people i knew.

"Where do you have to go? Do you have any money? Do you know how to contact these people? Do you need any help?"

I told her that i had just found out what was happening and that i was just going to have to play it by ear, slipping and sliding for a while until i could make contact.

"Girl, are you crazy? You militants ain't got no sense! Would you take that shit off your head and sit down so I can talk to you!" She always referred to me and my comrades as "you militants." She was a militant too, but at the moment she was not active, not out on Front Street, as she called it.

"Do you have this address written down anywhere or this phone number?"

"No, nobody even knows who you are or that we even know each other." Luckily, i had never made a habit of writing too much down, and since things had gotten so hot, i had put most of the numbers that i had for contacts in code. I knew all of my friend's numbers by heart, so that was no problem. I had never even called her from the 138th Street phone at my last place. I told her that as far as i knew there was no way i could be traced to her.

"Then relax, fool. It don't make no sense for you to be out

there in the street moving around right now. You've got to relax and get your head together."

"Look," i told her. "I don't want to impose on you. This is my thing, not yours, and i don't want to involve you in my stuff."

"Woman, will you please shut up? This ain't your thing, this is our thing. You done involved me in it already, and if I didn't want to be bothered, I wouldn't have opened my door. I'm your friend and I trust you and love you. I'll hide you out any old time. Where did you think you were gonna hide out, anyway? On the moon?"

I stared at her in amazement. I had never really known her. A real sister. Tough, critical, a bit too cynical, but a real stand-up woman.

"Here," she said, handing me a knife and some onions and potatoes, "make yourself useful. Even y'all militants got to eat."

I just sat there grinning. Grinning and peeling potatoes. Talking and feeling really at home.

It's early in the morning. I have to move. The move has got to be made with care since my picture has just been plastered all over the newspapers. Wanted posters of me are everywhere, and somebody had told me that the police have a photograph of me in the space over the glove compartments of their cars. Carefully, i arrange my disguise. It has been designed not to stand out, something that will help me blend in with the other people who will be on the subway early in the morning. I stare at myself in the mirror, debating whether to look like a secretary or a maid. It's too early in the morning for secretaries. I decide to look like a poor Black woman. Thick, ugly stockings, run-over black oxfords, beat-up plastic pocketbook, hand-me-down–looking plaid jacket, and, of course, lord-have-mercy–looking wig. My puffy morning face, smudged with a dab of awkward-looking eyebrow pencil and lipstick, are perfect for the look.

I walk down to the subway, stopping to buy the paper. I stand on the platform waiting for the train. I thumb the newspapers, making sure that no familiar photographs appear. I skim the headlines to find the usual assortment of right-wing half-lies, distortions, and scandal stories. The headlines, as usual, are offensive: "Commies Land in Outer Space." "Cops Nab Lightbulb Bandit." "Hubby Ties Knot with Country Gal." Finally, the train comes. I scan the cars as they pass, looking for the transit cop. Seeing none, i move toward the front of the train. I plop down in a vacant seat and immediately stick my head into the newspaper. Carefully, i look around to see who is riding in the car with me. In an instant i'm reproaching myself for leaving too early in the morning. I have an eerie feeling that something is wrong, but i can't put my finger on it. The subway car has a twilight zone air to it. With the exception of a few white men who look like they are going to factory jobs, the rest are Black women. One has on a nurse's uniform, another looks like she is going to church, hat and all, and the rest of them look more or less like me. I keep staring at them. And it registers. Without one exception, every one of these sisters is wearing a wig. It feels so spooky. I am hiding my beautiful, nappy hair under this wig and hating it, hiding my stuff to save my life. I, who have had to give up my headwraps and my big, beaded earrings, my dungaree jackets, my red, black, and green poncho, and my long African dresses in order to struggle on another level, look out from under my wig at my sisters. Maybe we are all running and hiding. Maybe we are all running from something, all living a clandestine existence. Surely we are all being oppressed and persecuted. I imagine the headlines: "Nigger Woman Nabbed for Nappy Hair." "Afro Gal Has Tangled Hair." "Militant Mom Bares All." It is really too much to comprehend. Such horrible things have been done to us. A whole generation of Black women hiding out under dead white people's hair. I have the urge to cry, but i don't. It would draw attention. I keep from getting up until my stop comes. I pray and struggle for the day when we can all come out from under these wigs.

CURRENT EVENTS

i understand that i am
slightly out of fashion.
The in-crowd wants no part of me.

Someone said that i am too sixties
Black.
Someone else told me i had failed to mellow.

It is true i have not
straightened back my hair.
Nor rediscovered maybelline.
And it is also true
that i still like African things,
like statues and dresses
and PEOPLE.

And it is also true
that struggle is foremost in my mind.
And i still rap about discipline—
my anger has not run away.

And i still can't stand ole
el dorado.
And i still can't dig no
one and one.
And i still don't dig no
roka fellas.
And i call a pig a pig.
And a party, to my thinking,
happens only once in a while.

Anyway, i'm really kind of happy
being slightly out of style.

Chapter 17

Over the next few years, home became a lot of places. I traveled quite a bit and met up with some really beautiful people, people so beautiful they restored my faith in humanity each time i passed through their station. Like most of us back in those days, i was new at this, learning about clandestine struggle as i lived it. I didn't have many fixed ideas at first about what i thought armed struggle within the confines of amerika should be like. I had done a lot of reading about it in other places, but i had no concrete idea how to apply the lessons from those struggles to the struggle of Black people within the United States.

It was clear that the Black Liberation Army was not a centralized, organized group with a common leadership and chain of command. Instead, there were various organizations and collectives working out of different cities, and in some of the larger cities there were often several groups working independently of each other. Many members of the various groups had been forced into hiding as a result of the extreme police repression that took place during the late sixties and early seventies. Some had serious cases, some had minor ones, and others, like me, were just wanted for "questioning."

Sisters and brothers joined these groups because they were committed to revolutionary struggle in general and armed struggle in particular and wanted to help build the armed movement in amerika. It was the strangest feeling. People i used to run into at rallies were now in hiding, sending messages that they wanted to hook up. Sisters and brothers from just about every revolutionary or militant group in the country were either rotting away in prison or had been forced underground. Everyone i talked to was interested in taking the struggle to a higher level. But the question was how. How to bring together all those people scattered around the country into an organized body that would be effective in struggling for Black liberation.

It became evident, almost from the beginning, that consolidation was not a good idea. There were too many security problems, and different groups had different ideologies, different levels of political consciousness and different ideas about how armed struggle in amerika should be waged. On the whole, we were weak, inexperienced, disorganized, and seriously lacking in training. But the biggest problem was one of political development. There were sisters and brothers who had been so victimized by amerika that they were willing to fight to the death against their oppressors. They were intelligent, courageous and dedicated, willing to make any sacrifice. But we were to find out quickly that courage and dedication were not enough. To win any struggle for liberation, you have to have the way as well as the will, an overall ideology and strategy that stem from a scientific analysis of history and present conditions.

Some of the groups thought they could just pick up arms and struggle and that, somehow, people would see what they were doing and begin to struggle themselves. They wanted to engage in a do-or-die battle with the power structure in amerika, even though they were weak and ill prepared for such a fight. But the most important factor is that armed struggle, by itself, can never bring about a revolution. Revolutionary war is a people's war. And no people's war can be won without the support of the masses of people. Armed struggle can never be successful by itself; it must be part of an overall strategy for winning, and the strategy must be political as well as military.

Since we did not own the TV stations or newspapers, it was easy for the news media to portray us as monsters and terrorists. The police could terrorize the Black community daily, yet if one Black person successfully defended himself or herself against a police attack, they were called terrorists. It soon became clear to me that our most important battle was to help politically mobilize, educate, and organize the masses of Black people and to win their minds and hearts. It was inconceivable that we could survive, much less win anything, without their support.

Every group fighting for freedom is bound to make mistakes, but unless you study the common, fundamental laws of armed revolutionary struggle you are bound to make unnecessary mistakes. Revolutionary war is protracted warfare. It is impossible for us to win quickly. To win we have got to wear down our oppressors, little by little, and, at the same time, strengthen our forces, slowly but surely. I understood some of my more impatient sisters and brothers. I knew that it was tempting to substitute military for political struggle, especially since all of our aboveground organizations were under vicious attack by the FBI, the CIA, and the local police agencies. All of us who saw our leaders murdered, our people shot down in cold blood, felt a need, a desire to fight back. One of the hardest lessons we had to learn is that revolutionary struggle is scientific rather than emotional. I'm not saying that we shouldn't feel anything, but decisions can't be based on love or on anger. They have to be based on the objective conditions and on what is the rational, unemotional thing to do.

In 1857 the u.s. supreme kourt ruled that Blacks were only three-fifths of a man and had no rights that whites were bound to respect. Today, more than a hundred and twenty-five years later, we still earn less than three-fifths of what white people earn. It was plain to me that we couldn't look to the kourts for freedom and justice anymore than we could expect to gain our liberation by participating in the u.s. political system, and it was pure fantasy to think we could gain them by begging. The only alternative left was to fight for them, and we are going to have to fight like any other people who have fought for liberation.

I wasn't one who believed that we should wait until our political struggle had reached a high point before we began to organize the underground. I felt that it was important to start building underground structures as soon as possible. And although i felt that the major task of the underground should be organizing and building, i didn't feel that armed acts of resistance should be ruled out. As long as they didn't impede our long-range plans, guerrilla units should be able to carry out a few well-planned, well-timed armed actions that were well coordinated with aboveground political objectives. Not any old kind of actions, but actions that Black people would clearly understand and support and actions that were well publicized in the Black community.

Chapter 18

After my acquittal in the Queens bank robbery case in Brooklyn Federal Court on January 16, 1976, i was brought back to new jersey, placed in the basement of the middlesex county jail for men, in solitary confinement, and held there for more than a year until the jersey trial was over. Lennox Hinds, then the head of the National Conference of Black Lawyers, together with the other members of the defense team, filed a civil suit against the state, charging that my conditions were cruel and inhuman. After a long, drawn-out court battle, both sides agreed that a hearing officer should review my jail conditions and make a ruling. The hearing officer was a man named Ploshnik, who was appointed by the state. We had no say whatsoever in who was appointed and, therefore, expected the decision to be favorable to the state. But he surprised everybody and ruled that my conditions of imprisonment were indeed inhuman and recommended that they be changed at once. But through a series of appeals and legal maneuvers, the state succeeded in keeping me confined in that basement. When the government finds it convenient to follow its own laws and administrative procedures, it does. And when it finds that these same laws are inconvenient for their own purposes, it simply ignores them.

I decided that i wanted Stanley Cohen and Evelyn to work together on the case. This turned out to be a mistake, since they were not exactly in love with each other. Neither Stanley nor Evelyn was a new jersey lawyer and we had to get a new jersey lawyer to be on the case. Ray Brown was busy with other commitments and couldn't possibly do it. Stanley asked a young white new jersey lawyer named Stuart Ball, and, after some reservations, he agreed to be the admitting lawyer. Stanley also wanted a young lawyer, Lawrence Stern, to act as his assistant. Even though Evelyn was involved in the defense and Lennox was handling the civil suit around my prison conditions, the Conference of Black Lawyers assigned a young Black lawyer from Mississippi named Lewis Myers to work on the case. I was delighted. Everyone knew that the new jersey trial was the big one and that my chances of receiving a fair trial were about slim to none. So the strategy was to try to surround the defense team with as much resources and expertise as possible.

It sounded like a good idea, but if there was ever a case of too many cooks in the kitchen, this case was it. Almost from the beginning the defense team was beset by personality conflicts. The problems were magnified greatly by the fact that nobody was being paid. The lawyers were having problems covering even their bare expenses. It seemed like every other month one or another of the lawyers was asking the judge to be relieved from the case.

We were in dire need of experts. We needed to find a ballistics expert and a forensic chemist, among others, to refute the state's charges. We were also in desperate need of an investigator to locate some of the doctors who had treated me while i was hospitalized and other potential witnesses. We fought and harped on this point until finally the judge, Theodore Appleby, issued an order that the state pay for the experts. But once we got the order, we found that we were in the same position that we started from. Without exception, everybody that we went to for help turned us down. The types of experts we needed almost always are police or are working for police agencies. Because my case involved the murder of a police officer, none of them would touch the case. The most crucial part of the prosecutor's case was the "scientific testimony" alleging that i had huge amounts of the dead state trooper's blood on me. We wanted someone who knew what they were doing to go over every inch of those clothes, to check out what was on them and also to check out what had been done to them. But we could not find one forensic chemist to work for us, let alone testify for us. If they had, they would never again have been able to work in peace for any police agency. People never hear about this side of a trial. But there is no place a defendant in a criminal trial can go to find "experts" in sciences commonly known as "police sciences." The police can virtually write up a report saying anything they want, and there is no way of refuting it. And there have been cases where "experts" have been double agents: working for a defendant while secretly working with the prosecutor.

One of the amazing things was the number of student supporters who gave their time and energy to help us. They volunteered to index and organize past transcripts and, together with political activists, did a survey of prospective jurors in Middlesex County. Members of the defense committee published a bulletin to keep people informed about what was happening in the case and also did speaking engagements and fundraising. People circulated petitions and demonstrated in front of the kourtroom. They volunteered to do typing, handle the telephones, etc. Entertainers like Harry Belafonte, Ossie Davis, and Ruby Dee performed at fundraising benefits. Poets like June Jordan, Audre Lorde, and Sonia Sanchez, among others, gave poetry readings. Political activists like Angela Davis and Amiri Baraka worked hard to educate the people about what was happening in new jersey. When Angela Davis came to new jersey to do a speaking engagement on my behalf, the new jersey prosecutor's office ambushed her and her party, harassing them until the moment they left the state. She tried to visit me at the jail, and not only did the judge forbid her to visit me but he stopped all of my other visits as well.

One of the most moving statements i have ever heard was a speech Judge Bruce Wright made at a fundraising rally for me. Judge Bruce Wright is a Black judge who was removed from the criminal court bench in New York because he was too fair and honest, and he did something that was unforgivable—he set poor people's bail at amounts they could afford to pay. The kourts will never be anything but a tool of repression until there are judges like Bruce Wright presiding over Black people's trials.

There were many, many people who i never got to meet, even though they worked so hard on my behalf. And even though i never got a chance to thank all the Black people, white people, Third World people, all the students, feminists, revolutionaries, activists, etc., who worked on the case, i thank you now.

A lot of the pretrial conferences had to do with nothing more than the defense making motions and the judge denying them. Every time we went to kourt the judge made a point of reading into the record that i had refused to stand up for him. He was one of those racist white dogs who really believed he was massa. He really took that "your honor" stuff seriously. If he could have made people bow to him and kiss his hand he would have done it. He claimed that he was a "stickler for the decorum of his courtroom." Plenty of decorum but not a bit of justice. Stand for him? It was out of the question. He was a real died-in-the-wool craka. The kind they could send to wipe out the "natives" in Africa, make Central

America safe for United Fruit Company, or run a sterilization center in Puerto Rico.

Stanley Cohen came to see me. He was excited and upbeat. His good news was that he had found an investigator, an old friend of his who owed him a favor. His friend had contacts with the new jersey state police and thought they might be able to come up with some information on Harper, the police officer who was the main witness. He was also making progress in finding a forensic chemist. We both felt that at least some of the scientific reports had been fudged by the new jersey state troopers. We talked about this and a million things before the visit ended. He was so positive. He said he had a plan, something he wanted to check out, but he didn't want to discuss it and raise my hopes prematurely. That was the last time i saw Stanley Cohen.

A few days later i received a phone call. Stanley was dead. His body had been found in his home with evidence of trauma. Nobody, with the exception of the police and Stanley's family, knows to this day the cause of death. The newspapers stated Stanley died of natural causes. But a friend of Stanley's, a doctor, told me he had talked to the coroner's office and had been given conflicting stories. No one knows for sure how Stanley died and we probably never will. The one thing we do know is that after his death, all the legal papers on my case came up missing. Evelyn talked to Phyllis, Stanley's widow, and she gave her every legal paper she could find that had something to do with my case, but the bulk of the material was still missing. Finally, Evelyn found out that the New York City police had my legal papers. "How did they get them?" i asked her. "I don't even want to think about it," she answered.

I could hardly believe all this was happening. It felt so strange. The New York police claimed they had taken my legal papers from Stanley's house as evidence. "Evidence of what?" i asked Evelyn. Apparently, my legal papers were the only property the New York Police Department had removed from his house. It took more than a month to get some of them back. Some were never recovered. None of the notes about the investigator or the forensic chemist were found. All the notes on trial strategy we had mapped out were missing. It was weird. I thought of Stanley's family and what they must have been going through. The circumstances of his death were so strange. I walked around with an empty feeling in my stomach for a long time.

After Stanley's death, William Kunstler joined the defense team. The first thing the judge did after admitting Kunstler to the case was to rescind the order for state-paid experts, claiming the lawyers had failed to move fast enough to get them. I became more suspicious than before. I couldn't understand why Appleby, all of a sudden, was so anxious we not have expert witnesses. It was obvious that without some financial help i would never be able to afford expert witnesses. I didn't have a thin dime to my name.

Appleby's strategy was to completely intimidate the lawyers, to harass them, threaten them until they became fearful of mounting any significant opposition to the legal lynching that was supposed to be my trial. Since there were no funds to pay for anything, the defense committees and the lawyers were forced to launch a fundraising campaign. The first time Bill Kunstler spoke in new jersey, Appleby attempted to have him thrown off the case, charging him with "improper conduct" and "conduct that was prejudicial to the administration of justice." The improper conduct was giving a lecture at Rutgers University during which he said that we needed money for expert witnesses, that the conditions of my confinement were detrimental to my aiding in my defense, and that under the law i was presumed innocent until proven guilty.

Appleby's *Order to Show Cause* why Bill should not be thrown off the case accomplished what it intended. Instead of preparing for trial, the lawyers were forced to spend time and energy preparing for the two-day hearing that would determine whether or not Bill stayed on the case. Appleby finally decided Bill would remain, but only after we had spent a month dealing with that madness. The implication of the hearing was clear. Any attempt the lawyers made to defend me would be met with the judge's hostility. Appleby threatened every single one of the lawyers with contempt, not once or twice but regularly. Lew Myers attended a fundraising cocktail party at which Angela Davis spoke. Someone sent a letter to the U.S. Treasury in Washington and, approximately ten days later, he was under investigation by the Internal Revenue Service. Evelyn was repeatedly harassed by Appleby. Not one day went by when the so-called impartial judge failed to show his hostility to the defense team.

The lawyers uncovered evidence that the offices across from the courthouse that they and the defense team were using were bugged. Motions for an investigation were denied. During a press conference, Lennox Hinds had the courage to call the trial exactly what it was, "a legal lynching and a kangaroo kourt." Appleby cited him for contempt and an effort was made to disbar him. Only after he took his appeal to the highest kourt in new jersey was he permitted to continue practicing as a lawyer in the state of new jersey.

The trial began on January 17, 1977, the same day Gary Gilmore was shot in Utah. Gary Gilmore was the first person legally executed since the death penalty was struck down by the u.s. supreme kourt in the early 1970s. His execution set the climate for the trial. The judge had denied almost every one of our motions, including my right to defend myself and act as co-counsel, a change of venue, a motion to review Harper's police record, a motion to introduce evidence that i had been victimized by the government's counterintelligence program (COINTELPRO), etc. Even though the National Jury Project had done a study of Middlesex County and had found that eighty-three percent of the people had heard about my case in the media and seventy percent had already formulated an opinion about my guilt, the kourt maintained that i could receive a fair trial. The judge said he would question the jurors and make sure they were "fair and impartial."

Appleby took great pains to avoid asking potential jurors whether they thought i was guilty, electing to ask them instead whether they could "put their opinions aside." He carefully avoided asking their opinions about me, the Black Liberation Army, the Black Panther Party, Black militants, or anything else that had been negatively and biasedly reported in newspapers. The trial lawyers had no right to question jurors. Appleby's voir dire was designed to make sure the most hypocritical, opinionated jurors stayed on the jury. Here are two examples taken directly from the transcript:

Q. And have you heard about this case?
A. Yes, I have.
Q. From what source may you have heard about the case?
A. Newspapers.
Q. And have you discussed it with other people?
A. Occasionally.
Q. And based upon whatever you may have heard from any source whatsoever, do you feel that you have already in your own mind formed an opinion as to the guilt or innocence of this defendant?
A. Well, to be perfectly honest, I think I would be a little biased.
Q. Let me ask you another question. In the event that you were to be chosen to serve, do you feel that you could sit and listen to all the evidence in the case and then judge it fairly and impartially and apply the law that the judge gives to you and put aside completely

any previous opinions or conceptions or ideas about anything in the case and then do you believe that you could render a fair verdict as to the guilt or innocence of this defendant?

A. I think I could.

Q. Do you believe that you could?

A. I think so.

Example number two:

Q. Do you feel that based upon whatever information you may have accumulated about the case from any source whatsoever that you have already formed an opinion in your mind as to the guilt or innocence of this defendant?

A. I would think—yeah, I would think that she was guilty, yeah.

Q. You feel that she's guilty?

A. Yes.

Q. And let me ask you another question. In the event that you might be selected to serve as a juror in this case, do you feel that you could sit and listen to the evidence and judge it impartially, apply the law the judge gives you, set aside this opinion that you have already formed?

A. Yes, I probably could.

Q. And then still judge impartially whether she's guilty or innocent?

A. Yeah. Depending on the evidence and all that.

These were typical of the answers given. The judge refused to remove the above two jurors for cause (on the basis of bias that would prevent them from being fair and impartial jurors) and our peremptory challenges were quickly exhausted. Remaining on the final jury were two friends, one girlfriend, and two nephews of new jersey state troopers. The so-called jury selection process was the biggest farce in legal history.

About halfway through the so-called jury selection process i was ready to call it a day. As bad as this jury sounded, it looked even worse. I didn't want to participate. But almost everyone on the defense team thought not participating was a mistake. "If you don't, we'll never get anything on the record. You'll never even be able to convince an appeal court of anything. You've got to get up there and tell your side of the story. We can prove by the medical testimony that you were shot in the back with your hand raised in the air. We can prove that Harper shot first. We can prove that after you were shot, your hand was paralyzed and, from the location of his gunshot wound, it would have been impossible for you to have shot him with your left hand. We can prove that Harper shot first. We can prove this if you take the stand. We can prove. . . ."

I was tired of this case. I damn sure didn't believe that any appeals kourt was going to free me or that any racist white, prejudiced jury was either. It was obvious i didn't have one chance in a million of receiving any kind of justice. The financial problems, expert witness problems, personality problems among the lawyers, in addition to rotting away in solitary confinement, had taken their toll on me. Every day when i entered the kourtroom i felt like i was entering the theater of the absurd. I wanted no part of it. The lawyers said that i could create a political climate which, they thought, would force the appeal court to give in if i participated in the trial and put on the record the fact that i was innocent. They were convinced that at the last minute the forensic chemist they were trying to locate in Canada was going to come in and save the day. I didn't put any stock in that, but i knew that keeping the momentum going around what was happening was important. I decided to remain and participate, even though it was killing me.

The trial went absurdly on. An all-white jury was selected, based on the advice of Kunstler and the Jury Project, who decided that even though the jurors seated in the panel were horrible, the others were worse. Not only did the judge deny my motion to act as co-counsel, he refused to permit the lawyers to read my opening statement to the jury. The defense team's headquarters, located in New Brunswick, was broken into, papers rummaged through and stolen, and the judge refused to investigate, calling the motion "frivolous." The state's witnesses, almost all of whom were pigs, got up and said whatever they were told to say. We had no expert witnesses to refute or even evaluate their testimony. The main witness, Harper, the state trooper i was supposed to have shot, testified he had told an "untruth" on direct examination but denied it was a lie.

I spent most of the trial looking up at the ceiling and hating myself for sitting there in the first place. When the time came for me to testify, i was shocked. I had thought i would be able to go into everything—being a fugitive, how i became a fugitive, the entire political scenario that led to being in the kourtroom. But then they told me something about "opening the door." Opening the door, it was explained, was like opening Pandora's box. If i gave the political reasons for my being a fugitive, the prosecutor could then introduce all kinds of prejudicial "evidence" that had nothing to do with what happened on the turnpike in order to show my "criminal intent." If i "opened the door," the prosecutor would be able to introduce manuals of guerrilla warfare and a whole stack of other material they found in the car that had nothing to do with this trial. In the absence of political witnesses (whose subpoenas for their appearance the judge had refused to issue) who would have testified about COINTELPRO's systematic attack on the Black Liberation movement, and on Blacks in general, my testimony would have been distorted. I wanted to back out completely, denounce the trial, but it was too late. The only way out was to testify, get my side of what happened on the record, and avoid "opening the door." The year of solitary confinement had made me almost mute. As i testified, i held on to a small picture of my child.

When i sit back today and examine why i participated in that trial, i think i must have been crazy. I guess i had been through too many trials and gotten too many acquittals and let that stuff go to my head. (Three other indictments had been dismissed. One in Queens state supreme court, charging me with killing policemen, was dismissed because the judge, after examining the grand jury minutes, determined there was not even enough evidence for me to have been indicted. The other two, one in Brooklyn supreme kourt and the other in supreme kourt in New York County, were dismissed for failure of the state to bring me to trial for six years after the indictments had been returned.)

Participating in the new jersey trial was unprincipled and incorrect. By participating, i participated in my own oppression. I should have known better and not lent dignity or credence to that sham. In the long run, the people are our only appeal. The only ones who can free us are ourselves.

Chapter 19

I was transferred on April 8, 1978 to the maximum security prison for women in alderson, west virginia, the federal facility designed to hold "the most dangerous women in the country." I had been convicted of no federal crime, but under the interstate compact agreement any prisoner can be shipped, like cargo, to any jail in u.s. territory, including the virgin islands, miles away from family, friends, and lawyers. Through the device of this agreement, Sundiata had been transferred to marion prison in illinois, the federal prison that was the most brutal concentration camp in the country.

Alderson was in the middle of the west virginia mountains, and it seemed as if the mountains formed an impenetrable barrier between the prison and the rest of the world. It had no airport, and to reach it, days of travel were necessary. The trip to alderson was so expensive and difficult that most of the women received family visits only once or twice a year.

I was housed in the maximum security unit (msu) called davis hall. It was surrounded by an electronic fence topped by barbed wire, which in turn was covered by concertina wire (a razor-sharp type of wire that had been outlawed by the Geneva Convention). It was a prison within a prison. This place had a stillness to it like some kind of bizarre death row. Everything was sterile and dead.

There were three major groups in msu: the nazis, the "niggah lovers," and me. I was the only Black woman in the unit, with the exception of one other who left almost immediately after i arrived. The nazis had been sent to alderson from a prison in California, where they had been accused of setting inmates on fire. They were members of the aryan sisterhood, the female wing of the aryan brotherhood—a white racist group that operates in California prisons and is well-known for its attacks on Black prisoners.

Hooked up with the nazis were the manson family women, sandra good and linda "squeaky" froame. Sandra had been sentenced to fifteen years for threatening the lives of business executives and government officials, and froame was serving a life sentence for attempting to kill president gerald ford. They were like the Bobbsey twins and clear out of their minds.

They called themselves "red" and "blue." Everyday "red" wore red from head to toe and "blue" wore blue. They were so fanatic in their devotion to charles manson that they wrote to him everyday, informing him about everything that happened at msu. They waited for his "orders," and you can be sure that if he told them to kill someone they would die trying to do it. Also hooked up with the nazis were the hillbilly prisoners: an obese sow who never bathed and walked around barefoot and a tobacco-chewing butch who acted like she was in the confederate army. There was one "independent" nazi who had fallen out with the others. She sported a huge swastika embroidered on her jeans.

Luckily, Rita Brown, a white revolutionary from the George Jackson Brigade, a group based on the West Coast, was among the four or five "niggah lovers." She was a feminist and a lesbian, and helped me to better understand many issues in the white women's liberation movement. Unlike Jane Alpert, whom i had met in the federal prison in New York, and whom i couldn't stand either personally or politically, Rita did not separate the oppression of women from the racism and classism of u.s. society. We agreed that sexism, like racism, was generated by capitalist, imperialist governments, and that women would never be liberated as long as the institutions that controlled our lives existed. I respected Rita because she really practiced sisterhood, and wasn't just one of those big mouths who go on and on about men.

I'm sure that a lot of prison officials thought i'd never leave the place alive. It was the perfect setup for a setup, and i dealt with the situation seriously. I didn't look for trouble, but i let the nazis know that i was ready to defend myself at any time, and that if they wanted ass (like they say in prison) they would have to bring ass. I made it clear to them that i hated them as much as they hated me, and that if anybody's mother had to cry it would be theirs, not Ms. Johnson. After a few run-ins, the nazis stayed out of my way.

After i had been at alderson for a while, we learned that the msu would be closed down because it had been declared unconstitutional. A phase-out stratification program was implemented that enabled those in msu to leave it during the day and to participate in the same activities permitted those in the general population. I got a job working on the general mechanic's crew, was allowed recreation, attended classes, and was able to eat and visit with the other women in general population.

Many of the sisters were Black and poor and from D.C., where every crime is a violation of a federal statute. They were beautiful sisters, serving outrageous sentences for minor offenses. Similar to the situation that existed at the federal prison in New York, some women could not afford to buy cigarettes without forgoing necessities, while others had money, contacts, wore fur coats, and lived as if they were in a different prison. That small group of women had been convicted of drug trafficking. Rumor had it that they performed the same services in prison as they had on the street, only now they worked for the guards.

One day, as i was returning to davis hall, a middle-aged woman with "salt-and-pepper" hair caught my eye. She had a dignified, schoolteacher look. Something drew me towards her. As i searched her face, i could see that she was also searching mine. Our eyes locked in a questioning gaze. "Lolita?" i ventured. "Assata?" she responded. And there, in the middle of those alderson prison grounds, we hugged and kissed each other.

For me, this was one of the greatest honors of my life. Lolita Lebrón was one of the most respected political prisoners in the world. Ever since i had first learned about her courageous struggle for the independence of Puerto Rico, i had read everything i could find that had been written about her. She had spent a quarter of a century behind bars and had refused parole unless her comrades were also freed. After all those years she had remained strong, unbent and unbroken, still dedicated to the independence of Puerto Rico and the liberation of her people. She deserved more respect than anyone could possibly give her, and i could not do enough to demonstrate my respect.

In our subsequent meetings i must have been quite a pain in her neck, falling all over myself to carry her tray, to get a chair for her, or to do whatever i could for her. Lolita had been through hell in prison, yet she was amazingly calm and extremely kind. She had suffered years of isolation in davis hall in addition to years of political and personal isolation. Until the upsurge of the movement for Puerto Rican independence in the late 60s, she had received very little support. Years had gone by without a visit. For years she had been cut off from her country, her culture, her family, and had not been able to speak her own language. Her only daughter had died while she was in prison.

I supported Lolita a hundred percent, but there was one thing about which we did not agree. At the time we met, Lolita was somewhat anticommunist and antisocialist. She was extremely religous and, i think, believed that religion and socialism were two opposing forces, that socialists and communists were completely opposed to religion and religious freedom.

After the resurgence of the Puerto Rican independence movement, Lolita was visited by all kinds of people. Some were pseudo-revolutionary robots who attacked her for her religious beliefs, telling her that to be a revolutionary she had to give up her belief in God. It apparently had never occurred to those fools that Lolita was more revolutionary than they could ever be, and that her religion had helped her to remain strong and committed all those years. I was infuriated by their crass, misguided arrogance.

I had become close friends with a Catholic nun, Mary Alice, while at alderson, who introduced me to liberation theology. I had read some articles by Camillo Torres, the revolutionary priest, and i knew that there were a lot of revolutionary priests and nuns in Latin America. But i didn't know too much about liberation theology. I did know that Jesus had driven the money changers out of the temples and said that the meek would inherit the earth, and a lot of other things that were directly opposed to capitalism. He had told the rich to give away their wealth and said that "It is easier for a camel to go through the eye of a needle than for a rich man to enter into the Kingdom of God" (Matthew 19:24). I knew a little bit, but i had too much respect for Lolita to open my mouth carelessly. I decided to study liberation theology so that i could have an intelligent conversation with her.

I never got around to it, though. The maximum security unit closed, and i was shipped back to new jersey. Lolita is free now, and she is no longer isolated from what is going on in her part of the world or in her church. I know that wherever she is, she is praying and struggling for her people.

Chapter 20

My mother brings my daughter to see me at the clinton correctional facility for women in new jersey, where i had been sent from alderson. I am delirious. She looks so tall. I run up to kiss her. She barely responds. She is distant and standoffish. Pangs of guilt and sorrow fill my chest. I can see that my child is suffering. It is stupid to ask what is wrong. She is four years old, and except for these pitiful little visits—although my mother has brought her to see me every week, wherever i am, with the exception of the time i was in alderson—she has never been with her mother. I can feel something welling up in my baby. I look at my mother, my face a question mark. My mother is suffering too. I try to play. I make my arms into an elephant's trunk stalking around the visiting room jungle. It does not work. My daughter refuses to play baby elephant, or tiger, or anything. She looks at me like i am the buffoon i must look like. I try the choo-choo train routine and the la, la, la song, but she is not amused. I try talking to her, but she is puffed up and sullen.

I go over and try to hug her. In a hot second she is all over me. All i can feel are these little four-year-old fists banging away at me. Every bit of her force is in those punches, they really hurt. I let her hit me until she is tired. "It's all right," i tell her. "Let it all out." She is standing in front of me, her face contorted with anger, looking spent. She backs away and leans against the wall. "It's okay," i tell her. "Mommy understands." "You're not my mother," she screams, the tears rolling down her face. "You're not my mother and I hate you." I feel like crying too. I know she is confused about who i am. She calls me Mommy Assata and she calls my mother Mommy.

I try to pick her up. She knocks my hand away. "You can get out of here, if you want to," she screams. "You just don't want to." "No, i can't," i say, weakly. "Yes you can." she accuses. "You just don't want to."

I look helplessly at my mother. Her face is choked with pain. "Tell her to try to open the bars," she says in a whisper.

"I can't open the door," i tell my daughter. "I can't get through the bars. You try and open the bars."

My daughter goes over to the barred door that leads to the visiting room. She pulls and she pushes. She yanks and she hits and she kicks the bars until she falls on the floor, a heap of exhaustion. I go over and pick her up. I hold and rock and kiss her. There is a look of resignation on her face that i can't stand. We spend the rest of the visit talking and playing quietly on the floor. When the guard says the visit is over, i cling to her for dear life. She holds her head high, and her back straight as she walks out of the prison. She waves good-bye to me, her face clouded and worried, looking like a little adult. I go back to my cage and cry until i vomit. I decide that it is time to leave.

TO MY DAUGHTER KAKUYA

i have shabby dreams for you
of some vague freedom
i have never known.

Baby,
i don't want you hungry or thirsty
or out in the cold.
And i don't want the frost
to kill your fruit
before it ripens.

i can see a sunny place—
Life exploding green.
i can see your bright, bronze skin
at ease with all the flowers
and the centipedes.

i can hear laughter,
not grown from ridicule.
And words, not prompted
by ego or greed or jealousy.

i see a world where hatred
has been replaced by love.
and ME replaced by WE.

And i can see a world
where you,
building and exploring,
strong and fulfilled,
will understand.
And go beyond
my little shabby dreams.

Chapter 21

My grandmother came all the way from North Carolina. She came to tell me about her dream. My grandmother had been dreaming all of her life, and the dreams have come true. My grandmother dreams of people passing and babies being born and people being free, but it is never specific. Redbirds sitting on fences, rainbows at sunset, conversations with people long gone. My grandmother's dreams have always come when they were needed and have always meant what we needed them to mean. She dreamed my mother would be a schoolteacher, my aunt would go to law school, and, during the hard times, she dreamed the good times were coming. She told us what we needed to be told and made us believe it like nobody else could have. She did her part. The rest was up to us. We had to make it real. Dreams and reality are opposites. Action synthesizes them.

I was extremely pleased that she had come. Her air was confident and victorious. The rest of the family prompted her to tell me her dream.

"You're coming home soon," my grandmother told me, catching my eyes and staring down into them. "I don't know when it will be, but you're coming home. You're getting out of here. It won't be too long, though. It will be much less time than you've already been here."

Excited, i asked her to tell me about her dream. We were all talking, i noticed in a conspiratorial tone.

"I dreamed we were in our old house in Jamaica. I don't know if you remember that house or not."

I assured her that i did.

"I dreamed that i was dressing you," she said, "putting your clothes on."

"Dressing me?" i repeated.

"Yes. Dressing you."

Fear ran up and down my back. "Was i little or grown?"

"You were grown up in my dream."

I felt slightly sick. Maybe my grandmother dreamt about my death. Maybe she dreamt that i was killed while trying to escape. Why else would she be dressing me, if i wasn't dead? My grandmother caught my drift of thought.

"No, you're all right. You're alive. It's just as plain as the nose on your face. You're coming home. I know what I'm talking about. Don't ask me to explain it anymore, because I can't. I just know you're going to come home and that you're going to be all right."

I drilled her for more details. Some she gave and some she didn't. Finally, after i had asked a thousand questions, my grandmother let all the authority show in her voice. "I know it will happen, because I dreamt it. You're getting out of this place, and I know it. That's all there is to it."

My grandmother sat looking at me. There was a kind of smile on her face i can't describe. I knew she was serious. My grandmother's dreams were notorious: her dreams came true. All her life her uncanny senses have been like radar, picking up and identifying all kinds of things that we don't even see. My family and i just sat there vibing on each other. Talking and laughing, bringing up old memories and telling funny stories. Calmness rolled down my body like thick honey.

When i got back to my cell i thought about it all. No amount of scientific, rational thinking could diminish the high that i felt. A tingly, giddy excitement had caught hold of me. I had gotten drunk on my family's arrogant, carefree optimism. I literally danced in my cell, singing, "Feet, don't fail me now." I sang the "feet" part real low, so i guess the guards must have thought i was bugging out, stomping around my cage singing "feet," "feet."

"You can't win a race just by running," my mother told me when i was little. "You have to talk to yourself."

"Huh?" i had asked.

"You have to talk to yourself when you are running and tell yourself you can win."

It had become a habit of sorts. Anytime i am faced with something difficult or almost impossible, i chant. Over the years i have developed different kinds of chants, but i always fall back on the old one "i can, i can, yes, i can."

I called my grandparents a day or two before i escaped. I wanted to hear their voices one last time before i went. I was feeling kind of mush and, so as not to sound suspicious, i told them i wanted to hear some more about the family's history, tracing the ties back to slavery. All too soon it was time to hang up. "Your grandmother wants to say something else to you," my grandfather told me.

"I love you," my grandmother said. "We don't want you to get used to that place, do you hear? Don't you let yourself get used to it."

"No, grandmommy, I won't."

Every day out in the street now, i remind myself that Black people in amerika are oppressed. It's necessary that I do that. People get used to anything. The less you think about your oppression, the more your tolerance for it grows. After a while, people just think oppression is the normal state of things. But to become free, you have to be acutely aware of being a slave.

Carry it on now.
Carry it on.

Carry it on now.
Carry it on.

Carry on the tradition.

There were Black People since the childhood of time
who carried it on.
In Ghana and Mali and Timbuktu
we carried it on.

Carried on the tradition.

We hid in the bush
when the slavemasters came
holding spears.
And when the moment was ripe,
leaped out and lanced the lifeblood
of would-be masters.

We carried it on.

On slave ships,
hurling ourselves into oceans.
Slitting the throats of our captors.
We took their whips.
And their ships.
Blood flowed in the Atlantic—
and it wasn't all ours.

We carried it on.

Fed Missy arsenic apple pies.
Stole the axes from the shed.
Went and chopped off master's head.

We ran. We fought.
We organized a railroad.
An underground.

We carried it on.

In newspapers. In meetings.
In arguments and streetfights.
We carried it on.

In tales told to children.
In chants and cantatas.
In poems and blues songs
and saxophone screams,
We carried it on.

In classrooms. In churches.
In courtrooms. In prisons.
We carried it on.

On soapboxes and picket lines.
Welfare lines, unemployment lines.
Our lives on the line,
We carried it on.

In sit-ins and pray-ins
And march-ins and die-ins,
We carried it on.

On cold Missouri midnights
Pitting shotguns against lynch mobs.
On burning Brooklyn streets.
Pitting rocks against rifles,
We carried it on.

Against water hoses and bulldogs.
Against nightsticks and bullets.
Against tanks and tear gas.
Needles and nooses.
Bombs and birth control.
We carried it on.

In Selma and San Juan.
Mozambique. Mississippi.
In Brazil and in Boston,
We carried it on.

Through the lies and the sell-outs.
The mistakes and the madness.
Through pain and hunger and frustration,
We carried it on.

Carried on the tradition.

Carried a strong tradition.

Carried a proud tradition.

Carried a Black tradition.

Carry it on.

Pass it down to the children.
Pass it down.
Carry it on.
Carry it on now.
Carry it on
TO FREEDOM!

Postscript

Freedom. I couldn't believe that it had really happened, that the nightmare was over, that finally the dream had come true. I was elated. Ecstatic. But i was completely disoriented. Everything was the same, yet everything was different. All of my reactions were super-intense. I submerged myself in patterns and textures, sucking in smells and sounds as if each day was my last. I felt like a voyeur. I forced myself not to stare at the people whose conversations i strained to overhear.

Suddenly, i was flooded with the horrors of prison and every disgusting experience that somehow i had been able to minimize while inside. I had developed the ability to be patient, calculating, and completely self-controlled. For the most part, i had been incapable of crying. I felt rigid, as though chunks of steel and concrete had worked themselves into my body. I was cold. I strained to touch my softness. I was afraid that prison had made me ugly.

My comrades helped a lot. They were so beautiful, natural, and healthy. I loved them for their kindness to me. It had been years since i had communicated with anyone intensely, and i talked to them almost compulsively. They were like medicine, helping me to ease back into myself again.

But i had changed, and in so many ways. I was no longer the wide-eyed, romantic young revolutionary who believed the revolution was just around the corner. I still appreciated energetic idealism, but i had long ago become convinced that revolution was a science. Generalities were no longer enough for me. Like my comrades, I believed that a higher level of political sophistication was necessary and that unity in the Black community had to become a priority. We could never afford to forget the lessons we had learned from COINTELPRO. As far as i was concerned, building a sense of national consciousness was one of the most important tasks that lay ahead of us. I couldn't see how we could seriously struggle without having a strong sense of collectivity, without being responsible *for* each other and *to* each other.

It was also clear to me that without a truly internationalist component nationalism was reactionary. There was nothing revolutionary about nationalism by itself—Hitler and Mussolini were nationalists. Any community seriously concerned with its own freedom has to be concerned about other peoples' freedom as well. The victory of oppressed people anywhere in the world is a victory for Black people. Each time one of imperialism's tentacles is cut off we are closer to liberation. The struggle in South Africa is the most important battle of the century for Black people. The defeat of apartheid in South Africa will bring Africans all over the planet closer to liberation. Imperialism is an international system of exploitation, and, we, as revolutionaries, need to be internationalists to defeat it.

Havana. Lazy sun against blue-green ocean. A beautiful city of narrow, spider-web streets on one side of town and broad, tree-lined avenues on the other. Houses with peeling paint and vintage u.s. cars from the 40s and 50s.

It's a busy place, full of buses, people hurrying, kids in wine- or gold-colored uniforms walking leisurely down the streets swinging book bags. The first thing that hit me were the open doors. Everywhere you go doors are open wide. You see people inside their homes talking, working, or watching television. I was amazed to find that you could actually walk down the streets at night alone.

Old people strolling slowly, carrying shopping bags, stop to ask, "Qué hay? Qué hay en la mercada?" "What are they selling in the market?" Without a moment's hesitation they yell at kids to get out of the street. They stand with their hands on their hips, acting like they own the place. I guess they do. They're not afraid.

"Es mentira." my neighbors exclaim. "It's a lie." Qué mentirosa tu eres." "What a liar you are." My neighbors ask me what the u.s. is like, and they accuse me of lying when i tell them about the hunger and cold and people sleeping in the streets. They refuse to believe me. How can that be in such a rich country? I tell them about drug addicts and child prostitutes, about crime in the streets. They accuse me of exaggerating: "We know capitalism is not a good system, but you don't have to exaggerate. Are there really twelve-year-old drug addicts?"

Even though they know about racism and the ku klux klan, about unemployment, such things are unreal to them. Cuba is a country of hope. Their reality is so different. I'm amazed at how much Cubans have accomplished in so short a time since the Revolution. There are new buildings everywhere—schools, apartment houses, clinics, hospitals, and day care centers. They are not like the skyscrapers going up in midtown Manhattan. There are no exclusive condominiums or luxury office buildings. The new buildings are for the people.

Medical care, dental care, and hospital visits are free. Schools at all educational levels are free. Rent is no more than about ten percent of salaries. There are no taxes—no income, city, federal, or state taxes. It is so strange to pay the price actually listed on products without any tax added. Movies, plays, concerts, and sports events all cost one or two pesos at the most. Museums are free.

On Saturdays and Sundays the streets are packed with people dressed up and ready to hang out. I was amazed to discover that such a small island has such a rich cultural life and is so lively, particularly when the u.s. press gives just the opposite picture.

I'm being introduced at a party. The hostess tells me that the man is from El Salvador. I hold out my hand to shake his. A few seconds too late, i realize he is missing an arm. He asks me what country i come from. I'm so upset and ashamed i'm almost shaking. "Yo soy de los estados unidos, pero no soy yankee," i tell him. A friend of mine had taught me that phrase. Every time someone asked me where i was from i cringed. I hated to tell people i was from the u.s. I would have preferred to say i was New Afrikan, except that hardly anyone would have understood what that meant. When i read about death squads in El Salvador or the bombing of hospitals in Nicaragua, i felt like screaming.

Too many people in the u.s. support death and destruction without being aware of it. They indirectly support the killing of people without ever having to look at the corpses. But in Cuba i could see the results of u.s. foreign policy: torture victims on crutches who came from other countries to Cuba for treatment, including Namibian children who had survived massacres, and evidence of the vicious aggression the u.s. government had committed against Cuba, including sabotage, and numerous assassination attempts against Fidel. I wondered how all those people in the states who tried to sound tough, saying that the u.s. should go in here, bomb there, take over this, attack that, would feel if they knew that they were indirectly responsible for babies being burned to death. I wondered how they would feel if they were forced to take moral responsibility for that. It sometimes seems that people in the states are so accustomed to watching death on "Eyewitness News," watching people starve to death in Africa, being tortured to death in Latin America or shot down on Asian streets, that, somehow, for them, people across the ocean—people "up there" or "down there" or "over there"—are not real.

One of the first questions on the minds of Blacks from the states when they come to Cuba is whether or not racism exists. I was certainly no exception. I had read a little about the history of Black people in Cuba and knew that it was very different from the history of Black people in the states. Cuban racism had not been as violent or as institutionalized as u.s. racism, and the tradition of the two races, Blacks and whites, fighting together for liberation—first from colonization and later from dictatorship—was much stronger in Cuba. Cuba's first war for independence began in 1868 when Carlos Manuel De-Céspedes freed his slaves and encouraged them to join the army in the fight against Spain. One of the most important figures in that war was Antonio Maceo, a Black man, who was the chief military strategist. Blacks played a crucial role in Cuba's labor movement in the 1950s. Jesús Menéndez and Lázaro Peña led two key unions. And i knew that Blacks like Juan Almeda, now Commandante of the Revolution, had played a significant role in the revolutionary struggle to overthrow Batista. But i was most interested in learning what had happened to Blacks after the triumph of the Revolution.

I spent my first weeks in Havana walking and watching. Nowhere did I find a segregated neighborhood, but several people told me that where i was living had been all white before the Revolution. Just from casual observation it was obvious that race relations in Cuba were different from what they were in the u.s. Blacks and whites could be seen together everywhere—in cars, walking down streets. Kids of all races played together. It was definitely different. Whenever i met someone who spoke English i asked their opinion about the race situation.

"Racism is illegal in Cuba," i was told. Many shook their heads and said, "Aquí no hay racismo." "There is no racism here." Although i heard the same response from everyone i remained skeptical and suspicious. I couldn't believe it was possible to eliminate hundreds of years of racism just like that, in twenty-five years or so. To me, revolutions were not magical, and no magic wand could be waved to create changes overnight. I'd come to see revolution as a process. I eventually became convinced that the Cuban government was completely committed to eliminating all forms of racism. There were no racist institutions, structures, or organizations, and i understood how the Cuban economic system undermined rather than fed racism.

I had assumed that Blacks would be working within the Revolution to implement the changes and to insure the continuation of the nonracist policies that Fidel and the revolutionary leaders had instituted in every aspect of Cuban life. A Black Cuban friend helped me have a better understanding. He told me that Cubans took their African heritage for granted. That for hundreds of years Cubans had danced to African rhythms, performed traditional rituals, and worshipped Gods like Shango and Ogun. He told me that Fidel, in a speech, had told the people, "We are all Afro-Cubans, from the very lightest to the very darkest."

I told him that i thought it was the duty of Africans everywhere on this planet to struggle to reverse the historical patterns created by slavery and imperialism. Although he agreed with me, he quickly informed me that he didn't think of himself as an African. "Yo soy Cubano." "I am Cuban." And it was obvious he was very proud of being Cuban. He told me a story about a white Cuban who had volunteered twice to fight in Angola. He had received awards for heroism. "His case is not at all common in Cuba, but there are some who have problems adjusting to change."

"What was his problem?" I asked. "When the guy came home he caused a big scandal with his family. His daughter wanted to marry a Black man and he opposed the marriage. He said he wanted his grandchildren to look like him. It was a big argument, and his whole family got into it. This guy was so mixed up he went crazy when his daughter called him a racist. He wanted to fight everybody. He was out in the street, crying and kicking lamp posts. He didn't know what to do. All the time he was in Angola fighting against racism, he never thought about his own racism."

I agreed with him that whites fighting against racism had to fight on two levels, against institutionalized racism and against their own racist ideas. "What happened to the man?" i asked.

"Well, his daughter got married anyway, and his family convinced him to go to the wedding. Now, he baby-sits for his grandchildren, and he says he's crazy about them, but the guy is still not right in the head. Every time I see him, he's apologetic. I told him I don't want his apologies. Let him apologize to his daughter and her husband. As long as he supports the Revolution, I don't care what he thinks. I care more about what he does. If he really supports the Revolution, then he's gonna change. And, even if he never changes, his kids are going to change. And his grandchildren will change even more. That's what I care about."

The whole race question in Cuba was even more confusing to me because all the categories of race were different. In the first place, most white Cubans wouldn't even be considered white in the u.s. They'd be considered Latinos. I was shocked to learn that a lot of Cubans who looked Black to me didn't consider themselves Black. They called themselves mulattoes, colorados, jabaos, and a whole bunch of other names. It seemed to me that anyone who wasn't jet black was considered a mulatto. The first time someone called me a "mulatta," i was so insulted that if i had been able to express myself in Spanish, we would have had a heated argument right there on the spot.

"Yo no soy una mulatta. Yo soy una mujer negra, y orgullosa soy una mujer negra," i would tell people as soon as I learned a little Spanish. "I'm not a mulatto, but a Black woman, and I'm proud to be Black." Some people understood where i was coming from, but others thought i was too hung up on the race question. To them, "mulatto" was just a color, like red, green, or blue. But, to me, it represented a historical relationship. All of my associations with the word "mulatto" were negative. it represented slavery, slave owners raping Black women. It represented a privileged caste, educated in European values and culture. In some Caribbean countries, it represented the middle level of a hierarchical, three-caste system—the caste that acted as a buffer class between the white rulers and the Black masses.

I found it impossible to separate the word from its history. It reminded me of a saying i had heard repeatedly since childhood: "If you're white, you'r right. If you're brown, stick around. And, if you're black, get back." I realized that in order to really understand the situation i had to study Cuban history thoroughly. But, somehow, i felt that the mulatto thing hindered Cubans from dealing with some of the negative ideas left over from slavery.

The Black pride movement had been very important in helping Black people in the u.s. and in other English-speaking countries to view their African heritage in a positive light. I had never heard of any equivalent movement around mulatto pride and i couldn't imagine what the basis for it would be. To me, it was extremely important for all the descendants of Africans everywhere on this planet to struggle to reverse the political, economic, psychological, and social patterns created by slavery and imperialism.

The problem of racism takes on so many forms and displays so many subtleties. It is a complicated problem that will require much analysis and much struggle to resolve. Although, in some ways, Cubans and I approached the problem from different angles, i felt we shared the same goal: the abolition of racism all over the world. I respected the Cuban government, not only for adopting nonracist principles, but for struggling to put those principles into practice.

I held my breath as i waited for my aunt to pick up the phone. It had been five years since i had last spoken to her. Five years since i had been able to contact my family. Hopefully, she hadn't changed her number. A click. And then, at last, i heard her voice. I was so happy.

"Anty," i almost shouted. "It's me. Assata."

"Who?"

"Assata."

"Who?"

"It's me. Assata. I'm in Cuba. I'm in Cuba. Oh, i love you. It's so good to hear your voice. How are you?"

The voice on the other end was my aunt's, but it was so cold i could hardly believe it. "Oh. Really. Assata. Hm. Right. Well, I'm fine."

"What's the matter, Anty? It's me. Assata. Are you all right?"

"I'm fine."

"Anty. Oh, i missed you so much. It's all right. Everything's O.K. I'm fine. I'm fine. How's everybody? How's everybody there?"

Again the icy voice. "Everything is just fine. What do you want?"

"What do i want? What do you mean, what do i want? I want to talk to you. I love you. You sound so cold."

"Well . . . it . . . it . . . I . . ." There was a pause. And then, "Say something so I'll know it's really you. Something only you and I know."

Finally understanding, i said the first thing that popped into my head. "Anty, panty, jack o'stanty." It was a stupid childhood rhyme and nobody else could possibly know about it. I used to taunt her with it when I was a kid.

"It *is* you. Oh, my God, it really is you," she screamed. "Wait. Give me a second to catch my breath. How are you?"

"Fine," i said. "How's Mommy and Kakuya?"

"Your mother's fine. Oh, she's gonna be so happy when I tell her I've talked to you. Kakuya's fine, too. Your daughter is so big you won't recognize her. She's almost as tall as you are."

I told her i wanted to call my mother and Kakuya as soon as i finished talking to her.

"No. You call her tomorrow. Let me call her first, so she really knows its you. Where did you say you are?"

"Cuba. I'm calling from Cuba. I'm a political refugee here."

"Cuba?" my aunt repeated. "Cuba? Are you O.K. there? I mean, are you safe?"

"I think so," i told her. "I feel fine. It seems that way."

Talking to Kakuya and my mother the next day was like a dream. "Hi," this little voice said into the phone. It was the most beautiful voice i'd ever heard. I was nervous and happy. Sweating buckets.

"How are you?" i asked my daughter.

"Fine."

I felt like a pot boiling over. All the feelings i'd kept inside for so long came gushing out. I had a million things i wanted to ask her. A million things i wanted to say.

My mother and i made plans. She and my aunt and Kakuya would come down as soon as possible. It seemed too good to be true. And it was.

Month after month passed by. In order for Kakuya to get her passport, she needed a birth certificate. My mother told me that for ten years Elmhurst Hospital had refused to issue Kakuya a birth certificate. Finally, after months of hassling, Evelyn had to go to kourt to get a document proving that my daughter had been born.

Over the months that followed, i began to understand the kind of hell that the police and the FBI had put my family through. After i had escaped, the police had so persistently and brutally badgered my mother that she had had a heart attack. What they had done to Evelyn was beyond belief. I understood why Evelyn had reacted to my call the way she did. At one time, Evelyn's office telephone had ten intercepts on it. She and my mother had received phony notes in my handwriting. They had received telephone calls with my voice telling them to "come to the spot and bring some money." They had found electric eyes and all kinds of other devices in and around their houses. They had experienced strange break-ins where nothing of value was taken. But they had survived. And grown stronger in the process.

As the plane swooped down over Havana, it seemed that my heart was beating on my ribs to get out. My stomach hurt. My mouth was dry like cotton. It seemed like a million people poured off the plane before the tall little girl with the great big eyes started down the ramp. I could see my mother, looking frail, yet so determined. With my aunt behind her, looking triumphant.

How much we had all gone through. Our fight had started on a slave ship years before we were born. *Venceremos,* my favorite word in Spanish, crossed my mind. Ten million people had stood up to the monster. Ten million people only ninety miles away. We were here together in their land, my small little family, holding each other after so long. There was no doubt about it, our people would one day be free. The cowboys and bandits didn't own the world.